# Tilting at Windmills

## An Autobiography

*Charles Peters*

▲▼▲
**ADDISON-WESLEY PUBLISHING COMPANY, INC.**
Reading, Massachusetts    Menlo Park, California    New York
Don Mills, Ontario    Wokingham, England    Amsterdam
Bonn    Sydney    Singapore    Tokyo    Madrid    San Juan

B
P4472 P

Many of the designations used by manufacturers and
sellers to distinguish their products are claimed as
trademarks. Where those designations appear in this
book and Addison-Wesley was aware of a trademark
claim, the designations have been printed in initial
capital letters (i.e., Jell-O).

Library of Congress Cataloging-in-Publication Data

Peters, Charles, 1926–
  Tilting at windmills : an autobiography / Charles
Peters.
    p.    cm.
    Includes index.
    ISBN 0-201-05657-7
    1. Peters, Charles, 1926–    . 2. Journalists—United
States—Biography.   3. United States—Politics and
government—1945–
I. Title.
PN4874.P45A3 1988
070'.92'4–dc19
[B]
87-35903

Cover design by Marge Anderson
Text design by Joyce C. Weston
Set in 10-point Trump Mediaeval by DEKR Corporation,
Woburn, MA

ABCDEFGHIJ-DO-898
First printing, April 1988

*To my son, Christian*

# Contents

# *Acknowledgments*

I am grateful to my wife, Elizabeth Peters, and to Nicholas Lemann, James and Deborah Fallows, Phillip Keisling, Jonathan Rowe, Jonathan Alter, Gregg Easterbrook, Mickey Kaus, Michael Kinsley, Timothy Noah, and Joseph Nocera for reading and commenting on the manuscript. My debt is great to them all, but the first six deserve oak leaf clusters for having served as readers and critics of more than one version. I am especially grateful to Carol Trueblood for her help not only on the book but in my work over the years at the Peace Corps and at *The Washington Monthly*. I also thank my editors, Doe Coover and Ann Dilworth, for their guidance and encouragement.

# Preface

WHY write an autobiography if you aren't George Washington? I think that is a question that would naturally occur to readers who happen to pick up this book. I'm not famous, nor have I performed deeds that are widely celebrated. I did, however, found a magazine called *The Washington Monthly*, which embodies ideas and convictions about mankind, politics, and society that I want to persuade others to share. The best way I can see to explain those ideas and convictions is to tell of the life that led me to them, for the firmest of my beliefs is that thought cannot be divorced from experience.

—*Charles Peters*

# CHAPTER 1

# Hometown

THE South and the Midwest meet in Charleston, the small city in West Virginia where I was born. It is 100 miles from Virginia, and 50 miles from Ohio. The mountains that separate the two regions end here, and the valley of the Kanawha River begins to broaden into the great plain that stretches from Ohio to Colorado. Here also the Kanawha becomes navigable. For the early pioneers headed westward, reaching Charleston meant the end of the arduous journey over the mountains and the beginning of the much easier water route—down the Kanawha to the Ohio and the Mississippi, to places like Cincinnati and Louisville and St. Louis, and from there further west on the Missouri or north to Minnesota or south all the way to New Orleans. By the time I was born in 1926, the great steamboats no longer made regular visits to Charleston, but occasionally an excursion steamer or Captain Billy Bryant's showboat would come along to recapture for a moment the look of the river during most of the nineteenth century. And the remains of an abandoned dock

1

could still be found less than a hundred yards from my house. I used to play there.

The arrival of the automobile made it easier to cross the Appalachian Mountains from Virginia to Charleston, but the trip still was no picnic for a boy as susceptible to car sickness as I was. The road eastward from Charleston was one tight curve after another as it climbed to its high point near the Virginia border. I preferred the relatively level trip west. There were a few hills, but they were much easier on the stomach than the Appalachians.

From both directions—from Virginia and from the West—came attitudes and values that strongly influenced Charleston. From the West, enthusiasm and optimism and a sense of unlimited possibility. From Virginia, the romance of Robert E. Lee and the Lost Cause, which said that life was a losing battle, one to be fought with gallantry and skill, to be sure, but with defeat and broken hopes at the end.

Snugly seated between green hills, Charleston was an attractive and comfortable place to live in the thirties. The downtown was a real downtown, a compact center of the community. The movie theaters, the banks, the department and ten-cent stores, the hotels, the courthouse, the library, the mayor's office, the police station, and the post office were all in an area of roughly twenty square blocks. I lived just five blocks from the center of downtown, so it was an easy walk, which I made even shorter by mastery of all feasible shortcuts through alleys and backyards. If I was feeling lazy, I could board a trolley (which was replaced, alas, by a bus in the late thirties).

Ten blocks east of downtown was the state capitol, a slightly less majestic but more graceful imitation of the one in Washington. It was the building we all were most proud of. Second came the Kanawha Valley Bank building, our eighteen-story skyscraper, and then the Union, Security, and Kanawha Banking and Trust buildings.

2

They were twelve stories—still impressive in West Virginia. My father's law office was in the Security building.

Between the capitol and downtown was the east side residential area, where I lived. It was shaded by elms and lined along Kanawha, Virginia, and Quarrier streets with the homes of the town's upper crust. The most impressive houses were on Kanawha, which faced the river.

Across the street was the kind of riverbank that brought joy to the heart of a boy. It was full of hidden nooks and beaches—as well as that abandoned steamboat dock—in which we could play pirates and plot mischief. We would run like rabbits whenever we encountered tough-looking hobos in the thickets. When the river iced over during the winter, we raced our sleds down the bank and out onto the ice. The embankment was steep, and I was scared every time.

While Charleston itself was attractive, when you drove out of town to the east or west you had to go by giant chemical plants that belched smoke and noxious fumes. The smell was terrible. You knew the air you were breathing was far from pure, but people seldom talked about the problem except as a nuisance. Employees of the plant, especially the executives, heatedly denied that there was any danger. Environmental hazards were accepted as something you couldn't do anything about. Likewise the horrible scars that coal mining had gashed into the green hills south of the city.

Most of the owners of the mines and plants did not have to breathe the air or look at the scars. West Virginia was an economic colony. Most of the profits from coal, our main resource, went to people who lived outside the state. Outsiders also owned the chemical companies and most of the land. Neither they nor the local rich were excessively burdened by a sense of social responsibility. One result that wasn't good at all for a boy like me was that no one had bothered to give land for public parks in

Charleston. When I was growing up, we didn't even have one large enough for a baseball diamond.

× × ×

MY father and mother were both born on the farm. Mother near a little town about thirty miles from Louisville, Kentucky, called Turner's Station, named for one of her maternal ancestors. Papa was from Monroe County, West Virginia, just across Peters Mountain from Virginia. The mountain and a small town in the county called Peterstown were named after a paternal ancestor, Christian Peters, who had discovered the area while heading south to fight for the colonial side during the Revolutionary War.

Papa's family prospered in the agricultural boom that began around 1900, and they continued to do well through World War I, well enough to send him to college at Hampden-Sydney and to law school at Washington and Lee. He served in World War I, rising from enlisted man to captain, and was involved in heavy fighting during the battle of the Argonne Forest. He remained highly patriotic throughout his life, but he was never sentimental about war. As a child, the war stories that I heard were not about derring-do but about fear and blood and agony. Papa could make you hear those artillery shells thundering like freight trains overhead and feel the mud and damp of the trenches. His favorite story was about the time a German bullet struck him and he was sure he was bleeding to death. It turned out that the bullet had glanced off his holster and he had wet his pants in fright.

After the war Papa settled in Charleston and began to practice law. He lived in a boarding house. Such places, usually offering room and meals, were an important social institution of that era. They provided an affordable alternative to renting a house or an apartment. The meals meant that young people busy making a living did not

4

have to bother with cooking or pay the cost of larger quarters that included a kitchen.

A typical house had twelve boarders who ate their meals there and an equal or smaller number who also lived in the house. Often it was operated by a widow whose only source of income was the home she was left when her husband died.

Boarding houses played a vital social role. They gave single men and women a place to meet and get to know one another under natural circumstances. If you ate dinner with members of the opposite sex every day and sang songs or played bridge in the parlor or sat on the front porch chatting, you got to know one another in a relaxed way that is almost impossible today. If the widow was respectable, it was perfectly permissible for single men and women to live in the same boarding house—separate bedrooms, of course. In addition, the regulars were always bringing guests. And you might dine once or twice a week at other boarding houses so that your circle of friends could steadily grow and the likelihood of your meeting Mr. or Miss Right could increase.

Actually, Papa didn't meet mother at a boarding house—they were introduced by a mutual friend—but the boarding houses were where he met many of his lifelong friends and created the network of acquaintances that was essential to a young lawyer's success.

By the early thirties, Papa had established himself as a successful trial lawyer in the firm of Mohler, Peters, and Snyder. Neither of his partners was good at trial work. Jack Snyder was a brilliant researcher and appellate brief writer, and Dan Mohler, who later became president of the Charleston National Bank, was the firm's rainmaker, the one who brought in the clients. So Papa spent a lot of time in the courtroom.

Trial law is hard work. You have to consider simultaneously what might be going on in the minds of the judge, the opposing counsel, the jury, and the witness on the stand, while thinking as well about how appellate judges might react if someday they review the case. The strain and the tension can be almost unbearable. There is exultation when you win but gloom and self-reproach when you lose. My father tried cases almost every week for thirty years.

When he came home from the office, he was usually tense. He would fix himself a bourbon and water and sit down to read the paper. He would have a second bourbon before dinner, but he was seldom completely relaxed by the time we sat down at the table. He could be upset easily, and when he was, his temper was hot. So I always tried to act as if I wasn't there, ate very quickly, and excused myself before the storm broke. If the storm was averted during dinner, Mother and I would feel safe for the rest of the evening; after dinner there was the distraction of gathering around the radio to listen to Lowell Thomas give the day's news, followed by "Amos 'n Andy," which always left Papa in a benign mood.

Mother and I thought Papa's temper was caused by his drinking, and we were constantly appealing to him to give up his modest ration of bourbon. When he was in his eighties he finally told me what he thought was behind the temper. It was fear, of failure—fear that a country lawyer wouldn't be able to compete successfully with the sophisticates of Charleston. He was ashamed of the fear, so he could not tell his wife and his son what was really troubling him.

When he was relaxed, Papa was warm, understanding, full of good humor, full of life. My most treasured moments with him were when the circus came to town. Usually it would arrive in Charleston on Sunday. If it didn't, Papa would take the morning off. We'd drive out several miles from Charleston to a place where there was a good view of the railroad tracks and wait for the circus train to pass by. In those days the ornate red and gold circus wagons were loaded on open flat cars and made a gorgeous spectacle. We would follow the train to the railroad yard and watch it unload. From there we'd walk alongside the elephants to the circus ground. By the time we arrived, the workers would have spread the canvas and would be rhythmically pounding the stakes into the ground. Then the elephants would pull up the great centerpoles and the canvas would rise to become the main tent. Soon the tents for the animals and the performers and the side show would be raised. What had been an empty field a few hours earlier had been transformed into a small city.

I was fascinated by this magic and by the backstage life of the circus, from the cooks preparing lunch in the cook tent to the performers putting on their costumes for the parade downtown. The parade—an institution that ended with World War II—was how the circus drummed up business for its afternoon and evening performances. It began around 11 A.M., leading off with the band and ending with the calliope. In between were horses, camels, elephants, and, in brightly painted wagon cages, lions and tigers and leopards and panthers, at least some of which could be counted on to produce menacing growls. And there were the clowns—always including the woeful bum. He had been created by Emmett Kelly for Ringling Brothers, but every circus had an imitation. After the morning parade the actual performance always seemed anticlimactic.

Mother's maiden name was Esther Teague. She had a lot of distinguished ancestors, but unfortunately they were no longer around when she was growing up. She was orphaned as a small child, and her early life was hard. Some of the relatives she lived with were poor. Some didn't love her. Her sanity was probably saved by her beauty—the world tends to be a lot nicer to attractive children—and by her grit, of which she had a very great deal.

She worked her way through a business college in Bowling Green, Kentucky, and arrived in Charleston in 1921 with a letter of introduction to the local Studebaker dealer, Charles Ellison. He gave her a job and also took her into his home. She became very close to his wife and four children. Ellison and his wife died young, and, I'm sure because of her own experience as an orphan, my mother became a second mother to their children.

In 1925 she married my father. She was twenty-six. He was thirty-five and was doing well enough that she no longer had to work. But she now had the responsibility of creating a social life that would enhance my father's prospects. Because both she and Papa were country folk, this was not easy. In the early years of marriage she also did all the cleaning and cooking. But by the mid-thirties, she had a servant to do the housework. The going rate for a full-time maid ranged from eight to twelve dollars a week. She also had a part-time handyman, either John Arnold or Columbus Presley, to fix things in the house and work in the yard at twenty-five to fifty cents an hour. They were the lucky ones among the hundreds of desperate men who came to the kitchen door begging for work, often asking for only a meal in exchange. Groceries were ordered by phone and delivered to the house. Each morning the milkman brought the milk and the iceman brought the ice—until we got a refrigerator in 1932. Trucks picked up and returned laundry and dry cleaning. A thirties housewife could make a career out of answering the doorbell.

The events of Mother's day were a bridge club luncheon, or a visit to the beauty parlor, or going shopping. I read practically every movie magazine ever published while waiting for Mother to have her hair done. And the idea of going shopping still makes my legs ache with the memory of hours spent trudging through department stores. I was sustained only by the hope of a rest stop at the soda fountain or a visit to Woolworth's or Kresge's, both of which had excellent toy sections.

There was no sense that this was the life of leisure. By the late afternoon of such days Mother would say she was "worn out"; her maid would cluck, "Miz Peters, you just gotta stop overdoing," and Mother would take to her bed for a nap.

Only her volunteer work with charities and political campaigns made use of her mind. Later she would become very active in the League of Women Voters. But that was after I had left for college. One good thing about all her spare time was that she spent a lot of it with me. I knew Mother loved me, and this, I think, is the single most important thing in a man's life, just as the love of a father is most important in a woman's life. Men and women who don't know they have this love often lack a sense of self-worth. There is no foundation under their lives.

Many people striving to make it, as my mother and father were in the twenties and thirties, turn their backs on those they have left behind. But my parents continued to identify with the poor farmers and with the down and out generally. At the dinner table, Papa would rail against high interest rates. They probably helped him personally, by making it possible for him to earn more from his investments, but they hurt the people on the farm.

Papa took me to a company store in the coal mining area to show me how coal companies used scrip to keep the miners in bondage. Scrip was a private currency that the companies used to pay the miners. It could be spent only at the company store, where most of the goods were overpriced. I got the point when I was charged ten cents for a nickel pack of gum.

My parents' concern for the down and out included

their relatives, of whom there were many. Papa had eight brothers and sisters and Mother had four, and both had innumerable nieces and nephews. Almost all of them were poor during my childhood. During the twenties, the agricultural prosperity that had sustained both families began to collapse. By the early thirties, most farmers were desperate. I remember spending the night at one farm where there was just one bed, one table, and a handful of chairs. The children slept on the bare floor. People were leaving for the city as fast as they could scrape together the price of a train ticket. Unfortunately, there weren't nearly enough jobs in the city to take care of all the refugees from the farms.

A steady stream of relatives shared my bedroom or slept in the living room while they sought work in Charleston. They were able people—during World War II and thereafter they all prospered—but in the thirties they couldn't get work or had to take jobs considerably beneath their talents. I knew it was not their fault. From then on I could never accept the fundamental tenet of American conservatism that anyone who really wants to can get a job and get ahead.

Of the relatives who lived with us, my mother's brother, Lloyd Teague, stayed the longest—from 1937 until he went into the navy in 1942. Uncle Lloyd had been educated as an engineer, but the Depression meant that he had to take whatever work he could get. During the early thirties, he had one of the most heartbreaking jobs imaginable—collecting mortgage payments from farmers and foreclosing when they couldn't pay. It was a tribute to the kind of man he was that most of the farmers liked him even though he represented the hated bankers.

In 1937, Uncle Lloyd got a chance to go into the insurance business in Charleston and came to live with us. Unlike most of my elders, he always talked to me as one adult to another. He also never had the axes to grind that parents invariably have as they try to guide your behavior and worry about how you're going to turn out. I was completely at ease with him. Whenever he wanted to do something with me, whether it was to take me to a ball game or for a drive on a summer night, I leaped at the chance.

The two women who shared our house—their apartment occupied the second floor—weren't members of our family but were closer to us than most of our real relatives. They were a mother and daughter named Mabel and Ella Anderson. I called them Mimi and Pud. Mimi was in her sixties and Pud in her thirties when I was born. Both treated me as if I was their own son. They were from Staunton, Virginia, and thought of themselves as ladies of the Old South, which indeed they were. Their apartment was filled with Confederate memorabilia; framed photographs of Lee and Jackson and Longstreet and Beauregard lined its walls. The apartment was far from luxurious—Mr. Anderson, who had been an engineer on the Chesapeake and Ohio Railroad, had died before the days of pensions and social security—but for me it was a warm and happy place where I always found love and kindness, and some of the most delicious southern cooking I've ever tasted.

The house we shared at 25 Brooks Street was a modest dwelling with no central heat—there were gas stoves in each room—and the floor of my room, a converted side porch, was covered with linoleum. I had to walk through my parents' bedroom to get to the bath, as did the various relatives who lived with us during the Depression and either shared my room or slept on the sofa in the living room.

× × ×

MY memories of the house on Brooks Street are short on the unpleasant experiences from which many of the bet-

11

ter autobiographies are carved. Not only was I a loved only child, I was also the beneficiary of much kindness from the relatives who lived with us, and especially from Mimi and Pud. I was, of course, spoiled by all these attentions, but I may have been saved from unbearable self-regard by the rough-and-tumble world that I shared with the many children who lived in the neighborhood. Most of them were clearly my superiors in the skills that are important to boys. They could run faster and throw a baseball harder. I may have been the crown prince within the world of 25 Brooks Street, but outside I was just another kid.

There were both white and black children in the neighborhood. There was a black ghetto in Charleston, but blacks who were servants often lived in quarters to the rear of the white people's homes where they worked. On my block, the largest colony of black children was the eight sons and daughters of Lulu and Octavia, who lived in the basement of their employers' house on Kanawha Street.

Octavia's children were the closest to me in age. Julia was a year or so older, Briscoe (or "Brick," as we called him) was my age, and June (a boy) was a year or so younger. Octavia's employers, Mimi and Silas Pickering, had a son three years younger, also named Silas, who was my close friend until he died in 1973. Other white friends of mine included James and Hoople Heffernan, who were Catholic; Sherwood Rubenstein and Stanley Webster, who were Jewish; and Thelma Jean Stambaugh, who, at age seven, was the star of a backyard nudist show that I, also age seven, produced after having seen Sally Rand at the Chicago World's Fair.

The Heffernans and Sherwood and Stanley were important figures in my boyhood because my affection for them helped save me from the anti-Semitism and anti-Catholicism that prevailed among my fellow Protestants, who were overwhelmingly in the majority in Charleston. My own appearance, which was distinctly Mediterranean, also helped. Both my parents were fair, but I was dark, and at various times was called a wop, a dago, a spic, and a kike. Once, when Uncle Lloyd asked at a newsstand whether his nephew had picked up the paper, he was told, "The only kid that's been in here was a little Syrian boy."

Another neighborhood child was Emma Payne Littlepage, whose grandfather was the only rich man on our block. He took me to the games of the local minor league baseball team, the Charleston Senators, in a chauffeur-driven Packard. I felt like Orphan Annie with Daddy Warbucks, an impression enhanced by his penchant for adventures such as flying to Shanghai on the *China Clipper* at a time when few Charlestonians flew anywhere. His chauffeur, Arthur, used to let me help wash the car. I had immense respect for Arthur, and this, along with my friendship with the black—we called them "colored" then—children of the neighborhood, helped me escape, to some degree at least, the racial prejudice of the times, which was even worse than the religious bigotry.

I say "to some degree" because I recall one day when Briscoe and I got into a fight and his mother came out the kitchen door to break it up. I appealed to her to accept my version of what caused the trouble, and I expected her to side with me. When I saw the angry look on her face, I knew that she knew I was counting on her to defer to the white boy. As she turned to take Briscoe into the kitchen, I was troubled, knowing I had done something wrong but not quite sure what it was.

I had probably been reflecting my parents' attitude, which was that blacks were fine people as long as they knew their place. Amos and Andy in Harlem were lovable fellows. The good side of this attitude was its freedom from hatred. The bad side was the assumption that, if a black hit a white, the black was at fault unless proved otherwise.

After Emma Payne Littlepage's grandfather and the Pickerings, my father was probably the block's most prosperous citizen. His income from the practice of law was rising steadily. Although our house was modest, we lived comfortably. But for most of our neighbors, money was a constant problem. Mrs. Heffernan, a widow, made about twenty dollars a week as a clerk in a store. Mimi, who clerked in a dress shop, and Pud, who worked as a cashier in a restaurant, made no more than that and maybe less. But for us children, money was not important. The Saturday afternoon cowboy movie and serial—Flash Gordon was our favorite—cost only ten cents, and a nickel would buy enough penny candy to last the afternoon.

× × ×

THOUGH I liked the other kids in the neighborhood, I never minded playing by myself. My favorite toys were the little tin soldiers you could buy at Kresge's or Woolworth's for five cents each. I must have collected more than 200 by the time I was ten. I used them to stage World War I battle scenes that my father had told me about or that I had seen in the movies. In my imagination, the same tin doughboys could serve as Crusaders and Saracens, cowboys and Indians, Union and Confederates. I also had Naval Academy midshipmen and West Point cadets that I lined up in football formations and crashed into each other in re-creations of Army–Navy games. If I wasn't playing with my soldiers, I was out in the yard throwing a baseball or a football into the air and running to catch it. I also read a lot.

My reading list was about as far from John Stuart Mill's as one could imagine. I began with the Big Little Books. Then came the comic books. At first they were reruns from the Sunday newspaper. *Famous Funnies*, for example, featured four or five Sundays' worth of such standards as "Dick Tracy" and "Little Orphan Annie." Then, around 1938, came *Action Comics* and *Detective Comics*, with original strips. *Action* had Superman and *Detective* had Batman. They were exciting because you hadn't read them before and their heroes could do things that even Dick Tracy couldn't. During the same period, I listened faithfully to the "Jack Armstrong," "Little Orphan Annie," and "Tom Mix" radio shows. Fascinated by such heroes as Baseball Joe and Harold Hackney, Halfback, I also began to read hardcover sports novels, which you could borrow from the library or buy for half a dollar.

The movies were a major influence in my life. On Saturday afternoons, I went to the Rialto with the gang from the neighborhood, but at other times I often went by myself. There were six theaters in downtown Charleston, and I was in one or another at least twice, and often three times, a week from the time I was seven through my high school years.

I liked comedies the most—Laurel and Hardy, Wheeler and Woolsey, the Marx Brothers, Our Gang, the Three Stooges, Joe E. Brown, Harold Lloyd, W.C. Fields, and, even, God help me, the Ritz Brothers. I was enchanted by actresses who combined spunk and a sense of humor—women like Carole Lombard, Myrna Loy, Jean Arthur, Katharine Hepburn, Rosalind Russell, and Claudette Colbert. Jean Arthur was my favorite. *Mr. Smith Goes to Washington,* starring her and James Stewart, helped shape my image of the life I wanted to lead and of the kind of person I wanted to be.

If one thing consumed more of my time than the movies, it was, as my reading preferences would suggest, the world of sports. My interest in football came from my father. When I was five or six he began taking me to the annual game between his alma mater, Washington and Lee, and West Virginia University, which took place in Charleston every fall during the thirties. I believe my sympathy for the underdog may have begun with W&L's team, for which I rooted and which always lost. I also rooted for West Point because my father had been in the army, but in those days it didn't do much better than W&L. Perhaps to have at least some connection with a winner (or maybe through the influence of the Heffernan boys) I became an avid Notre Dame fan, too. Although he did not share my passion for the Fighting Irish, Papa was kind enough to take me to South Bend to see Notre Dame play. And once I got to go to the game that to most boys of my era was the biggest of them all: the Army–Navy game in Philadelphia. The event fell a bit short of my dreams. A blizzard had dumped a foot of snow on the stadium the night before, and the windchill factor must have been minus ten or twenty. Papa and I were both miserable, but we tried to act as if we were having a grand time.

Uncle Lloyd was responsible for my interest in baseball and horse racing. He took me to my first Kentucky Derby in 1935 and to more than ten Derbies thereafter. For Uncle Lloyd, who made barely enough money to live on, the Derby was his one excursion into living like the rich. We had a box in the area of the grandstand, where the wealthy and famous sat. I felt very important as I casually strolled within inches of a movie star.

I was eight on my first visit to the Derby. With two dollars to bet, I ended up winning six out of eight races and the fabulous sum of twenty dollars. My parents, doubtless sensing that they had a prodigy in the family, asked me the secret to my success. I explained that I inspected the horses in the paddock before each race, looking for the one with the biggest legs. If one of the Budweiser Clydesdales had been there, I would have put my entire bankroll on him.

16

Uncle Lloyd was a Cincinnati Reds fan. It was the major league team nearest to the town where he grew up in Kentucky. It was also the team nearest to Charleston. The big events were the doubleheaders on Sunday afternoons when the team was at home and you might get a chance to see Johnny Vandermeer and Bucky Walters pitch. We had to get up at 2:30 A.M. to catch the 3:30 train to Cincinnati. My excitement would mount as the dawn broke while the train raced along the banks of the Ohio River. We would be sitting in the dining car, which in those days on the Chesapeake and Ohio was quite elegant, and I would be breakfasting on pancakes and hot chocolate.

When we reached Cincinnati we would walk through the giant art deco train station and catch a cab to the Netherland Plaza Hotel. We went there not to get a room—we would return to Charleston on the evening train after the second game—but to see the visiting team, which always stayed there. It was also where the man who provided our tickets stayed. He was Henderson Peebles, a Charleston insurance man who had learned that one of the secrets of success was to be a source of tickets for sporting events his clients might like to attend. But he was also one of the most generous men I have ever known. Neither Uncle Lloyd nor I was likely to become a major client, but he continued to come up with tickets, even when I was in college. I can still see him in his suite at the Netherland Plaza being shaved by the hotel barber. This seemed very grand to me. To have a suite in a large hotel was impressive enough, but to be able to summon a barber to your room on Sunday morning was really something!

I enjoyed playing baseball and football as much as I enjoyed watching them. The trouble was that I wasn't very good at it. The only plays I could perform well were catching passes and stealing bases. (The latter, I suspect, had less to do with my skill than with the ineptitude of the catchers, who, in sandlot baseball, were usually the neighborhood fat boys.) So I was usually a coach or a manager. This was to become a pattern in my life: I was a leader because I was ill-equipped to be anything else.

Since Charleston had no public playing fields or parks, we usually played in someone's backyard. My mother threw us out of ours after one muddy football game during which we eradicated most of the lawn and all of her flower beds. The yards were always too cramped, often bisected by brick or concrete walks on which we could crack our heads in a slide or a tackle, and surrounded by houses whose windows were sometimes shattered by our balls. On those occasions, I would take up a collection, march into Mrs. Pickering's (she was the most tolerant of the neighbors), and hand her fifty cents, which she would treat as full payment for the damage that had been done.

Sometimes we would be short a player or two and I would be pressed into service, which I welcomed if the game was baseball or touch football but not if it was tackle. I remember one bitterly cold day when the ground was frozen so solid it felt like concrete. We were playing a team whose members must have been six inches to two feet taller than I was and at least twenty pounds heavier. From the moment the fullback trampled me on the first play, I never prayed harder for a game to end.

× × ×

BOTH my mother and father were active workers in the Democratic party. They worshipped Woodrow Wilson. Mother cried when Al Smith lost to Herbert Hoover. When I was six years old, they took me to the county fair and gave me fifty cents to spend. I spent it all on a tinted photograph of FDR. During election campaigns, I loved to visit Papa at the party headquarters, where I imagined that important strategy was being plotted. I spent the afternoons after school plastering bumper stickers on cars and handing out campaign buttons all over the East Side. I followed the political news in the papers as avidly as I did the sports results. It's not hard to see why I was ripe for *Mr. Smith Goes to Washington.*

By 1936, my father had become a prominent figure in state Democratic politics. He was managing the campaign of the man who was elected governor that fall. When he went to the national convention in Philadelphia, he rode in the current governor's limousine to Grafton, where he and the governor boarded the B&O's National Limited for the remainder of the trip to Philadelphia.

This trip excited my imagination not only because of my passion for politics but also because of another passion—trains. I must have acquired this fascination from Pud, whose father had been an engineer on the Chesapeake and Ohio. She loved to talk about the train trips she had taken. By the time I was eight, I had a collection of timetables that filled a small closet. From the Great Northern to the Southern Pacific, the Seaboard to the Rock Island, the Boston and Maine to the Wabash, I had them all, and I used them to plan trips to every part of the country. My enthusiasm was in no way diminished by the improbability of some of my more elaborate itineraries.

When I wasn't perusing my timetables, I was hanging around the railroad station. Late in the afternoon I would ride my bike to the New York Central station, which was just five blocks from my home. Between 4:30 and 5:00, three trains came in and one departed. They were minor league trains, with only two or three cars and not very glamorous destinations, such as Columbus, Grafton, and Roanoke. But I imagined all the travelers as great adventurers coming and going from long distances on matters of grave importance. And even though the trains were short, their great engines were a stunning sight as they thundered into the station amidst clanging bells and clouds of steam. Coming home at 5:00 P.M., as I was riding up Brooks Street, I could see the C&O's Fast Flying Virginian leaving its station (which was across the river) for New York. Here was a really important train—eleven cars long, with sleeping and dining cars and a genuinely glamorous destination. I always stopped to watch it pass along the river.

Because my father's law practice was prospering, and because I was an only child, he and my mother were able to afford to take me on some of the trips I planned. The grandest was a two-week trip to the West Coast in 1935. There were so many stops and changes of railroad that our tickets were about a yard long. The train we took from Chicago to Los Angeles was called the Chief and had the kind of observation car with a rear platform where politicians made campaign speeches and travelers, sitting in canvas captain's chairs, could contemplate the receding horizon. A bright little girl on the train quickly became my favorite companion. We spent hours together leaning over the rail that surrounded the platform, watching the track hurtling beneath us and shouting to one another above the clatter of the train whenever we spotted a jackrabbit or an Indian or someone who remotely resembled a real cowboy.

× × ×

THE schools I attended while I lived on Brooks Street, Mercer Elementary School and Thomas Jefferson Junior High, were both within easy walking distance of my house, close enough to come home for lunch every day. At Mercer, the students ranged from well-off to poor, but there were a lot more of the poor, from the local orphanage and from one of the roughest neighborhoods in town.

Yet, amazingly, there were only a couple of real delinquents. The rest were as well behaved as you would want kids to be.

I was better off materially than all but a handful of my fellow students. Since the principal was also a friend of my parents, I was at risk of becoming a teacher's pet. I could not bear the thought of being cast in that role, so I began to develop a rebellious streak that has stayed with me through the years. It has tended to make the respectable establishments of my life—whether school faculties, employers, or the leaders of business, government, and the press—somewhat wary. Except for this problem, school was easy for me.

This was true until I entered junior high school and had to take courses called Wood Working and Sheet Metal. I was terrible at both. I couldn't make the simplest bookends or ashtrays, and I had my first encounter with sleeplessness, worrying about my ineptitude. I passed the courses, but only because some kind friends hammered some judicious licks on my behalf whenever the instructor's back was turned.

Sunday school at the First Presbyterian Church was an important part of my education. In the first half hour, from 9:45 to 10:15, groups of about a hundred children met for a prayer or two, a scripture reading, a couple of hymns, and a short sermon by the adult leader. This part of the program was pretty tedious, redeemed only by such rousers as "Stand Up for Jesus" or "Lead on O King Eternal," for which I acquired a lifelong affection.

Then we broke up into sections of ten or so, each taught by a young adult. Here I found something that was missing from all but a handful of classes in my primary and secondary education—spirited, even heated, discussion and debate. The subject usually was the application of Christianity to daily life. The hottest sessions dealt with Germany's treatment of the Jews. The gassing hadn't started, but Jews were already being beaten, robbed, and sent to concentration camps. One of my classmates enthusiastically supported these actions. I did not, so we argued constantly. Most of the others in the class were torn between their dislike of brutality and their distaste for Jews.

I was not very religious—my prayers tended toward requests that Papa be inspired to take me to the Army–Navy game or that the Democratic ticket win the next election—but I believed in God until I was eighteen. In my early childhood he was Robert E. Lee; then he became FDR. The last time I recall reading the Bible as a believer was the day Roosevelt died. But I have continued to believe in the Golden Rule and in the idea of Christian love and that the only real test of those convictions is how we act in our daily lives.

My anti-Nazi sentiments led me into a terrible mistake when I was thirteen. I was finishing eighth grade when the Germans overran the Low Countries and France. By midsummer, Henry Luce's magazines were full of stories of how the Germans were now poised to cross the Atlantic—illustrated with frightening drawings of a curved arrow sweeping from Europe through French North Africa to Brazil and right on to our own shores. This threat was, needless to say, a good deal easier for a *Time* magazine artist to convey than it would have been for Hitler to carry out. But I thought it was real. I decided I would have to prepare to defend my country. The only way I could see of doing that was to go to military school. My parents, perhaps worried about my rebellious streak— the most recent manifestation of which had been the explosion of a firecracker in Miss Chenowith's arithmetic class—also seemed to think military school was a good idea.

So off I went to Kentucky Military Institute, near Louisville. What no one had told me was that many parents of that era regarded military school as a kind of private reformatory where they dumped their more unruly adolescent sons. There were some really good cadets, as we were called, but there were some really bad ones, too.

One of the latter became my tormentor. He was bright and could be charming, but he had another, much less happy side. One of his typical tricks happened one night before a crucial exam—he slit my pillow, scattering thousands of feathers all over my room. With room inspection due first thing in the morning, I had to spend the entire evening picking up each feather, frantically pursuing those that wafted into the air an inch ahead of my outstretched hand. He did something along these lines every week or so. The nightmare was that I couldn't do anything about it. He was bigger than I was, and the unwritten code forbade tattling to the authorities. I simply had to endure. I didn't even tell my parents, but they divined that something was wrong and mercifully raised no protest when, after sticking it out through the 1940–41 school year, I announced that the threat of Nazi invasion was sufficiently diminished that I could return to Charleston High School the next fall.

CHAPTER **2**

# Conscious Happiness

**I**F happiness is rare, conscious happiness is even rarer. Yet it was mine for my three years at Charleston High School. After the miserable year at military school, Charleston High was like stepping from darkness into golden sunlight. Each morning I awakened to confront these delicious facts: I wasn't at KMI but in my own bed in my own home; I could walk to school, and my tormentor would not be there.

Except that it was lily-white, Charleston High was very close to a perfect democracy. All social classes—at least all that there were in Charleston—were represented. A very few of the wealthy sent their children away to private school, but seldom before the eleventh grade. Students were not judged on the basis of social position. Popularity was determined by physical attractiveness, athletic skill, and—unlike those attributes or money or social position, all of which you were born with—by something called "personality," which you could develop on your own, without any assistance from your parents. Clothing had to conform to prevailing fashion, but prevailing fashion did not require anything expensive—in marked contrast to the seventies and eighties, when Esprit, Reebok, and Calvin Klein became standard equipment for the young.

The quality of instruction at Charleston High was uneven, but there was at least one excellent teacher in each major subject. My favorite was Miss Lake Caldwell, who introduced me to the *New Republic* in the tenth grade. Its liberalism was an important antidote to the steady stream of Republican propaganda in *Time* and *Life* and the *Saturday Evening Post*, the other magazines I read regularly, and in the rest of the press, which was overwhelmingly conservative. It would be hard for a young person today to believe how rare the liberal voices in journalism were at that time or how joyous I felt in finding a magazine that enthusiastically supported FDR. If it criticized him, as in the case of his brief alliance in 1942 with the Vichyite Admiral Darlan, it did so from the point of view of the Left, not the Neanderthal Right.

Because my schoolwork was not very demanding, I maintained an A average with less than an hour's study a day. This left lots of time for other pursuits. The most time-consuming of these was thinking about girls. I seemed to be in an almost perpetual state of arousal. Like more than one adolescent male before and since, when the bell rang to change classes, I had to rise very carefully from my chair, maneuvering my notebook to conceal the bulge in my trousers.

All this heat produced little of the consummation I devoutly wished for. Nevertheless, scandal attached itself to my name early in my junior year. As my date and I walked home after a school dance one Saturday night in November 1942, snow was falling. It became heavier as we trudged up the hill. I now lived in a part of town called South Hills, to which my family had moved in 1941, and she lived there, too. We managed to make our way to my house, where we planned to ask my father to drive us the rest of the way. But he said the snow was too deep for his car. So it was decided that my date would spend the night in our guest room. That's all that happened. But by noon on Monday, everyone at Charleston High had heard we'd spent the night together. Since the story endowed me with a reputation that was not without positive aspects for a young man, I'm afraid that I was less than zealous in seeking to correct it.

There were other times when my reputation for mischief was deserved. On Students Day, when high school students got to serve as municipal officials, I was the chief of police. The real chief asked me what I would like to do. Never thinking he would agree, I said, "Send a squad car to Charleston High and arrest Eddie King, the gym teacher."

"Done," the chief replied as he pushed a switch on his squawk box and said, "Sergeant, send a car to Charleston High and pick up Eddie King." I gulped. Everyone liked King, but he had a quick temper. It was easy to imagine his red-faced reaction to the arrest. After King was handcuffed and escorted to the squad car, the chief radioed the officers that it was a hoax. King did not laugh. I was in trouble.

I survived this episode with a reprimand from Mr. Richardson, the principal. But he now was on my case. Hearing that I was to be the producer for the Class Day show, he went on Red Alert. And when, during the performance, a young lady in a grass skirt ran across the stage pursued by a young man with a lawn mower, he ordered the curtain rung down.

This sort of thing did not set well with some of the faculty. At the end of our junior year, when the time came to choose students for the National Honor Society, I was blackballed by a teacher on the selection committee, who said, "We've got to teach this young man a lesson." The lesson was not specified, nor was the reason I needed it. Everyone on the committee understood.

Next to girls, my favorite diversion was hanging out at a local pool hall called the Strand—not because I liked to play pool but because I could follow the major league baseball scores there. The Charleston radio stations did not broadcast major league baseball until the late forties. So unless you could bear to wait for the morning paper— and my interest was far too intense for that—the only solution was to go to the Strand.

In its gloomy back room, which reeked of stale beer, there were six pool tables, a Western Union ticker (which brought the scores every half inning), and a blackboard where the scores were posted. It usually took around ten minutes to play half an inning, so suspense mounted as the clock ticked past that time and you began to hope that your team was scoring or to worry that the other team was. The ticker might confirm that something was indeed afoot by announcing a pitching change or a home run during the course of the half inning. But sometimes thirty or forty minutes would go by and then a zero would come in on the ticker. The pitcher might have walked the bases full, which takes a lot of time, and then escaped being scored on, possibly through equally time-consuming strikeouts. You never knew these details until the next day's paper, unless you had a friend with a radio that could pull in the stations broadcasting the St. Louis and Cincinnati games.

My parents were less than enthusiastic about my home away from home at the Strand. It was prudent to avoid being too obvious about my daily visits. In this regard, an ideal situation arose during the summer between my junior and senior years, when I worked as a messenger at the Kanawha Valley Bank. My daily trips to the Charleston Clearing House took me down an alley that afforded access to the rear entrance of the Strand. So, going and coming, I could check the scores, unobserved by my parents or by my superiors at the bank.

There is another virtue to messenger jobs. Most of the time you're free to think about anything you want, which is far better than having your mind chained to something other people want you to think about. If you can't find work you love and you don't need much money, try being a messenger.

That same summer, my friend Bill Buchanan and I began to talk about rewarding ourselves for our labors with a trip to New York. We estimated that we could save sixty-five dollars each from our earnings, so that was our budget. Over bag lunches in the library of my father's office, we pored over hotel brochures and ticket and restaurant information. We recruited four friends to join us. We bought train tickets (twenty-two dollars each, round trip); made reservations at the Hotel Picadilly on 45th street, just off Times Square (three of us in a room for $1.50 each per day); and ordered tickets for seven plays, all at the minimum price, which was $1.20 or $1.80. They included *Oklahoma*, which had just opened; *Harriet*, with Helen Hayes; and *Something for the Boys*, with Ethel Merman, whose brassy charm captivated me so absolutely as to dim even the luster of *Oklahoma*, which I knew I was supposed to like better. We discovered Barbetta's, an Italian restaurant on 46th Street, where the food was good and cheap. We went to a nightclub called Cafe Society Uptown, which featured Teddy Wilson's trio, with a great drummer named Big Sid Catlett. There we had our first hard liquor in the soft form of a cocktail called an Orange Blossom. Sixty-five dollars and fifty cents covered it all, including subway and bus fares.

Choosing to see seven plays in four days may seem excessive, but my interest in theater had grown steadily from the time I was putting on my backyard shows and going to the circus with my father. By the time I reached high school, I always read the drama section of the *New York Times* and the theater reviews in the *New Yorker*.

I also was active in the high school theater group, usually working backstage, which I enjoyed the most, but occasionally performing. My acting triumph was as a New York sightseeing guide in a play called *Two on an Island*. A native New Yorker happened to attend one of the rehearsals and collapsed in laughter at my southern-accented delivery of the guide's spiel.

I held one other job during high school. In my junior year, just after I turned sixteen, I was hired as a page by the state senate. I had to arrange to keep up with my schoolwork at night and on the weekends, because the job took most of the day. In the morning I ran errands for members and distributed copies of the daily journals of each house and of the bills that had been introduced the day before. Somewhere between noon and 2:00 P.M., depending on how much legislative business was on the day's calendar, the session would begin. Since my duties during the sessions were few—if a senator wanted to introduce a bill or an amendment, I would run to his desk and take the document to the clerk—I could observe the proceedings with a minimum of distraction. I had a ringside seat on a marble step at the foot of the rostrum, from which the senate president, the clerk, and the parliamentarian presided over the thirty-two senators.

The West Virginia state senate of 1943 was fortunate, as legislative bodies go, in possessing only one numbingly dull orator, and even his speeches had a kind of drama. He invariably was drunk when he delivered them, so there was a degree of suspense about whether he would still be standing when he finished. On one occasion he wasn't, and the sergeant-at-arms and the doorkeeper had to carry him from the chamber. (The prospect of a similar misadventure may explain why some incumbents now oppose the televising of legislative proceedings.)

Most of the senators were undistinguished—not very good, not very bad. There were three, however, whose votes either were for sale to the highest bidder or were, in a remarkable series of coincidences, always cast in favor of the side with the most money.

I liked trying to predict the vote on major bills, guessing where each senator would come out on the basis of his record and the interests of his friends and supporters. By the end of the session I had become quite skilled at this. Unfortunately, the votes I predicted seldom were the ones I would have made myself. I was a liberal Democrat, and the senate was dominated by a coalition of Republicans and conservative Democrats. Although most were not for sale for cash, they could be powerfully influenced by the sense that their general prosperity—as lawyers, insurance agents, or whatever else they were when the legislature was not in session—was likely to be enhanced by a conservative voting record.

I was fascinated by the intricacies of parliamentary procedure and by the flowery language of the senators. The Charleston High School student council was the victim of my attempts to display my mastery of these arts. I had been elected to the council the previous fall. I later ran for president but came in second (which meant I was vice-president) to my old Sunday school adversary, the Nazi. America's entry into World War II had had a salutary effect on his political philosophy, and he no longer railed about the fiendish plots of international Jewry.

Although my interest in politics, from the student to the state and national levels, was shared by only two or three of my friends, I was on the whole more like than unlike the other young people with whom I was growing up. For example, the pleasures of politics could not compare with the euphoria I felt one morning in Miss Knight's English class when Libby Holliday, whom I had been trying to get up the courage to ask to a dance, slipped me a note asking me to ask her. Then there was the high of the adolescent laughter into which we would collapse as we relived the Eddie King and Class Day episodes, laughter that was so intense and pure that I have found myself yearning for it years later.

And there was touch football. Bill Buchanan and I always managed to be on the same team. He was a gifted passer and, despite my small hands, I was a good receiver. I really didn't care whether we won or lost, so long as we had exciting, high-scoring games and Bill and I played well, with a couple of diving catches to add a little drama. A typical contest would be called for darkness with the score 42–42. There have been few times that life seemed so sweet as when I walked home in the cool autumn twilight from one of those games.

In this life the bad times were rare. Probably the worst came the day I was student chief of police. After we had arranged the gym teacher's arrest, the real chief took me on a tour of the station, showing me the jail and introducing me to the other officers. He seemed to like me, and his tone became increasingly confidential. When we returned to his office, he said, "Son, would you like to see how we take care of niggers?" He must have thought I nodded, for he proceeded to open a door, revealing a closet full of bloody garments. He had kept them as souvenirs of the beatings he and other policemen had given blacks. I was sickened by the sight and by the fact that the chief obviously was trying to honor me with his confidence, to show that he thought I was adult enough to understand how real men dealt with real problems.

So there was a dark side to life in Charleston, but the episode with the police chief was one of the few times I had to face it. With the exception of that miserable year at military school, my life was good.

× × ×

PEARL Harbor came during my first year at Charleston High. Thereafter, the war dominated the newspapers. We

32

were all very patriotic. At football games our band would play not only "The Star Spangled Banner" but "Anchors Aweigh," "Off We Go into the Wild Blue Yonder," "The Caissons Go Rolling Along," and "God Bless America." I deserted Baseball Joe for books about the war, like *Guadalcanal Diary*, and movies like *Purple Heart*, in which the Japanese cold-bloodedly executed American prisoners of war, sending you out of the theater ready to charge. In such an atmosphere, it was only natural that I enlisted in the army in the spring of 1944 and that all but one— he had flat feet—of my closest friends joined up during the next year.

I was hoping to be placed in an army program designed to produce graduates who could understand the people of Japan and speak their language. I saw myself interrogating Japanese prisoners on the battlefield and, after the war was won, leading the conversion of Japan into a democracy. This represented a shift from my ambition to become a navy carrier pilot, dive-bombing Japanese battleships. That dream evaporated when I failed the test for the navy pilot program. It was heavily weighted toward math and physics, which weren't my strong points academically.

So, naturally, the army, instead of putting me into the Japanese studies program, sent me to Ohio University in early July for an engineering course emphasizing math and physics. I liked the school and the little town of Athens, where it was located. The trouble was that to get through chemistry, physics, analytical geometry, calculus, and electricity, I had to study hard for the first time in my life. Often I would go down to the cafeteria to continue working after lights out. By dint of effort, not aptitude, I did well. I still brag about my A in calculus.

The library at Ohio U. is where I discovered *PM*, the left-wing tabloid that Marshall Field and Ralph Ingersoll had founded a few years earlier. *PM* was even more rabidly pro-Roosevelt than the *New Republic*, which was just fine with me. FDR was seeking his fourth term and was opposed by Thomas E. Dewey. The big issue in my mind was whether we would have a strong international organization after the war to replace the League of Nations, whose spinelessness had encouraged Hitler and Mussolini and the Japanese. I thought we needed an international police force to control future aggressors. Dewey was against it but Roosevelt was for it, which was further proof to me of his greatness.

After completing the Ohio engineering program, I was ordered to Camp Atterbury, Indiana, from which I would be assigned to an infantry basic training center. The main occupation at Atterbury was praying that you would be sent to some nice post—near San Francisco, say—and would escape the kind of dreary desert that Camp Fannin, Texas, was reputed to be.

At Atterbury I continued to display a knack for irritating first sergeants that had first surfaced with Sergeant Moon at Ohio U. Moon's face reddened when he was riled, and when I was around it was usually deep crimson. For the life of me I cannot recall a specific incident of misbehavior; I think the problem was my general tendency to observe rules in a somewhat irregular way. For instance, rather than stand in a long line, I would loll in the grass reading or chatting until the line was down to one or two people and the door about to close. At that point I would make a last-minute dash, arriving just in time. This was enough to send Sergeant Moon into a slow burn.

When I arrived at my barracks at Camp Atterbury, I noticed that there was an empty private room at the end of a long room with about forty bunks in it. I decided that I preferred privacy to the company of thirty-nine, so I took up residence in the private room. Around midnight, the door burst open, the light switched on, and a voice bellowed: "What the hell do you think you're doing here?" It seems the room was reserved for noncommissioned officers, and the voice—it belonged to another sergeant—went on to convey the owner's view that only a smartass wise guy could possibly have concluded otherwise.

For basic training I drew Fort McLellan, Alabama. It wasn't San Franciso, but I thought it was a cut above Camp Fannin. As it turned out, for the next six weeks I yearned for that dry Texas desert. I arrived at Fort McLellan in late January, and it rained every single day until well into March. And it was cold. The tar-paper huts that served as our barracks obviously had been designed by someone who thought Alabama was the tropics. In the summer it is, but in the winter, temperatures in the forties are common.

The army did not call off training events because of rain and cold. We did whatever was on the schedule regardless of the weather. And we probably did more of it than any trainees in the history of the army. The Battle of the Bulge, which had ended just a few weeks earlier, had so severely depleted the supply of infantry replacements that recruits were being sent overseas with as little as eight weeks' training. We were scheduled for sixteen weeks, but the officers were determined that we would be adequately trained even if the time had to be cut in half again. As a result, a typical training day lasted from 5:30 or 6:00 in the morning until 6:30 or 7:00 at night. There were frequent night exercises—including one memorable all-night march in the rain—with no time off the next day.

Around the middle of March, however, the rains stopped and the balmy Alabama spring began. Training remained hard, but life at least seemed bearable, except for my new first sergeant. There are some people you rub the wrong way simply by looking at them. He was one.

Standing fifty feet away from me on the steps of the company clerk's office, he would shout, "Peters, your shoelaces are tied wrong." This was more than a casual observation, since it usually was followed by something like, "That means you're latrine orderly this weekend." The other form of punishment, KP (scrubbing pots and pans in the company kitchen), was only slightly preferable. I had latrine or KP duty all but two weekends of basic training.

Except for the first sergeant, I got along well with my fellow soldiers. Every social class and many different occupations and home states were represented, but most of the men were farmers from Georgia, Alabama, and Mississippi. They had been exempt from the draft because agriculture had been deemed essential to the war effort. But by the beginning of 1945, the army was scraping the bottom of the nation's manpower barrel, and they were being drafted. In my hut, everyone except me was a farmer. They were older than I was, some by more than ten years, but I liked most of them and they were kind to me.

One day, after we had returned to the hut exhausted from a long march, I discovered that my fountain pen was missing. It was a good one, worth about fifteen dollars, a lot of money in those days. As I left to go to the shower room, the other men knew I was upset. When I returned, there were fifteen crumpled one-dollar bills spread over the top of my bunk. Our pay was only fifty dollars a month.

During the long, hard days of training, we dreamed of weekends off when we would surely meet a beautiful girl whose passion would, if anything, exceed our own. I continued to dream on most of the weekends—in either the kitchen or the latrine. But one Saturday, after a week during which I had miraculously escaped the sergeant's attention, another private and I managed to secure passes and get away from the post around 7:30 P.M. We took a bus to Atlanta, arriving after midnight. There were no bars open, or at least none that we could find. Worse, there were no girls, passionate or otherwise, on the streets.

And there were no hotel rooms. Finally, one desk clerk said he thought he would have a room around 4:30 A.M., so we slumped in chairs in the lobby and waited. Finally, a laughing couple emerged from the elevator and handed their key to the clerk, who handed it to us. Their still-warm bed was as close as we came to attaining our dream. That afternoon we had to catch the bus back to Fort McLellan so we could arrive before our passes expired at 7:00 P.M.

On April 12, a long day ended with a ten-mile march that brought us back to our company area. We were all red-faced and weary and looking forward to a good shower as soon as we were dismissed. But instead of giving us the order to fall out, the captain mounted the steps of the company clerk's office and said that he had an announcement: President Roosevelt had died that afternoon in Warm Springs, Georgia.

I was devastated. A lump quickly came to my throat, and I knew I was going to cry. I wanted to be alone, so when we were dismissed I walked to my hut, got my Bible from the footlocker under my bunk, and went to the coal shed next to the shower room. I turned to the Twenty-third Psalm and tried to read it, but my eyes were filled with tears and I could barely see the page.

The following week, one of our regular runs over the obstacle course was on the schedule. For most of my life I had not been very strong or athletic, but in my last two years at Charleston High we had a rigorous physical workout every day. The army had a similar program at Ohio U. and a much more demanding one at Fort McLellan. I could do more than 50 pushups and 500 situps and leg lifts. I was in such good shape that I was beginning to think of myself as a Tarzan. On this obstacle course run we would be carrying, for the first time, full field packs on our backs and a rifle strapped to our shoulders. I raced through the course with no problem until I came to the last obstacle, a thirty-foot-high platform with wooden ladders leading to it. On the platform was a railing from which was draped a cargo net. I swiftly climbed the ladder, put one hand on the railing, confidently jumped over it, and reached with the other hand for the cargo net. I never touched it.

I hit the ground with a terrific thud, landing on my rear as the rifle slung over my shoulder crashed hard against my head. I was conscious and felt no pain, but I knew I must be injured. From the looks on the faces of the men gathered around me, I could tell they had reached the same conclusion. Soon I heard a siren, and within minutes I was lifted onto a stretcher and into an ambulance, which rushed me to the hospital.

After being x-rayed, I was placed in a private room in the orthopedic ward. This did not strike me as promising. Privates, as I had learned at Camp Atterbury, did not get private rooms. Then the doctor instructed an orderly to stay with me and prick the sole of my foot with a pin every half hour or so. My reaction was, "Jesus Christ, I'm going to be paralyzed!" But I tried to appear calm when I asked the doctor what was wrong. He said one of my vertebrae was fractured and the two on either side of it were dislocated. I was sorry I had asked and started to wonder what life in a wheelchair would be like. Then, suddenly, I began to feel pain. It hurt like hell, but pain never was so sweet. I figured, as long as I'm feeling something, I can't be paralyzed. I don't know if that was medically sound reasoning, but it turned out to be right. Two weeks later they put me in a body cast and the pain ended, never to return. The cast was uncomfortable at first—it covered my trunk from neck to thigh. But within a few weeks I had adjusted to it and, except for the itching produced by the Alabama heat during the summer, it didn't bother me at all.

During the two painful weeks, when the doctor thought my situation a bit on the precarious side, my little private room was crowded with hovering attendants. There was Sergeant Maughm, a forty-five-year-old medic who said he had been J.P Morgan's butler; a very pretty nurse named Bonnie; and two German POWs who had been captured in North Africa when Rommel's troops surrendered. One, Fritz, was a giant of a man. He could easily lift me out of bed, cast and all. He was the good German, always cheerful and always kind. The other, whose name I no longer remember, was a sly, mean, effeminate little Nazi. Even at this point, when the war in Europe was almost over, there was still an active cell of Hitlerites among the prisoners.

While the pain was severe I was given morphine, enough that I came close to getting addicted. I remember begging Bonnie for just one more shot. Fortunately, she resisted. I did, however, acquire another addiction—cigarettes. I had managed to get through high school without smoking. But I realized that the substitutes I used for oral gratification—chewing gum and pencils—were not very attractive. I thought smoking would seem more sophisticated. I probably would have tried it earlier if I hadn't been afraid that my first attempts would look awkward. The private hospital room—and the free cigarettes provided by the Red Cross—gave me the chance to learn to smoke unobserved and without risk of embarrassment. In a matter of weeks, I was up to a pack a day.

After my injury, I received orders to report to the University of Chicago for the Japanese program. But it was clear that I wasn't going anywhere but the hospital for the next few months. It is fortunate that my injury intervened before I could singlehandedly lose the war in the Pacific. What my high scores on the army's language aptitude test didn't reveal was, as I discovered when Fritz tried to teach me German (and later when I tried to learn French in college), that I have a terrible ear for language. This left me with considerable skepticism about using written tests as the decisive factor in peoples' lives.

Joseph Burkholder Smith, who did join the Japanese program (and later became a member of the CIA), occupied a bed adjoining mine when I moved from the private room to the ward. Joe became my literary mentor. He started me off with the Studs Lonigan trilogy by James T. Farrell. There was enough steamy sex (for that era) to keep me turning the pages quickly and to convince me that Joe was an authority to whose counsel I should attend. Next he launched me on another trilogy, *USA* by John Dos Passos. Soon I was reading Fitzgerald, Sinclair Lewis, Sherwood Anderson, Faulkner, Hemingway, and practically all the plays of Eugene O'Neill.

The hospital's information and education officer, a lieutenant from Oberlin, introduced me to a writer named George Seldes, the iconoclastic leftist who published a small newsletter called *In Fact*. Seldes made me aware for the first time of the American press's tendency to suppress news that would disturb its advertisers, especially big ones like the tobacco companies.

Sometime during this period, I became a socialist. Seldes was certainly influential in the process, as was the moving description of Eugene Debs in *USA* and a book by John Strachey called *The Coming Struggle for Power*.

My socialist beliefs did not endure for more than a year or two—with one exception. And that was based not on what I read but on what I observed firsthand about medical care in the army. At Fort McLellan it was excellent. Good doctors had been drafted. Though their salaries were modest compared to what they could have been making in private practice, they were diligent and conscientious.

The care was even better at Ashford General Hospital, to which I was transferred in October 1945. Before the war, Ashford had been the Greenbrier Hotel, a beautiful mountain resort in West Virginia, a hundred miles east of Charleston. The army commandeered it and turned into a showplace hospital. Severely wounded soldiers were flown there from France and Germany, and it was where the brass came for rest and recuperation. One day I found myself standing next to Dwight Eisenhower in the lobby. Because there were so many higher-ups around, the place was run much more the way a hospital should be than the way most really are.

I became an advocate of a national health service, in which good doctors would be required to participate as they did during the war and which would give the same quality care to rich and poor alike, as was the case with the privates and generals at Ashford. I believe in this form of socialism because I saw it work.

# CHAPTER **3**

# A New York Snob

I WAS discharged from the army in January 1946 and immediately went to New York City to enter Columbia College. While in the hospital, I had read *Teacher in America* by Jacques Barzun, one of the luminaries of the Columbia faculty. Barzun's description of the college was seductive. It was not gigantic, like the university of which it was a part, but had only 1,750 students and small classes, averaging twenty students or so. More surprising, those small classes were taught, even at the freshman level, by the brightest stars of the faculty—people like Barzun and Lionel Trilling and Mark Van Doren—rather than by the graduate students my friends who went to other prominent universities often got stuck with.

As Barzun's book implied, teaching was important at Columbia. In the fall of 1946, for example, Trilling taught eleven hours a week. Today's average in the Ivy League is more like five hours. And, as Barzun explained, this teaching served an overall educational objective, which was to make sure that every student was introduced to the basics of Western civilization. All students were required to take courses that introduced them to the major works of literature, art, and music as well as to the thought of the great philosophers, economists, and historians. Having leafed through the bulletins of other colleges, which listed a bewildering array of electives with no discernible purpose, I welcomed this deprivation of free choice.

As an intellectual experience, Columbia more than met my expectations. Most of the classes *were* small; most of the teachers *were* outstanding. But I had come to Columbia not just to be educated but to live the life of a New Yorker. I had access to that life because it was cheap. Even a student of modest means could enjoy the city. Tuition was $225 per term. A glass of beer cost a dime, so you could have a full evening of intense discussion and fairly intense drinking for a dollar or so. The subway was only a nickel as 1946 began. One snowy night in late January, I took the IRT from the Columbia stop at 116th and Broadway to Greenwich Village, getting off at Sheridan Square and buying a copy of the *Daily Worker*. I felt deliciously radical with my upturned coat collar and my scarf blowing in the wind. Later, in April and May, the same nickel would buy a ride on an open-topped double-decker bus that would take you down to Washington Square or up to the Cloisters—a perfect answer to those warm spring afternoons when you weren't going to get any studying done anyway. There were lots of inexpensive French and Italian restaurants, like Le Champlain, La Fleur de Lis, and Barbetta's, where dinner with a glass of wine could be had for less than three dollars.

Watching classic films in the theater at the Museum of Modern Art cost forty cents. Eddie Condon's jazz concerts at Town Hall were little more than a dollar. You could spend an evening at clubs like Jimmy Ryan's or the Three Deuces on 52nd Street for only two dollars or so.

Theater, concert, opera, and ballet tickets could be had for less than two dollars if you didn't mind sitting at the top of the balcony, and I didn't mind at all. Any time I wanted to hear the New York Philharmonic or another great orchestra, I could get into Carnegie Hall free, courtesy of Norman Eliason, who was an usher there and lived on the same floor I did in John Jay Hall. Betty Combs, a voice student and my first New York girl friend, gave me a free introduction to *Der Rosenkavalier* and her other favorite operas. This did not take place at the Met but by listening to records in her teacher's studio apartment in a brownstone in the West Sixties, which he let us use Friday and Saturday nights. I liked the music, but my main interest was Betty. To be alone with a pretty girl in a brownstone apartment in New York, even though our behavior was relatively chaste, was, like buying the *Daily Worker* in Sheridan Square, very close to the heart of what I had hoped life in the city would be.

And of course there was the theater. In just my first term at Columbia, I saw Gertrude Lawrence in *Pygmalion*, the then-unknown Marlon Brando playing Marchbanks to Katherine Cornell's Candida, Paul Douglas and Judy Holliday in *Born Yesterday* (their first starring roles), and Ethel Merman in *Annie Get Your Gun*. The following season I saw the original production of Eugene O'Neill's *The Iceman Cometh*, Lerner and Loewe's *Brigadoon*, and *The Importance of Being Earnest*, with John Gielgud as Worthing and Margaret Rutherford as Lady Bracknell.

The 1947–48 season brought the original production of *A Streetcar Named Desire*, with Marlon Brando playing Stanley Kowalski. I saw a Saturday matinee performance, and that evening I tried to play Brando with my date, who proceeded to walk indignantly out of my life.

The next year came *South Pacific*, *Kiss Me Kate*, and the original *Death of a Salesman*, with Lee J. Cobb as Willy Loman. Remember, all these shows opened in just the three and a half years when I was a student at Columbia College. I do not believe that there has been a comparable period of creativity in the history of the American theater.

One of the most impressive things about Columbia in the late forties was the brainpower of its students. They were, for the most part, not from the social elite—Jason Epstein was the only person I knew who had gone to prep school. They were drawn largely from two groups. One was World War II veterans. Several of them were my friends: Bob Williams, who had endured the frightening disintegration of the 106th Division during the Battle of the Bulge; John Uhl and Don Kirchoffer, who had served in the navy; and Ned Gatchell, who had been a bomber pilot and had flown those hair-raising daylight missions over Germany. I was nineteen when I entered Columbia, but most of the other veterans were two to six years older and therefore more mature and much less likely to waste time than the average college student. They were tough competition.

Only a little less tough, however, was the next largest group of students, the bright high school graduates from New York City, like my friend Steve Marcus. Because there were so many applicants from the city, they were subjected to more demanding admission standards than the rest of us. Columbia had a Jewish quota then, which meant that if you were from New York *and* Jewish, you had to be even brighter to get in. To those of us who were their less diligent classroom competition, these New Yorkers seemed demonic in their devotion to academic excellence—they'd get off the subway at 8:00 A.M., go directly to the library in South Hall, and stay there, except for meals and classes, until it closed, studying every minute. Norman Podhoretz, who later became editor of *Commentary* and a leading neoconservative, was a member of this group.

I knew Podhoretz as someone who attended a class with me, not as a friend or even an acquaintance. The course we took together was in twentieth-century fiction, taught by Harrison Steeves. Since the lures of life in New York often left me less than prepared for the morning's discussion, I sat in the back of the room. Podhoretz sat in the front and was always prepared. He was constantly waving his hand, constantly talking, constantly trying to impress the professor.

The problem was that Podhoretz was a Jew from Brooklyn and Steeves was a snobbish old Wasp with little patience for the upwardly mobile. However brilliant Podhoretz might be, Steeves would not give him the recognition he so avidly sought. Steeves bestowed his regard, instead, on one Donald Maher, a reserved young man with the right accent.

The juxtapositon of Podhoretz and Steeves was hilarious to those of us on the back benches. But our laughter did not reflect personal animosity (as Podhoretz suggests in his book, *Making It*). Indeed, most of us were grateful to him for deferring the dread moment when Steeves might ask, "Well, Mr. Peters, you haven't said much lately. Why don't you tell us what you think Proust is trying to say?"

Several of my other classmates later made their marks on the world. One who did, and who probably influenced me more than anyone, I met on an October afternoon in 1946. I was with about twenty other students in Trilling's Humanities 3 class, discussing William Blake's *Songs of Innocence*. I noticed that some of the most thoughtful observations were being made by a dark, slight young man who was sitting in that day.

When the class broke up, I wanted to ask him about some of the things he had said, and I spoke with him as we walked out of Hamilton Hall, around to 116th Street, and on to the Amsterdam Avenue bus stop. Apparently we were headed in the same direction, for, still talking, we boarded the same bus. The conversation continued until I reached my stop. "I get off here," I said. "So do I," he said. We walked from the bus stop to my apartment building at 200 West 92nd Street. "Well this is where I live," I said. "So do I," he said. It was time to introduce ourselves. His name was Allen Ginsberg. He lived on the second floor; I lived on the fourth.

Allen and I became friends. He opened up a new world for me, introducing me to people like Jack Kerouac and Neal Cassady, people who were much more open and much less careerist than the typical Columbia student of that time. Sometimes I thought they were crazy, but more often I found myself liking their unconventionality.

One of the most appealing aspects of their unconventionality was that they didn't push it. Once, at a party, Kerouac took me into a bedroom to show me pictures of Arab boys in various postures of sexual abandon. It was obvious that Jack thought they might stimulate certain thoughts in my mind. But when I asked him instead about an attractive girl in the front room, he cheerfully put away the pictures and told me, "She works for United Press and is from Mt. Airy, North Carolina. I'll introduce you."

I liked Allen best. When you talked to him you knew he really heard what you were saying. The barriers of pride and self-image that inhibit real communication between people were so slight in Allen that he could strip them away instantly when you were trying to get through to him. In his gentleness and his indifference to material things, he was almost otherworldly. One day we went to the Frick Museum, where, directly opposite the El Greco that occupies the most prominent position in the main room is a St. Francis by Bellini, and we stopped to look at it. As we stood there I thought, of course there aren't saints any more, but Allen comes closer than most of us. I may have idealized Allen and Jack and Neal—Jack and Neal, in particular, had tormented undercurrents in their lives that I was unaware of—but my idealized version provided what was, for me, an important alternative to the Podhoretzes and the veterans, who were all preparing to don gray flannel suits.

The reason I was living on 92nd Street was that toward the end of my first term I had decided I didn't like life in a dormitory. The rooms were tiny and institutional, and, worst of all, women were not permitted above the ground floor. So Bob Williams and I launched an apartment search that consumed most of our afternoons for several weeks. Apartments were as scarce in New York in the spring of 1946 as they are today. I think the last time they were plentiful must have been in the thirties. We trudged along every street in the Village without success. Then we decided to go down Broadway, starting at 116th Street, where Columbia is, and stopping at every apartment building or real estate office along the way. At building after building and office after office, the word was "no vacancy" or "fully rented." Finally, at a 94th Street realtor's, there was good news. The agent told us that a Mrs. Goldhurst had come in that morning saying she wanted to rent two rooms of her apartment: "Maybe you'll find a couple of law students from Columbia for me." I said I was a prelaw student and that we were both from Columbia.

"Well," said the agent, "she's a very charming lady. Around forty-five, I'd say. Lives alone. I think she said she and her husband have separated. Anyway, here's her office phone number. I'm sure the apartment is very nice."

I had visions of a forties version of Mrs. Robinson, mature but still attractive, lonely, and lusting in her luxurious apartment. We called Mrs. Goldhurst immediately and arranged to meet at her place that evening. The address was 200 West 92nd Street.

As we approached the building, the luxurious part of my vision began to fade. The building was at the corner of 92nd and Amsterdam Avenue. It clearly had seen better days, and even then it had not been luxurious. Amsterdam Avenue was almost entirely Irish and almost entirely lower middle class or a step beneath; 200 West 92nd Street was a step beneath. We climbed a dark and dingy stairwell to the fourth floor. Mrs. Goldhurst opened the door. She was about five feet tall and must have weighed around 160 pounds. Her hair was steely gray, she had the shoulders of a linebacker, and her jaw made Dick Tracy's look weak.

She led us down the hallway to two modestly furnished rooms that looked out on 92nd Street. Then she showed us the bathroom, which had an old-fashioned chain-pull toilet and a tub of similar vintage. The kitchen looked as if it had been painted around the turn of the century and the fixtures bought about the same time. You could see the lathing through several gaping holes in the plaster.

This was not the apartment of our dreams, and Mrs. Goldhurst definitely was not Mrs. Robinson. She was better. Bawdy and full of life, she was a female Falstaff. She had us laughing in minutes, and within an hour we were enjoying ourselves so thoroughly that there was no question we would take the rooms. The rent was low, and Mrs. Goldhurst said that whenever we wanted she would cook dinner for us for a dollar each.

She became the central figure in my life for the next seven years. During most of that time I was either living in her apartment or dining at her table. From the spring of 1946 until the spring of 1948, I did both.

Her full name was Genevieve Gallagher Goldhurst,

but everyone called her Tiny. She was born to an Irish family in Scranton, Pennsylvania. She moved to New York to work in the early twenties and married a man named Harry Goldhurst.

Harry was on Wall Street, and in the twenties that meant doing well. Tiny and Harry settled in a prosperous suburb, Larchmont, in Westchester County. Soon there were four sons—Richard, William, Harry, Jr., and Peter.

Then came the crash and with it the discovery that Harry had been a pioneer in what might be called the Boesky-Levine approach to the science of investing. A term in a federal penal institution ensued. By the time Harry got out, the 1939 New York World's Fair was about to open. He figured the city would be flooded with tourists. So what was the smart thing to do? Get into the hotel business, of course. He settled Tiny and the boys in Redbank, New Jersey, bought a hotel on Times Square, and started planning how to spend all the money he was going to make. Unfortunately, the tourists never came, at least not to Harry's hotel. His only regular guests were a troop of vaudeville midgets, who did not rank prompt payment of hotel bills high on their list of priorities. The result was that Harry went broke. In fact, he was worse than broke. He owed a lot of money, and his creditors were in hot pursuit. Harry felt it would be prudent to disappear for a while.

When he resurfaced several years later, it was as Harry Golden, editor and homespun philosopher, of Charlotte, North Carolina. He had failed again with another improbable enterprise called Midas Mineral Spring Water. The brochure read: "Since 1608 Indians have known its restorative powers." Cynics suspected that the "spring" was a broken pipe. But Harry was not easily discouraged. He started a weekly newspaper called *The Carolina Israelite*. There weren't many Jews in North Carolina, so for a while it appeared that the Israelite would share the fate of his other enterprises. Then he had an inspiration: he created the Carolina Israelite Award and bestowed it on Bernard Baruch, the reknowned financier and presidential adviser. Harry suspected, reasonably enough, that Baruch was an egomaniac and probably couldn't resist coming to Charlotte to accept the award and address a dinner in his honor. His suspicion turned out to be well founded. The great man came to Charlotte, and the locals were impressed. They might not have heard of Harry Golden, but they had certainly heard of Bernard Baruch. Advertisers began to include the *Israelite* in their schedules. Harry wasn't rich by any means, but at least he could afford to send for two of his sons, Billy and Harry, Jr. They were in North Carolina at the time of my arrival at 92nd Street. Dick was in the army in Japan, and Peter, who was retarded, had just been placed in an institution.

During the war years, Tiny had supported all four boys. This had not left her feeling too kindly toward Harry. In fact, his multitude of failings, and those of his sister Clara, were the subject of many of Tiny's most hilarious stories.

One thing about Tiny's storytelling took a little getting used to. She would assume you knew all the characters. When she mentioned Sam, she did not bother to explain who he was. It usually took half the story to figure it out, and sometimes it took several stories over several months before you had him clearly in your mind. But you were never to interrupt with a question like "Who's Sam?"

Gradually, however, we got to know her regular cast of characters. Our favorite was Hazel, the nymphomaniac. When Hazel's name came up in a story, you always knew what she was doing or, if she wasn't doing it, you knew that she was thinking about it.

But Hazel was a minor character compared to Harry. However he may have wronged Tiny, he continued to occupy the center stage of her stories. I understood why when I met him in 1947. Expecting to dislike him because he had run out on his family, I was totally charmed. Within an hour or so we were singing "Stand Up for Jesus" together. Harry later wrote *Only in America* and several other best-selling books and achieved considerable fame.

So did some others who passed through Tiny's apartment as roomers or as frequent dinner guests, including Ginsberg and E.L. Doctorow, whom we knew as Eddie or Edgar. James Lee went on to Hollywood, where he wrote many movie and television scripts, including "Roots." But Tiny Goldhurst was the star of 92nd Street.

Of those who both lived and dined with Tiny over a considerable period of time, I was closest to Jimmy Lee and Dick Goldhurst, Tiny's oldest son. Jimmy had the kind of beguiling wit that made you not want the evening to end and an interest in women that was even keener than mine. Dick was warm and kind, with the soul of a poet and, like his mother, the body of a football player. His burliness was an important protection for the rest of us, because Quinn and Kling's, the neighborhood bar where we hung out, did not include among its many endearing virtues a guarantee that there wouldn't be a fistfight or brawl on any given night.

A typical evening at Tiny's would find two or three of us already seated at the table when Tiny arrived around 6:00 P.M. loaded down with bags of groceries and exhausted by a hard day's work as an office manager for a small printing company. After depositing the groceries in the kitchen, she would return to the dining room, which was also her bedroom, to sit wearily on the sofa, which was also her bed, and light a cigarette.

Her spirits would gradually brighten as she told us an amusing story about the competition between Harry and Martin, her two bosses, for the affection of the office blonde. Soon we would all be laughing, and Tiny would go to the kitchen to prepare the spaghetti and cheesecake, which was the menu at least every other night, while the rest of us continued talking. Tiny didn't have a television set, so we had to entertain ourselves.

The talk often turned to our fascination with the character of the incompetent confidence man played by Groucho Marx and W.C. Fields. Our favorite movies were *Duck Soup*, *A Night at the Opera*, *My Little Chickadee*, and *The Bank Dick*. Sometimes we created our own scenarios. One was about how Franz Kafka was really still alive, hidden in a Budapest attic by his literary executor, Max Brod. Brod, played in our imagination by Sam Levine, had taken advantage of the great writer's paranoia to convince him that he was his protector: "Franz, baby, I'm the only thing standing between you and all the schnooks in Buda, not to mention those in Pest." Brod would arrive each day in a limousine paid for by the proceeds of Kafka's books to give the writer a stale bagel and pick up the manuscripts that Brod would publish— "I feel it is my duty to share these posthumous literary discoveries with the world"—and for which he would piously pocket the royalty checks. If *The Producers* had been made back then, Mel Brooks would have been our God.

When we weren't talking, we were singing. I would lobby for my favorite hymns, but only Harry Golden and a few old Sunday school friends from Charleston really shared my affection for them. Gershwin, Porter, and Rodgers and Hart usually won out at 92nd Street.

And then there were the musical equivalents of Franz Kafka and Max Brod, with lyrics we came up with on our own. One was inspired by a fling Jimmy and I had playing the horses. To the tune of "Battle Hymn of the Republic," it went: "I have been to Hialeah, Narragansett, Churchill Downs, and you'll never catch me hanging 'round any trackless town. I have won the Daily Double and I'll win again today, as they come racing home. Take me, take me to Jamaica. Take me, take me to Jamaica. Take me, take me to Jamaica, I know I'll win today." (Jamaica was a New York race track of such singular unattractiveness that it was patronized only by those hopelessly addicted to the ponies.)

I had been interested in racing ever since Uncle Lloyd took me to my first Kentucky Derby at the age of eight, but I had never made bets except at the track. Now I had a bookie at 110th and Broadway.

I began with an academic interest in comparing the various handicappers employed by the New York papers. Gradually my focus narrowed to two: Frank Ortell of the *World Telegram* and Joe Gelardi of the International News Service. As I studied various combinations of their predictions, a remarkable pattern emerged: if Gelardi picked a horse to place and Ortell picked him to win, place, or show, a show bet on that horse would pay off often enough to produce a steady, if modest, profit.

I urged Jimmy to join me in pursuing this investment opportunity. We each put up ten dollars. I then inquired at neighborhood bars as to the whereabouts of a suitable bookie and soon located the gentleman at 110th and Broadway. The project was launched with two-dollar bets on Brags Rags and Northern Deb at Hialeah. Both finished in the money and they paid a total of seventeen dollars, considerably better than show bets usually do. I began to bet every day, the bookie's hangout being conveniently located between Columbia and my apartment. Incredibly, we continued to win—never as much as on the first day, but each week still produced a modest profit. Then the bookie stopped accepting our show bets and demanded that from now on we bet to win. Instead of getting out, we tried to do it his way and lost all our profits as well as our original twenty dollars.

We often had guests for dinner at 92nd Street—friends from Columbia or the theater or people like Doctorow, who went to Kenyon College with Dick and Billy. Occasionally, someone would just appear. One of these was Herbert Huncke, whom we knew through Ginsberg. Allen had met him in the Automat on 42nd Street between 7th and 8th Avenues, which was a headquarters for junkies and petty criminals. Herbert was both. He was slight, dark, and fine-featured. He moved, Kerouac once observed, like an Arab. You could easily picture him sneaking into a house or picking a pocket. When he appeared at 92nd Street, good fellowship was not his only motive. He was usually trying to sell us something, and that something, one suspected, often was not in the hands of its rightful owner. If he was especially impecunious, Herbert would ask for the empty bottles in the apartment, which he could sell for a few cents apiece. Tiny always gave him the bottles and occasionally bought his merchandise, although the buying was done with a mournful sigh and an upward roll of the eyes as she contemplated the current penalty for receiving stolen goods.

Allen's taste for minor criminals once nearly got me in trouble. Although I continued to eat at Tiny's, in April 1948 I moved to an apartment of my own. One night around 2:00 A.M., Ginsberg, Kerouac, and Huncke arrived for a visit. That wasn't unusual, except that this time they brought along an exotic young woman—I'll call her Susie instead of using her real name, since her life has subsequently taken a respectable turn.

Susie and I hit it off. The next night, she called and asked if she could come by and take a bath. I said fine. When she emerged from the bathroom, she said she had had an inspiration. My apartment would be a perfect place for her to use for scoring with johns. Susie, it seemed, was a prostitute. She had a notebook full of clients. All she needed was a place to do business—a "pad," as she put it. Although I was anxious to make a favorable impression on Allen's friends, I said no.

Allen was not as successful at avoiding trouble. A few weeks after Susie visited my apartment, I was on the subway, reading the *Daily Mirror* over the shoulder of the person standing next to me. When he turned to the back page, I saw a large photograph of four people staring out of the rear of a paddy wagon—Allen, Susie, Herbert, and their friend Little Jack Melody.

They had been driving around Queens with Little Jack at the wheel when they were stopped by a policeman who wanted to tell them they were going the wrong way on a one-way street. Little Jack, mindful of the possible misunderstanding that might arise from the fact that the car was stolen, did not wait to hear the officer out. Instead, he jammed the accelerator to the floor and sped off into the night. As he attempted to negotiate a sharp corner, the car turned over, and its occupants quickly scattered. Allen returned to his apartment on York Avenue. He opened the door, thinking he was safe at last, only to be greeted by several city officials in blue uniforms. It seems that Allen had left his diary in the car and that it contained his address. (I can't explain why he took his diary on a joy ride through Queens or, for that matter, why they chose Queens in the first place.) Allen had made another mistake: he had permitted Little Jack and Herbert to use his apartment for storage, and, you guessed it, among the stored goods there were few that were the legal property of either Herbert or Little Jack. To beat the rap, Allen had to commit himself to the care of psychiatrists at Payne Whitney.

There are dramatic differences between Charleston and New York, and by the end of my first year at Columbia, those differences were beginning to have an effect on me. Charleston is the small town where practically everyone knows you or your family. The good side of this is that it encourages you to behave thoughtfully toward others. If you're a clerk in a store and you're rude to Mrs. Jones, it is likely that she knows several people who know you and that she will tell them about it. Also, when people have known you well for your entire life, they aren't likely to mistake you for either the purest saint or the most evil sinner. Their knowledge of you is protection against unjust accusation as well as unwarranted praise.

But all this is limiting, too, which is why many people want to escape small towns. They want to be more than they have been. Someone in New York might hire them to do great things, while the small-town employer would know their limits all too well. In other words, the song's promise—"If you can make it there, you'll make it anywhere"—is misleading. Some people make it in New York because they *couldn't* make it back home. They never would have gotten the chance.

New York also offers anonymity. Your private life can be your own business and no one else's in a way that's impossible in a small town. But anonymity also means that, even after living in New York for years, you can walk all the way down Fifth Avenue and not be recognized by a single human being. This may explain why so many people who go to New York thinking that they want anonymity end up trying to be celebrities or envying those who are. Some even seek identity through contact with celebrities. The most extreme example is the horde of autograph-seekers that follows in the wake of anyone famous. Telling their friends about having seen a celebrity, and proving it by showing his autograph, endows them with importance and gives them something to talk about.

I was not immune to celebrityism. Having met a few of the famous during my years in New York—including Grace Kelly, John Huston, Ingrid Bergman, and William Faulkner—I became skilled at casually weaving these brief encounters into conversations with my friends and acquaintances. I could get a sense of importance even by knowing someone who knew a celebrity—"She's a close friend of Tennessee Williams, you know." A similar sense of self-importance can come—and this is especially so in the case of intellectuals—from knowing something others don't, from being among the first to divine what's in and what's out in literature and in the arts.

By 1947, I was getting pretty heavily involved in this sort of thing. In other words, I had become a snob. One reason was the transfer of my career interest from politics to the theater, which had happened the previous summer. In politics, snobbery is likely to lose you votes. In the arts, it can be viewed as evidence of your higher powers of discrimination.

But a more important cause in my case was insecurity. From the secure world of Charleston High School, where I was "most likely to succeed" in my class, I had entered a world where what I considered my exceptional promise was not instantly recognized. There were a lot of very bright students who were better prepared for Columbia than I was.

During my first term I puzzled over the phrase "perne in a gyre" in "Sailing to Byzantium." Should I confess, I wondered, that I hadn't a clue as to what it meant? Of course not—I would only confirm that I was a hick from West Virginia. So I slipped off to the library to consult *A Vision*, the book in which Yeats explains his philosophy. But instead of enlightenment, I encountered even greater obscurity in those bewildering diagrams of intersecting cones, and my anxiety became worse.

I finished the first term with two As and four Bs. Although a perfectly respectable record in retrospect, it opened a crack of doubt in my academic self-assurance. At Charleston High School I had gotten As without unseemly sweat. Now it was clear that I would not get many unless I became a grind. I enjoyed the pleasures of New York far too much to take that possibility seriously.

Instead, I gradually became a snob, trying to impress others not with my performance but with my awareness of what was intellectually chic. I could talk knowingly about the latest literary controversy or casually drop the names of the authors who were "in." In the library I would feign total immersion in Baudelaire, especially if a Barnard girl was sitting nearby. The only movie theater I would deign to enter was the Thalia on West 95th Street. It featured ancient classics as well as the work of the French and Italian directors who were fashionable in the forties and who seemed to have a special fondness for overexposed film and scratchy sound tracks.

This was a period during which you could not, as I secretly did, admire a Victorian house or the beaux arts splendor of Grand Central Station. Picasso was in, and so was Henry James. I liked neither, but I pretended that I did. The first minutes of an encounter with someone you wanted to impress were spent flashing your taste badges. And your worst fear was that you might flash the wrong one, that you might be praising last year's poet instead of this year's. So you made sure to keep abreast of those publications that could keep you informed of what was in and what was out—the *New Yorker* and the *Partisan Review* were the essential ones.

My grades began to plummet. I was afraid to commit myself to the effort that might produce an A and then have to face the fact that I couldn't make it even when I was really trying.

In January 1948 I got a call from the dean's office about my sinking grades. This resulted in a referral to a psychiatrist. I knew I had lost my way and needed help. I was turning into someone I didn't like at all, and I was ready to open myself to someone who wanted to come to my rescue. I was lucky enough to find a really kind and caring doctor.

At the same time that I was seeing the psychiatrist, another benign influence appeared in my life. That spring, Van Doren offered a remarkable course that began with Kafka's *The Trial* and *The Castle*, continued through *The Divine Comedy*, and ended with *Don Quixote*. It was a progression from lost bewilderment to what became my true faith—that I had to pursue my own vision even if the rest of the world thought I was only tilting at windmills.

During the worst of my snobbish period, I was fortunate to have friends like Tiny and Jimmy and Dick, who could laugh away my pretentiousness. And then there was Allen, who was constantly saying, "Come down," by which he meant strip away all the posturing that separates you from your true self. Allen himself was not above impressing people with his sophistication. And in that sense he was part of my problem. Occasionally, he would suggest that it was hip to smoke marijuana (he called it "tea") or to be gay, but most of the time when we talked, I felt that he was not trying to impress me and that I did not have to try to impress him.

Another factor in my salvation was sports. A baseball or football fan quickly discovers that the blue-collar worker sitting in the bleachers is just as likely to be able to discuss the finer points of the game as a Ph.D. from Harvard. It was the same lesson about people that I had learned in the army and at Charleston High, but during my most snobbish period, in 1947, its only reinforcement came when I went to Ebbets Field or Yankee Stadium.

A few years later, my interest in baseball may have saved my life. It was a Sunday afternoon—or maybe Labor Day—in early September 1951. The New York Giants and the Brooklyn Dodgers were locked in one of the great pennant races of the era, the one that ended with Bobby Thomson's famous home run. I was dating a young woman from Brooklyn whose father was not only hot-tempered but highly, and rightly, suspicious of my intentions toward his daughter. The one thing he and I had in common was baseball.

On this particular afternoon, he had gone to the beach and his daughter and I had the apartment to ourselves. We watched the Giants and Dodgers on the living room television for a few innings, but mutual affection soon led us into her bedroom. The situation was developing along natural lines when suddenly we heard the front door open and someone walk in. She whispered, "Oh my God, it's my father." This presented several problems, not the least of which was how we were going to get from the bedroom to the living room unobserved. There was a clear view from the front door down the hallway that we would have to cross, so it was not going to be easy. We were given a moment's reprieve when we heard the father go into the kitchen. In that moment, she slipped into her dress and rushed down the hall to greet him and keep him in the kitchen so I could put on my pants and shirt and sneak into the living room. By the time he entered the room, I was sitting before the television set absorbed in the game. He greeted me and sat down to watch, but I sensed that I was not yet out of the woods. For one thing, I had not managed to get my shoes on. The daughter's disheveled aspect, which I probably shared, might also arouse suspicion. But when the father complained that he had missed the last inning coming from the beach, I saw an opportunity to lay his suspicions to rest. I immediately launched into: "With the Giants leading two to nothing and one out, Snider doubled off Maglie, then Robinson tripled, scoring Snider, but with Robinson on third, Pafko hit a scorcher down the third base line. Thomson grabbed it, tagged Robinson, and threw to Lockman at first for a double play." Although he was disappointed that the Dodgers had blown an opportunity to tie the score, he was obviously reassured that I had been attending so closely to the game. This feeling, unfortunately, was not shared by his daughter, who realized that I had been listening while we were in bed. She refused to be comforted by my involved explanation of how the human mind can operate on two levels.

# CHAPTER 4

# From the Theater to Politics

**B**Y the spring of 1948, my elitism was crumbling. The final blow came as a result of a commitment I had made to start a summer theater in Charleston that summer. As the season drew closer, I was increasingly immersed in the real world of practical decision making. Earlier I might have tried to impress my friends in New York by talking about how "interesting" it would be to produce *The Dog Beneath the Skin* by W.H. Auden and Christopher Isherwood. I now had to focus not on what would make me seem sophisticated but on what would entertain the people I knew in Charleston.

I had become involved in the theater purely by chance a couple of years earlier. I had entered Columbia as a prelaw student, intending to go on to law school and then join my father's firm and embark on a career in politics. That plan was temporarily derailed in 1946 when I was offered a chance to work in a summer theater in Boylston, Massachusetts. The offer came about this way: I had gone to the Biltmore Hotel to see my parents, who were visiting New York. On my way out, I spotted two friends from Charleston—Angus Peyton and Bob Kearse—having a drink in the Palm Court. After chatting a while, they asked me to join them at a night club called The Blue Angel, where they were meeting Bob's sister, Maggie, and her husband, Don Richardson.

Maggie was an actress. She was playing a maid in *Life with Father*, one of the most successful plays of the forties. Her role may have been small, but I knew that getting on Broadway in any role was a considerable accomplishment, and I was impressed. Her husband, Don, had most recently served as assistant director of Robert Sherwood's *The Rugged Path*. That night he was full of stories about the play's talented director, Garson Kanin, its star, Spencer Tracy, and Tracy's girl friend, Katharine Hepburn. All this was very glamorous, so I made a point of keeping in touch with the Richardsons. It turned out that Don and I shared a passion for Shaw. We would take long walks in Central Park discussing the great man's ideas. That summer, when Don was hired as director of the Boylston Theater, he asked me to come along.

I was the assistant stage manager—not the most exalted function in the theater. My living quarters were even less exalted. Jimmy Lee and I (we first met at Boylston) slept in beds stretched across the lanes of a bowling alley in the basement of the theater. Nonetheless, I found life backstage fascinating. I also found that young women were just as fascinated. My experiences in summer stock lit up their eyes in a way that "prelaw" definitely did not. I decided to renounce law and politics in favor of the theater.

Another factor in this decision was that Harry Truman, the new president, was not the leader that FDR had been. I later changed my mind, but at the time he seemed much too dreary and lackluster to inspire anyone. There were none of the great causes, such as ending the Depression or winning the war, that had made public life seem so important when I was a kid. The world of *Annie Get Your Gun* and *The Iceman Cometh* seemed much more exciting.

When I returned to school that fall, I met Joe O'Reilly, a tall Arizonan who looked like a younger, skinnier Gregory Peck. He'd come to Columbia as part of a navy training program and had decided to stay on after the war. In addition to rooming with me at Mrs. Goldhurst's for one term, he got me involved, as stage manager, with the Columbia University Players, of which he was one of the principal powers. They were a talented group. Two of them—Dolph Sweet and Sorrell Booke—went on to become prominent character actors in the sixties and seventies. The director was a psychiatric student named Preston Munter. I don't know what kind of a therapist he turned out to be, but he was a very good director, gifted at getting the best out of young amateurs. I worked under him on *The Taming of the Shrew* and *Murder in the Cathedral* during the 1946–47 school year.

In the fall of 1947, Jimmy Lee and I began to talk about starting a summer theater. The dialogue was straight out of a Mickey Rooney–Judy Garland movie:

Charlie: "Why waste time trying to persuade someone else to give us jobs in summer stock? We can have our own company!"

Jimmy: "That's a great idea. We know the young talent better than most of the big producers."

Charlie: "Yeah, the whole gang from Boylston—they're all good."

Jimmy: "Joy Reese is prettier than half the ingenues on Broadway. Besides, she can act."

Charlie: "There are three or four hot talents at Columbia. Sorrell Booke is certain to be a great character actor."

Jimmy: "But what about money? We'll have to pay the Actor's Equity minimum—fifty dollars a week—and transportation from New York. Then we need sets and lighting equipment."

Charlie: "If we do it in Charleston, I'm pretty sure I can get sets and lights from the Kanawha Players. That's the little theater group I worked with when I was in high school."

Jimmy: "What about the salaries?"

Charlie: "We'll sell season tickets in advance. That's what the Players do. Maybe I can get their mailing list. They may even sponsor us."

In the summer of 1948 it all happened. Joy and Sorrell came down to Charleston, along with a set designer and five other performers from New York. Thanks largely to the intercession of my old neighbors, Mimi and Silas Pickering, who were the Lunts of the Charleston stage, the Players gave us their sets, lights, and sponsorship—and the mailing list, which produced enough season ticket orders to finance us through opening night. Individual Players volunteered their time, too, doing most of our backstage work as well as performing the roles our small New York cast couldn't fill. The last missing link was a theater. St. Matthew's Episcopal Church lent us its parish house, which had a serviceable stage and could seat an audience of about two hundred.

Our first play, definitely not by Auden and Isherwood, was a comedy called *John Loves Mary*. As we began rehearsals, we quickly discovered that we had a serious problem on our hands. The sixty-five-year-old actor we had hired to play Mary's father was more than a little deaf; he couldn't hear half his cues. Forty-eight hours before opening night, we faced up to the fact that we had to replace him. I called on Silas Pickering, whose wife already was cast as Mary's mother. But could Si learn the lines in just two days? He was a busy man with lots of other fish to fry. Rehearsals were interrupted constantly by phone calls about a contract he was negotiating between his company, Union Carbide, and a labor union. I was near despair the morning of opening night when I saw that he still didn't seem to know what act he was in, much less what he was supposed to say. But by the end of the last rehearsal at 5:30 P.M., he knew the part perfectly, and I went home to dinner optimistic about the night ahead.

Then at 7:30, just an hour before curtain time, there was a terrific thunderstorm, and all I could think was, "Nobody will come! We'll have to close tomorrow!" But the rain lasted only half an hour, people did come, and the play seemed to go well. The cast went to my house to await the review in the morning paper. It finally arrived at 2:30 A.M.: "Last night at St. Matthew's Parish House, a real cloudburst was followed by a cloudburst of laughter."

Of the remaining seven plays, all but one were successful. The failure was Molière's *Le Bourgeois Gentilhomme*. We decided to heighten its accessibility by adding songs by George Gershwin and Cole Porter, including "Of Thee I Sing," "Love Is Sweeping the Country," and "Friendship." The prospects for success of this possibly flawed aesthetic concept were not enhanced by the inability of most of the company even to carry a tune, much less sing at a professional level.

When much of the grim-faced audience departed well before the first performance was over, we decided to enliven the proceedings by having M. Jourdain, played by Jimmy, make his first entrance riding a bicycle from the back of the theater down an aisle and up a specially built ramp onto the stage. The problem was that the stage was only fifteen feet deep, which meant that Jimmy had to slam on the brakes the split second he went over the top of the ramp. One night his timing was a bit off. Fortunately, his injuries were minor.

From the summer theater experience, I learned how

hard it is to make a business work and developed a lasting respect for the entrepreneur who manages to survive. We were lean. We didn't even permit ourselves the luxury of a regular telephone—we had a pay phone in the office with a nickel taped to the wall beside it in case of an emergency. The result was that ours was the only summer theater in West Virginia and one of a handful south of the Mason-Dixon line that managed to break even.

I also learned to respect the energy and idealism of the young people in our company who worked every day of the week from 10:00 A.M. to 11:00 P.M. for miserable wages. This had a major effect on the rest of my life. I learned from them the importance of loving the work you do—and the importance of ignoring money whenever it is an obstacle to doing that work. I never loved the theater as much as they did. But when I found the work I did love, I remembered the lesson.

1948 was a good year for me. My academic decline halted in the spring term. The summer theater was a success. And though some traces remained, the worst of the snobbery period was over.

× × ×

LIFE was by no means perfect, however. My main problem was women. One of the most painful shared memories for men of my generation—those of us who reached maturity during the forties and fifties—has to be that of the young women we had known but not known. We were so exclusively concerned with impressing them, with scoring, with making out, that we seldom took the time to find out who they really were. They, in turn, seldom truly got to know us because we were determined to appear to be something we were not—cool and in control, when we were in fact scared to death.

Sometimes a girl would be real enough to break through to whatever was real in me. I remember those who did with special warmth but also with pain, because I fled from them far too quickly—usually in a matter of months.

By the time I was twenty-five I had become aware of this tendency and had begun to fight it. Two relationships followed: the first lasted more than a year, the second more than three years. I was still tempted to flee and still didn't understand why, but I was at last hanging in there long enough to really know and understand the other person—enough so that with parting came the agony of lost love. That pain finally drove me to figure out my problem. I had been looking for perfection, not because I felt I deserved it but because I thought I needed it. The young woman had to be perfect because I wasn't.

I had what I have come to call the Gable anxiety. The typical film hero of my formative years was practically flawless—strong and handsome, with an engaging personality and an appealing sense of humor. He could ride a horse, shoot a gun, or make love to a woman with equal style and skill. There was practically nothing he couldn't do. Preeminent among these leading men was Clark Gable. In my childhood and early teens, the Gable anxiety was no problem. After all, I was still a kid. But as I became a young man, I felt I had to be as flawless as Gable. What would girls think if they found out I couldn't skate or ski? I really used to worry about things like that.

My anxiety was highest during the early phase of a relationship—or, more precisely, during what I considered the crucial moment of that phase. Every good general knows there is a moment to be seized, when a bold move must be made or the tide will turn against him. A similar truth governs matters of the heart. The key moment—or so I thought during most of my teens and twenties—was the first kiss. I devoted an immense amount of psychic energy to the timing of this move. The process of courting involved first saying the right thing and then doing the

71

right thing. Once the right things had been said, once rapport had been established, it was time to do the right thing—namely, kiss the girl. When I failed to do so, it seemed to me that she knew the moment had passed (in fact, a series of cues from her had been part of the buildup), and she'd be frustrated and disappointed that I had not seized it. These feelings, as I sensed them, began to erode my confidence, and I became less and less likely to either say or do the right thing. A promising evening—often a promising relationship—would go into decline, all for want of a simple kiss at the right time.

If, on the other hand, I did kiss her at the right moment, her expectations were satisfied and my confidence was enhanced. We would both go on saying and doing the right things, and the relationship would flourish.

Sometimes the physical circumstance of the occasion would create problems. One time a young woman came to my apartment, an action that in those days was a favorable omen in itself. But I had not anticipated a major difficulty: the chair where she sat was low and deep, and it was seven or eight feet away from where I was sitting. As we talked, I was increasingly distracted by such thoughts as "Why doesn't the damn place have a sofa?" and "How am I going to bend over that chair suavely, or at least without falling down?" As I debated the pros and cons of telling her to "stand up" or "come here"—since she had made the gesture of coming to the apartment, it would be graceless to treat her as if I took her compliance for granted—the conversation became disjointed and uncomfortable. It was clear that the moment had passed.

Looking back, I realize that I greatly overestimated the importance of the right moment. I was wrong to ruin an evening berating myself as a cowardly wretch for not seizing it. Still, my advice to young men is this: When in doubt, kiss her. It is always best to act on the assumption that the person you like likes you. Some may not, and you may therefore suffer momentary embarrassment, but certainly that is preferable to never finding out about those who do.

Freud may have attached too much significance to sex. But surely he was right about its importance to one kind of person—the male in his teens and twenties. The importance I gave the kiss is just one example. Perhaps the most compelling evidence in my life was why I decided to go to graduate school.

One night in early 1949, during my senior year at Columbia, I got a call from Frederick Burkhardt, the president of Bennington College. He said that he was looking for someone to teach dramatic literature and direct the student theater at Bennington and that I had been recommended by Joseph Wood Krutch.

Seldom has my imagination been so stirred. This will be hard for readers of the eighties to understand, but in the forties, Bennington, a women's liberal arts college in Vermont, occupied a very special place in American higher education. It was legendary as the school where girls did it—in an era when most girls most definitely did not do it. They were even allowed to have men visit their rooms, which was also unheard of at the time in women's institutions of any kind.

Naturally, I expressed keen interest in this opportunity. Burkhardt then began to question me about my credentials. Here, alas, a problem arose. Professor Krutch, whose wit and wisdom made him my favorite teacher, was extremely vague about the details of life. He thought I was a graduate student when I was actually only a college senior. As my true academic status became clear to Burkhardt, his tone changed from eager interest to "Well, we'll certainly have to get together next time I'm in New York. Nice to have talked to you, Mr. Peters."

As I ruefully reflected on the care and dedication I would have brought to the casting process, I resolved that should this cup ever pass my way again, I would be ready to drink. This meant that I had to go to graduate school. So in the fall of 1949, I enrolled in Columbia's master's program in English drama and the dramatic arts.

× × ×

THE program involved studying the literature of the theater and also learning the practical side of play production. Since I was fairly well informed in both of these areas, there was a considerable rest cure aspect to this period of my life. The same appeared to be true of most of my fellow graduate students, who seemed to be marking time, trying to delay facing reality. It was possible to finish the program in one year, but most took longer. I managed to stretch it out for a little more than two years.

The only academic project that really engaged me was my master's essay on *Death of a Salesman*. It was an attack on the play's symbolism, which involved blaming society for the problems of the individual. There was, however, another, more personal, reason the play disturbed me. In the words of its author, it "touched a fear that one has lied to oneself over a period of years in relation to one's true identity and what one should be doing in the world."

I had been lying to myself about my commitment to the theater. Even though I continued to work in it, I was beginning to realize that it was not right for me. There had been a number of clues. I had turned down invitations to be the producer of the Columbia Varsity Show in 1947 and the Equity Library Theater's *The Show Off* in 1948. Each would have given me an opportunity to display my talents to a New York audience. If I had been truly serious about the theater, I would have leaped at both chances. I also would have run the summer theater again in 1949.

Instead, I spent that summer in Charleston doing nothing. I played a lot of tennis and generally enjoyed coasting on the local reputation I had earned with the previous summer's success.

I have seen this pattern in others who are doing work that is not right for them, especially when the work endows them with respectability or glamour. What drives them is not love of their work but the desire for that glamour or respectability. My affection for the theater was real, but I was beginning to realize that it wasn't enough to motivate me to consistent hard work.

× × ×

I was also realizing that my interest in politics had not gone away. I stayed up all night listening to the returns in November 1948 when Truman upset Thomas Dewey. During the months before the election, as I read about the strength of the Democratic senatorial and gubernatorial candidates around the country—in Illinois, for example, Paul Douglas was running for the Senate and Adlai Stevenson for governor—I had begun to suspect that an upset was possible. I also felt that as people came closer to the choice, Truman's hick quality, which so many people found embarrassing, would seem less important than his warmth and humanity, which was striking in contrast to Dewey's cold aloofness.

I wasn't for Henry Wallace, even though I had been fairly far to the left when I first came to Columbia. My first roommate, if not a member of the Communist party in fact, certainly was in spirit, and I was in enough agreement with him that at first this didn't bother me. But gradually the crack of doubt that had been opened in my mind by the Nazi–Soviet pact of 1939—as a twelve-year-old totally uniformed about Marxist doctrine, I was nevertheless suspicious of anyone who would make a deal with Hitler—was expanded and deepened by Russian postwar behavior in Eastern Europe. For me, the final disillusionment came with the communists' brutal takeover of democratic Czechoslovakia in March of 1948. The different positions my roommate and I were taking at this time reflected the great split that was occurring in the American liberal movement in the period 1946–48. One faction remained sympathetic toward communism and the Soviet Union, as almost the entire left had been during the war. The other faction—of which one of my teachers, Lionel Trilling, was a leader—refused to ignore what the Russians were doing in Eastern Europe.

The two factions clashed repeatedly: in the split between the Liberal and the American Labor parties in New York; in connection with a conference of intellectuals at the Waldorf; at an American Veterans Committee convention in Des Moines; and, most visibly, in the 1948 presidential campaign.

I remember a Wallace rally at the MacMillan Theater on the Columbia campus. Van Doren spoke movingly, as did Wallace, but all of the other speakers delivered harangues in the numbingly predictable idiom of conventional Marxism, which I could not bear. I doubted that the rest of the country could bear it either.

So I began the election night of 1948 with a little more hope than most Democrats but still fearing that defeat was probable. As the returns came in, I became increasingly excited. I remember my frustration around 5:00 A.M. when the result became clear and there was no one I could call to share my joy. None of my New York friends cared enough about the election to stay up that late.

In the spring of 1949 I volunteered to work for Franklin Roosevelt, Jr., who was running in a special election for Congress from the Manhattan district where I lived. His headquarters was in the the Graystone Hotel, at Broadway and 91st, just around the corner from Tiny's. I handed out leaflets and performed other lowly tasks. What was memorable about the campaign was the magnetism of FDR Jr., then young, handsome, vigorous, and endowed with the aura of the magic name. Children followed him in the streets. He could attract large crowds within moments of stopping at a corner. He won by a wide margin. Eleven years later, I saw him in West Virginia, campaigning for John Kennedy. Roosevelt had become a drunk, and now Kennedy was fulfilling FDR Jr.'s once bright promise.

In 1951, I worked in the campaign of Rudolph Halley for president of the New York city council. And in 1952, I was swept up in the enthusiasm for Adlai Stevenson. Again, I was mostly handing out leaflets. This is not easy to do in New York. Almost everyone lives in apartment buildings with locks and buzzer systems to keep out strangers. Even when I found a way to get into the buildings, there was the problem of persuading people to open their doors. Countless evenings I ended up hoarse from shouting through closed doors to tenants who were too suspicious to open up but curious enough to be willing to listen if I was willing to shout. Unfortunately, the noise often brought the super charging down the hall to evict me.

My father remained active in politics during my years in New York. His greatest moment came in 1949, when he sponsored a bill in the state legislature to control air pollution in West Virginia. With tireless support from my mother, who mobilized the League of Women Voters, he got the bill passed by the House of Delegates, but it was killed in the Senate by the lobbyists for DuPont, Union Carbide, and the other companies that were doing the polluting. Still, I thought my father had made a magnificent effort—this was twenty years before the Environmental Protection Agency came into existence—and I had a nagging sense that what he was doing was far more important than my work in the theater. Two years later, in 1951, something happened that transformed this nagging sense into a conviction that politics was in my blood and would be my life.

Louis Kronenberger, the theater critic for *Time*, was teaching Restoration drama that year at Columbia. He offered to recommend me for a job at Time-Life. I was completely unqualified, having had no experience in journalism. Still, I was fascinated by the possibility and pursued it through the fall of 1951, gradually realizing that my desire for the job reflected the continuing strength of my old interest in politics and public affairs. After a series of four or five interviews, the competition finally narrowed down to a fellow who had been an editor of the *Yale Daily News* and me. He got the job, but I knew then that I was going to find some way of following in my father's footsteps.

In the meantime, I had to get a job, and the only experience I had was in the theater. Advertising agencies, because they produced most television programs in those days, were among the few employers interested in people with backgrounds like mine. So, early in 1952, I went to work for J. Walter Thompson.

Madison Avenue occupied a peculiar position in American culture at that time. It had recently been "exposed" in a best-selling novel, *The Hucksters*. Yet when the book was made into a movie, its adman-hero was played by Clark Gable, and women like Deborah Kerr and Ava Gardner were attracted to him. In other words, one had the sense that this might not be the worthiest of enterprises, but it was certainly glamorous and exciting.

There were no Gables or Kerrs or Gardners at J. Walter Thompson. Instead, there were a lot of very nice people, most of whom spent their day in a state of fright that made them behave like sharks. The reason for the fright was that everyone knew that clients could make irrational decisions. An agency might have devised a perfectly good campaign, but the client's president could go to a cocktail party and meet someone from another agency who would seduce him with charm and cleverness. Or perhaps his sales would slip for reasons having nothing to do with advertising. In either case, the agency could get the ax.

The resulting insecurity trickled down from the account executives to the lowliest-of-the-low, like me. For the first time in my life, I had the classic symptoms of an ulcer. I went to see a doctor whose office was in Tudor City, just a few blocks from Madison Avenue, and who had a lot of patients from the world of advertising. He talked to me in the kind of human way that doctors rarely do, describing the tormented lives of his other patients and urging me to get out while I still had a stomach lining. It turned out that I didn't have to quit—it was done for me.

After serving as a messenger and as a script reader for the "Kraft Television Theater," I was assigned to the "Lux Video Theater" as a production assistant. This meant going out for coffee (and the producer's Jell-O), laying out the floor plan with chalk, and sitting around a lot. Soon after I was assigned to the show, one of those terrible events beyond the control of the agency happened. This time it was the fault not of the client but of the network. CBS, in the person of a vice-president named Hubbell Robinson, decided to move the Lux show, which had had perfectly respectable ratings, to a time slot opposite NBC's "Dragnet," the blockbuster program of the day. Everyone was terrified of what this would do to our ratings, so the producer decided to go with a prestige author for the first night of the new time slot. He commissioned William Faulkner to write a script based on Faulkner's short story, "The Broach." I admired Faulkner

79

immensely, but I thought that the script was bad and made the mistake of saying so.

When the show aired, our ratings plummeted. The producer decided that I had demoralized the actors with my negative thoughts about the script, causing them to perform so ineptly that viewers by the millions switched to "Dragnet". I was fired. I thought the producer was crazy, but the truth is that like most young employees in any organization, I regarded the boss as a cardboard figure. I had no empathy for the fear he must have felt, and I failed to give him even a hint of the support he must have needed as he saw his career threatened.

But even if I had behaved with consummate tact and understanding, I still might have been fired. As countless historians have since noted, organizational life in the fifties demanded conformity. It was amazing how quickly the organization-man ethic took hold. As late as 1948, a hit Broadway play could praise rebellion. When Ensign Pulver threw the tyrannical captain's palm tree overboard as the curtain fell on the last act of *Mister Roberts*, the audience exploded into approving applause. Just five years later—in 1953, the year I was fired—they were applauding Barney Greenwald in *The Caine Mutiny Court Martial* for saying that Ensign Keith should not have rebelled against the tyrannical Captain Queeg, that authority must be understood, respected, and lived with.

CHAPTER **5**

# The Great
# Defender

**B**Y the time I left J. Walter
Thompson in May 1953, I had
made up my mind to go to law school. It was not that I
wanted to be a lawyer; I wanted to get into politics, and
I saw law school as the tried and true way.

It was too late to apply for that fall, so I decided to
enter the following year. The delay gave me time to earn
enough money for tuition, which in those days wasn't all
that much. I was embarrassed to ask my parents for the
money, since I had so smugly assured them seven years
earlier that the theater was my true vocation. Yet what I
did during the next fifteen months—working at the Bucks
County Playhouse in Pennsylvania, collecting unemployment insurance, taking reservations for American Airlines, reading manuscripts for a literary agent, and assist-
ing the producer of the Newport Casino Theater in Rhode
Island—paid me barely enough to live on, and I saved
practically nothing.

One of the few good things about this period was my
relationship with Theron Baumberger, the producer at the

Bucks County Playhouse. He wasn't a big-time success—his only Broadway hit had been *Heaven Can Wait*, years earlier—but he had become one of the great impressarios of what was called "the straw hat circuit" and had turned the Playhouse into one of the best summer theaters in the country. My main assignment was as Theron's driver and companion. He was in his late sixties and suffered from hypertension, and he clearly did not have much time left (in fact, he died in September 1953, just a week after the season ended). But his life had endowed him with a rich store of experience that he took delight in sharing with me. I responded with warmth and affection, perhaps out of guilt for my failure to give my boss at J. Walter Thompson any understanding or maybe just because Theron's humanity was irresistible.

The producer at Newport the next summer, Sarah Stamm, was another case altogether. I don't think she had a warm thought for anyone other than herself. In August, near the end of the season, she fired me. Whatever her shortcomings, the experience was sobering. Since I had also been fired by the literary agent, I had managed to irritate, to the point of my dismissal, three employers in the space of just fifteen months. I was beginning to suspect that I was not born to work for others.

I left Newport for Charlottesville, where I entered the University of Virginia Law School in September 1954 at the age of twenty-seven. I chose Virginia because the common law of Virginia and West Virginia is quite similar and because Virginia's Law School was better than West Virginia's at that time. The cost was a bit higher than at West Virginia, but my parents, grateful that the GI Bill had financed the rest of my higher education and delighted that at last I was going into a respectable line of work, were more than glad to foot the bill.

Virginia was very different from Columbia. The university was as conservative as the state, which was ruled by the Byrd machine and preparing to embark on a campaign of "massive resistance" to integration. There were only a handful of blacks, other than the handymen, waiters, and cleaning women, on the campus.

When I went to register the first day, it was warm, and I was wearing an open-necked shirt. A woman in the dean's office took me aside to tell me that tie and jacket were required. Most of the students were Waspy and conventional. But they were bright, so the classroom discussion was intelligent and, because they were ambitious, spirited as well. Competition was intense, especially during the first year, when we were trying to qualify for the law review. Making the review was essential if you hoped to join a major New York or Washington firm, or if you wanted to practice elsewhere but do so knowing you *could* have gone to New York or Washington.

The classroom was enlivened not only by the students but by the teachers, who during the first year were excellent, and by the beginning courses—contracts, torts, property, and criminal law—which raised basic issues of law and society in a way that I had never thought about. There were other pleasures to that first year, including the delight of walking to the law school through Jefferson's Lawn and spending weekends with my girl friend, Helen Parker, whom I had met at the Bucks County Playhouse. She had moved to Washington, which is just two hours by train from Charlottesville by way of Culpepper and Manassas.

It was a happy time for me, but not, I soon realized, for many of my classmates. Roughly half of them clearly did not like the law. Why, then, were they there? As I got to know them, I realized that for most it was that they wanted to do something respectable, usually to impress their parents or their friends, and they couldn't think of anything else.

There was and is, however, a legitimate reason why

people who don't like the law go to law school. It teaches them how to think. There is no reason people could not be taught to think in an undergraduate course in literary crticism as easily as in a law school class in contracts, but they rarely are. So law schools have to do the job.

I did well enough the first year to be invited to try out for law review, and I managed to make it after a fairly brutal competition. But by that time, roughly two months into my second year, I had had enough of law school. The second- and third-year courses were more specialized, less interesting, and less well taught than the first year's. The law review was one of the redeeming features of this period, but even it had its bad as well as its good side.

The good side of the law review was that your work was subject to the rigorous scrutiny of your colleagues. On matters of style, their judgment, like that of most lawyers, was hideous. But on the soundness of your analysis, their criticism was often accurate and bracing. What was bad about the law review was that originality not only wasn't encouraged, it was aggressively discouraged. The law's reverence for precedent—what someone else has already thought—was heightened by the conformity of the fifties. This wasn't good news for those of us who were inclined to dissent. An article I wrote was not printed because it disagreed with the prevailing wisdom on the establishment-of-religion clause of the First Amendment. It also opposed the argument that had just won two Virginia law professors a major victory in the Virginia Court of Appeals, a source of great pride to the school. The dean attempted to get me to change the article's main point. He called me into his office and told me that my position would help parochial schools. Then, leaning closer, he confided that Chief Justice Arthur Vanderbilt of the New Jersey Supreme Court had recently warned him that the Catholics were taking over the country.

My theory of the establishment clause was that it did not forbid government action that helped or harmed religion, so long as that action did not single out religions generally or one religion in particular for help or harm. I thought it would be fine for the government to tax church property as part of a program of taxing property generally. While most constitutional lawyers of that era thought the GI Bill would not survive a test of constitutionality in the court, I disagreed. I thought it was fine for the government to finance a veteran's education at Notre Dame, so long as he was free to attend other colleges, sectarian or nonsectarian, instead. This position, though unconventional at the time—it later gained respectability when it was advanced by Philip Kurland of the University of Chicago—was nonetheless rational and had historical support in the debates of the Founding Fathers.

My salvation during this period was a professor named Hardy Dillard. He was courtly, charming, and—like my favorite teacher at Columbia, Joseph Wood Krutch—an irresistibly amusing storyteller. He so reeked of southern aristocracy that when he launched into an anecdote about "my horse Major," all of us in the lecture hall assumed that he had come to class straight from a morning gallop around his plantation in the manner of Scarlett O'Hara's father in his better days.

In fact, Hardy did not have a horse of any kind—we later learned that Major was an example from Williston and Corbin's *Restatement of the Law of Contracts*—and his plantation was a small Charlottesville lot with unmown grass and a house that was a miniature version of Tara *after* the war. But he was a brilliant man, and I basked in signs of his regard.

His office was just off the main reading room of the

law library, and one day, while I was studying, he opened the door and beckoned me in. Hardy, like some of the other law professors, had an outside practice, and after we were seated he proceeded to tell me about a case he had been working on that he couldn't see any way to win. I saw things from a different angle, he said; perhaps I could come up with a new approach. I failed Hardy on this one, but I don't know how I would have survived law school without his faith that whatever originality I possessed was a virtue not a vice.

Unfortunately, there were many areas of the law to which my originality did not extend. Not only was I incapable of coming up with new ideas, I couldn't understand the old ones. An example was income taxation. The one time I tried to prepare my own tax return, I overpaid by $900. My ineptitudes are worth thinking about in appraising our system of licensing lawyers. Once I had graduated and passed the bar exam, I was, like all lawyers, licensed to practice every kind of law. Yet I was good at only some kinds and not at all good at others. I could try cases but not compute taxes. On the other hand, I have watched an excellent tax lawyer bungle the trial of a case. Why not license lawyers only for those areas of practice in which they are truly competent?

Regrettably, this line of reasoning did not occur to me at the time, and I accepted the notion that I should be an all-around lawyer, good at everything, just as I had accepted the Clark Gable ideal of the kind of man I should be. So I worried that I couldn't do taxes, just as I had worried that I couldn't ski. This concern, combined with the rejection of my law review article—which, by the way, was accompanied by one editor's suggestion that I resign from the review—reawakened the anxieties that had come from the three firings, and I went into the only real depression of my life during the winter of 1956–57.

Breaking up with Helen that December did not improve the situation. Even the political events of the fall of 1956 seemed to be conspiring to make things worse. In early November, Russia's suppression of the revolt in Hungary came right on the heels of Anthony Eden's insane invasion of Suez. And then there was the second defeat of Adlai Stevenson. On election day, I buttonholed voters on Stevenson's behalf outside the Albemarle County courthouse, where the gentry who owned the estates surrounding Charlottesville voted. Ninety percent of them were smugly indifferent to my arguments. This hardly seemed a promising beginning for a career in politics.

This depression lasted until the end of March. My road back began in a setting not generally associated with spiritual uplift—a fraternity party. I was a member of a legal fraternity, Phi Delta Phi. I had joined not because I liked fraternities—I had not belonged to one in high school or college—but because this was one to which only those at the top of their class in their first year were invited, and I thought I had better grab the recognition before my academic standing declined, as I correctly anticipated it would.

I seldom went to fraternity social events, but for this occasion, a party in March 1957, I would have had to pay a fine if I didn't go. As I walked through the door, my eyes immediately alighted on a stunning blonde surrounded by a half-dozen of my classmates. I spent the rest of the evening in a futile attempt to get close enough to talk to her. The next day I was describing the party to Joan Dillard, Hardy's daughter, over lunch in the cafeteria, when who should walk in but that same young woman—accompanied by a retinue of what must have been the only hippies in Charlottesville in 1957. Was it possible that she not only was beautiful but would also understand why I liked Ginsberg and Kerouac? I pointed her out, and Joan said, "Why I know her. That's Beth Hubbell." Joan arranged a date.

Beth turned out to be intelligent and to have a first-rate sense of humor as well. We discovered that we had a lot in common. We both lived in the country several miles from Charlottesville, in houses that were fewer than a hundred yards apart, separated by woods that had kept us from running into each other. We both had had recent romances that had failed—hers with a West Point cadet she met while she was attending Vassar. And we both had abandoned careers in the arts. Beth had gone to New York in her early teens to study at the School of American Ballet. Then, at age seventeen, she had decided that the life of a dancer was not for her.

The most important thing we shared was our fears. Beth's were worse than mine because they were much deeper. Her mother, an army wife married to a major stationed in Hawaii, had fallen in love with a dashing general and divorced her husband when Beth was only five years old. The result was a childhood that ranged from lonely to miserable. Trying to help her helped me to get over a dangerous preoccupation with myself; in making the case to her that she could overcome her fears, I began to overcome my own.

My depression had come from a fear of failure. But as I talked with Beth, I began to see that failure was bound to be part of life and that in many ways it would be beyond our control. What was within our control was the effort we made to do the right thing and to serve the right causes. Failing to make that effort was the only failure one should truly fear. Perfection wasn't necessary; trying was.

But I knew that trying might demand sacrifice and that it might lead me down a path I couldn't foresee. So the night I proposed to Beth, I said, "Ordinarily, marrying a young lawer would mean that you would be increasingly well off as the years went by. But I know that the road I'm on may take me away from the law and into something else. Suppose I decided to start a newspaper in some town where we wouldn't have a chance of making money. All we would do is barely get by doing something we love. Are you willing to do that?" The answer was yes. We were married on August 3, 1957.

× × ×

WITH marriage I acquired a family of in-laws. The central figure was Beth's mother, Sybil Fletcher Peyton. Sybil was meant to march with Betty Friedan and Gloria Steinem, but she was born in 1899 and she graduated from Vassar in an era when few women even entered college. She was a skilled sculptress and a talented writer. But the social pressures of her time forced her into an unhappy marriage with an army lieutenant named Reginald Hubbell.

Both she and Reg came from service families. Reg's mother was the granddaughter of the General Worth for whom Fort Worth is named. Sybil's father was Admiral Frank Friday Fletcher, who commanded the American fleet shortly before World War I and won the Congressional Medal of Honor at Vera Cruz in 1914.

During the twenties and thirties, Reg and Sybil lived a typical army life, stationed at posts from Paris, France, to Springfield, Missouri, including West Point, Manila, Governor's Island (where Beth was born), and Honolulu, where Sybil fell in love with that general. He was Phillip Bradley Peyton, who was a close friend of George Marshall and was expected to play an important role in World War II. Unfortunately, he had a heart attack in 1941, soon after he and Sybil married, and he had to retire.

But Sybil had a cousin, Frank Jack Fletcher, who did rise to high command during the war. He was in command at the Battle of the Coral Sea, the first time we turned back the Japanese, and was co-commander of the American forces at the Battle of Midway, the greatest U.S. naval victory of World War II. Yet hardly anyone knows his name. The reason is that after losing two carriers, the *Lexington* in the Coral Sea and the *Yorktown* at Midway, he was convinced that his bureaucratic enemies back in Washington were saying, "Fletcher may win battles but he might lose us the war." The United States had only four carriers left, and Frank Jack had two of them, both off Guadalcanal to protect the American ships that were supporting the marines locked in battle ashore. Intelligence told Frank Jack that a major Japanese air attack was coming. He was determined not to lose any more carriers, so he withdrew. The Japanese sank most of the remaining ships. In his effort to protect himself against backbiting about losing carriers, Frank Jack ruined his career. His name could have rung with Nimitz, Halsey, and the other heroes of the Pacific, but today the few who have heard of Frank Jack at all think of him as someone who ran away from a fight.

His cousin Sybil would never be accused of that. She was a combative woman and a tough mother-in-law. She knew every fault of mine and made sure that Beth did, too.

But she had a redeeming wit and was a wonderful raconteur. In fact, sometimes I suspected that she had lived her life for the sake of the stories she could tell. Each anecdote was a polished gem—so polished that I also suspected that where her life had not supplied the delicious detail that would make the story perfect, her own imagination was ready and willing to step into the breach.

Whatever suffering I endured at Sybil's hands has been more than made up for by her sister, Alice, who is a total delight—warm, loving, funny. Her New Jersey farm, near Clinton, is the center for an enormous extended family of old friends and relatives, of which I feel privileged to be a part.

× × ×

AFTER we were married, Beth and I moved into the upstairs apartment at 25 Brooks Street, where Mimi and Pud used to live, and I joined my father's law firm, Peters, Merrick, Leslie, and Mohler. Like most small-town firms, its practice was general and included almost every kind of legal problem. The older Mohler having died, his son Bill was now the junior partner, and my father was the firm's "rainmaker." But by the time I arrived, he was sixty-seven and no longer able to do much of the work he attracted. So he began turning it over to me, which meant that I had more responsibility than is usual for a beginning lawyer.

The disadvantage of being the boss's son was that my father was embarrassed to intercede on my behalf when salaries were discussed. This, along with my penchant for choosing work on the basis of its being interesting rather than its potential for generating income, meant that I got $250 a month to start and was making only $500 a month three years later.

I spent a third of my time on work that was dull and routine. The dullest of the dull was searching real estate records for defects in the titles to land that was being sold. This was not just tedious, it was a racket. The title to a lot in a subdivision that some other lawyer had searched thoroughly last year might take no more than ten minutes to bring up to date but was billed at the same rate as a title search for a farm ("bounded on the north by a line running from a persimmon tree to the left bank of Hans Creek"), which could take a week. The latter might be underbilled, which was how lawyers justified the racket to themselves, but the subdivision title, which was much more common, was always overbilled.

The interesting part of my practice was trying cases and the work I did for the *Charleston Gazette*. For the *Gazette* I reviewed articles that the editors thought might be libelous. It was a morning paper, so they usually called me in the late afternoon or early evening to check an article for the next day's edition. Since the paper would be going to press in a few hours, decisions had to be made fast, which gave drama to the occasion. The stories were interesting, as were the reporters and editors who worked on them. So I looked forward to these calls and, when summoned, would walk eagerly to the paper's office on Hale Street, a few blocks from our apartment.

The libel problem I remember best came up during the 1960 Democratic gubernatorial primary. One candidate for governor had given the *Gazette* a tape recording of a conversation in which another gubernatorial candidate offered to split the "take" if the first candidate withdrew from the race and threw his support to the second. (The take was the amount a governor could expect to be paid in return for state contracts, licenses, and franchises.) I knew both men and recognized their voices, so the story was published. It had no discernible effect on the election—the candidate who made the offer won. You have to understand the state of electoral morality in West Virginia at that time—the term Lever Brothers was used in reference not to the detergent manufacturer but to a family in Logan County that was particularly adept at manipulating voting machines.

The other legal work I liked was trying cases. Most were personal injury suits in which we represented either the plaintiffs or the insurance companies, which were usually the true defendants. Although they were fun to try, most of these cases struck me as crazy. They were the result of auto accidents, most of which really had been accidents, but to win you had to prove it was the other fellow's fault, which meant that each side had to fudge.

The first case I tried, however, was not like that. It involved clear right and wrong, and it showed how much we needed Ralph Nader back then. My client had been induced by a crooked lawyer to give him a note for $2,000 for a service the lawyer failed to perform. The lawyer sold the note to a crooked friend at a large discount. Even though the crooked friend had every reason to suspect that the note had been improperly obtained, he was now what the law calls a "holder in due course" and, as such, was entitled to collect the full amount. But because I was able to keep the two crooks on the stand long enough for the jury to begin to see through them, it became clear that I had a chance to win. Then the lawyer for the other side, a distinguished member of the bar in his early sixties, a former mayor of Charleston and a pillar of the community, asked me to step into the hallway, where he offered me a bribe to throw the case. I refused, and the jury found in favor of my client. But the law was the law, and the verdict was reversed on appeal. My client would have had to pay the $2,000, but I convinced the former mayor that I would never stop fighting. Since the fee he could charge for a $2,000 judgment was not enough to cover the series of retrials and appeals I was threatening to take him through, he gave up.

There are uses for tenacity. A young lawyer who is enthusiastic and determined can use it to overcome an older attorney who is experienced but has lost his taste for hard work. This is one of the few exceptions to the law's usual imbalance in favor of the rich and against the poor.

I also handled a lot of criminal cases, perhaps twenty in all. I came to criminal law with the image of *The*

*Wrong Man* in mind. Remember the Hitchcock film? The police arrest an innocent man, and his lawyer is the bright and brave young David who saves him from the prosecutorial Goliath. This is one of the great liberal myths, and I accepted it without question.

But I never *had* an innocent client. They were all guilty. The police seldom get the wrong man. In difficult cases, they seldom catch anyone. The people they do arrest are usually handing the television sets out the store window when a squad car happens to pass by.

Another liberal myth about crime is that all criminals can be rehabilitated. My experience was that, as a practical matter, this is true of about only half—and they are almost always young, nonviolent offenders or people who went for a gun or a knife during a family argument or a lovers' quarrel. But even some of them—the compulsive thief or the habitual wife-beater—are bad risks, meaning that probation should probably be given only to first offenders.

In my first criminal case, my client, Seattle Sid Frizell (the name is fictitious, the person was real), quickly convinced me that he was innocent of the burglary with which he was charged. In fact, he got me so fired up that even though there was a bit of evidence against him— several witnesses who had seen him commit the crime— I convinced the prosecuting attorney that I would put up such a fight that he would have to abandon all hope of going on his fall hunting trip. So the charge was dismissed. I called a friend in Pittsburgh, who promised to get Sid a job. I contributed a bus ticket to Pittsburgh and an old Brooks Brothers suit I had always resented for the accurate indication it gave of the width of my shoulders.

The morning after Sid's release, I picked up the *Gazette* and was confronted by a headline: "Break-In at County Jail." Seattle Sid had cashed in his bus ticket and pawned his suit—maybe he didn't like the narrow shoulders either—and bought a shotgun, which he used in an attempt to break into the jail and free some of his friends. The venture was unsuccessful, but I regarded it as so admirably quixotic that I once again came to Sid's defense. This time I argued that however unfortunate the episode might have been, it had not been anticipated by the state legislature. Thus there was no such crime as breaking *into* a jail. I don't know whether the prosecutor was impressed by my reasoning or wanted to attend a bar association meeting at the Greenbrier that week, but once again Sid went free.

The next I heard of him was in a news report from Texas. It seems that, shortly after being sentenced to the state penitentiary there, he had confessed to several crimes in West Virginia. I was puzzled, because Sid had not struck me as a man excessively burdened by guilt. Then a friend, who was more sophisticated about crime than I, explained that Texas was famous for having the toughest state penitentiary in the country and that prudent men, upon finding themselves within its walls, began to search their consciences for infractions committed in gentler jurisdictions. Confessing these misdeeds would, they hoped, lead to extradition to a slammer that had a little more class.

Thanks to the advice of my father and the help of Bill Mohler, who was a skilled trial lawyer, I lost only two cases. In one, my whole case depended on my client's having assured me during our pretrial conference that the defendant's car had approached from the right. When I questioned him on the witness stand, he said, "It was coming from the left." This is one of those moments when a lawyer needs the skills of the finest actor. My case had crashed, yet I had to proceed as if my client's cause remained overwhelmingly meritorious. The jury wasn't fooled.

In the other case I lost, my client was accused of

having had sexual relations with his fourteen-year-old stepdaughter. He was forty years old, with finely chiseled features and gray hair that gave him a man-of-distinction look. In reality, he was a sullen slob; I could hardly bear to be in the same room with him. The daughter, on the other hand, was adorable. As I questioned her in court, my mind was filled with fantasies about Juliet, Beatrice, and occasionally, I must admit, Lolita. These are not thoughts that produce hard-boiled cross-examination. As she left the stand, everyone in the court, including me, believed her story. But I had my duty to my client. So I launched into a final argument that rang every possible variation on the who-shall-cast-the-first-stone theme, trying to get the jury to admit to itself that, where sex is concerned, we have all sinned in our hearts if not in fact.

In the course of this oration, I came so close to confessing certain indiscretions of my own that I feared the sheriff might lead me away instead of my client. But I escaped. My client almost did, too. The jury let him off with just a year in prison, far less than he deserved.

The jury may have been too tender in this case, but I was amazed by the instinct for the right verdict that most juries have. When they do go wrong, it's usually because one side's lawyer is a lot better than the other's. The system's working depends on there being a level playing field, but the field isn't level when the rich can afford the best lawyers and the poor can't.

The simplest example of the role of money in the law is the case of the store that has sold you a defective refrigerator. If the store won't replace it or give you your money back, you should be able to go to court. The catch is that, since the refrigerator is worth only a few hundred dollars, the case does not involve enough money to yield an adequate fee for your lawyer. You can represent yourself before a justice of the peace or the small claims court, but often you will be met there by a skilled department-store lawyer who is well paid to handle hundreds of cases like yours. And the judge may be biased in favor of the store because it brings him more business (some courts are financed wholly or in part by litigant fees) or because it gave him a campaign contribution.

Money corrupts lawyers as well. Consider, for example, the way they let the meter run when they are representing a well-heeled client. Once I had a client who was definitely not well-heeled. A meeting was scheduled to discuss a settlement with the firm that represented the opposing party, who was rich. Three members of the firm came to meet with me. The meeting dragged on, and I kept looking at my watch as the other lawyers repeated over and over, with only slight variations, what they had already said.

I finally figured out what they were doing. They were running the meter, and with three of them there it was running in triplicate. As I went to the door to bid the three lawyers good-bye, I saw them get into a waiting limousine, which you can be certain the client was paying for, too.

In order to attract and hold on to a rich client, the lawyer cleverly plays on the client's insecurities to convince him that he would be helpless without the lawyer's brilliant advice. Subtly encouraging this dependence in nonlegal settings is a good way to woo clients. Lawyers often volunteer for positions on the boards of charitable institutions, where they labor earnestly to make themselves indispensable to their fellow members, who just happen to be the town's wealthiest citizens. Nothing makes a lawyer's stomach churn more than hearing his client say of another lawyer, "I just don't know what the board would do without him."

An important aspect of the immorality of the legal profession is what might be called "the cult of the pro." Still strong today, this cult was at its height in the fifties.

The sports pages were filled with accolades for the professional who was dedicated to doing his work well; Joe DiMaggio was a good example. There is really nothing wrong with this attitude when it is applied to sports. But in the law, it means that what counts is being a highly skilled practitioner and that the moral content of the work and the moral character of the client are irrelevant. You are to do a superb job for the highest bidder. If there are good people and good causes that cannot afford your skills, that is just too bad.

# CHAPTER **6**

# Two Winners in West Virginia

**O**NE day, after I had been practicing law for about fifteen
months, I was in the courthouse record room, mired in
the dreariness of researching real estate titles, when I was
called to the phone. It was an old high school friend, Bill
Brotherton. "How would you like to be my clerk?" he
asked. To the average person, this invitation might sound
unenticing, but Bill had been in the House of Delegates
for several terms and now was chairman of its most important committee, the Judiciary Committee. And from
my days as a page, I knew that the clerk was the committee's chief staff officer. I accepted immediately.

My main function was to prepare a summary and
analysis of each bill. This was often the only objective
view of a bill available to members of the committee,
whose information otherwise came from lobbyists with
axes to grind. I had considerable power, but it was power
that depended on my exercising it judiciously, never appearing to lobby but always being ready to expand on my
views when asked. I could not defeat a powerful lobby,
but if there was little lobbying interest or if the powerful

lobbies were on opposing sides, my advice often tipped the balance.

I enjoyed working in the legislature so much that I decided I wanted to be a member. In February 1960, I filed to run for the House of Delegates in the May primary.

West Virginia would be making its choice for the Democratic presidential nomination in the same primary. A few days before I filed, Matt Reese, who was second in command of the statewide group supporting John Kennedy, came to my office at the Judiciary Committee and asked me to run Kennedy's campaign in Kanawha County. Like a lot of Democrats, I had been impressed by Kennedy's near-miss of the vice-presidential nomination at the 1956 convention and by the overwhelming margin of his victory in the 1958 Senate race in Massachusetts. He had the smell of a winner. And after two straight Democratic losses to Eisenhower, that was important. Although I didn't like his failure to confront the Red-baiting of Senator Joseph McCarthy, I admired the courage he and his brother Robert had shown in taking on corruption in organized labor, a stand that distinguished them from most other liberals of the period. All in all, I thought Kennedy was better than the other candidates and stood a better chance of beating Richard Nixon, who appeared almost certain to be the Republican nominee.

I was also drawn to Kennedy because of his heroism in the South Pacific during World War II. What I had learned about war from my father, from Beth's family, and from the veterans I had known who had been in battle gave me immense respect for the bravery and the cool intelligence Kennedy had displayed when his PT boat was sliced in half by the Japanese destroyer. What was most impressive was Kennedy's concern for his men and the way he translated that concern into effective action to save their lives. The ability to perform in the clutch was essential, I believed, in an era when decisions about nuclear war might have to be made in a matter of minutes.

In addition, my mother was an ardent Kennedy supporter and had been working for him for several months. So it was not surprising that when Larry O'Brien, over breakfast in the Daniel Boone Hotel, again asked me to run the campaign for Kanawha County, I said yes.

There was not much to do at first. One night in February I picked up the senator at the airport and took him to the secretary of state's office in the capitol, where he filed for the election. Then I rented a headquarters in the Kanawha Hotel and began a series of meetings to attract volunteers. Kennedy helped by coming to Charleston for the opening of the headquarters in mid-March. We rounded up a small band and strung a ribbon for him to cut. Several hundred people came to watch, and many of them then signed up as volunteers.

After lunch I accompanied Kennedy to a series of television and radio interviews. It was during these interviews that I saw for the first time the man the country later got to know in those remarkable presidential press conferences. He answered questions with wit and intelligence—and with a stunning command of the facts and issues. I knew I was in the presence of a first-rate mind.

I was becoming a true believer, but not many other West Virginians seemed to share my enthusiasm. During the next three weeks, our prospects looked increasingly gloomy. The problem was Kennedy's religion. Only 4 percent of the state's voters were Catholic, and they were devoted to Kennedy—most of our 400 volunteer workers in Kanawha County had names like Callahan and O'Malley. But many West Virginians were anti-Catholic. Prejudice against Catholics has almost disappeared from this country today, but in 1960 it was still virulent among many Protestants, even, as I had discovered on the law review, among some highly educated ones.

In early April, the polls showed us trailing Hubert Humphrey 60–40. Although Kennedy had won the Wisconsin primary, he had not done well in the Protestant areas of the state. This meant that the religious issue would dominate our primary, which was next on the national schedule. West Virginia became the test of whether Kennedy could carry Protestant states.

In the early going, my own campaign looked equally unpromising. I was running against a field of veteran candidates. On top of that, ever since the county had adopted voting machines that listed the candidates in alphabetical order, no candidate with a last name beginning after "K" had been nominated on the Democratic ticket.

I knew that if I was to have a chance, I had to try to meet every voter in the county. During March I went to rallies almost every evening and to coffees organized by Democratic housewives almost every day. I also went door-to-door, handing out cards with my name and picture, and walked through the grocery and department stores, trying to talk to each voter long enough to be sure he or she would remember me on election day.

The experience of campaigning person-to-person is one reason why elitist theories of government have little appeal for me. The elitists argue that the public official should be insulated from the vulgar mob so that he can make decisions in the public interest objectively, without fear or favor. The trouble with this theory is that, if you don't know what the people's problems are, it's hard to come to the right decisions. The best way to learn about their problems is to meet people face-to-face and listen. And what could motivate you more to do that than the need to get elected?

Whatever its impact on my political theory, my shoe-leather campaign did improve my electoral prospects. By the beginning of April, I felt I had a chance. But I now had to devote most of my energy to the Kennedy campaign, which was in trouble.

So Beth took over my campaign. She put a big "Peters for House of Delegates" sign on top of our used Buick and proceeded to drive all over the county, attending coffees and rallies, handing out cards, and doing all the other things I had been doing in March. When the votes were counted, my best precinct was a black housing project that I had never visited but where Beth had knocked on every door.

On the Friday after the Wisconsin primary, five or six of us from West Virginia were summoned to Hickory Hill, Robert Kennedy's home in McLean, Virginia. Most of the key figures in the national campaign were there, including Ted Sorensen and Ken O'Donnell. The atmosphere was grim. The West Virginians were asked what could be done. I urged that Franklin D. Roosevelt, Jr., who was said to be a friend of John Kennedy's, be brought into the campaign, explaining that FDR was God to most West Virginia Democrats and that the approval of God's son might make it possible for them to consider voting for a Catholic. I was getting nowhere. Bobby looked bored.

Then Matt Reese, a giant in height and girth—and in political wisdom—spoke up: "Last week, I was in Logan [a small town in the southern West Virginia coal fields], and I was walking down the street with a friend when he stopped and said, 'Did you know Mrs. Roosevelt stood right here?' I said, 'I didn't know she had been here recently.' My friend said, 'Oh, I mean when she was here in 1934.'" At that, Bobby rose from his chair, left the room, and called FDR Jr.

Because West Virginia had become the crucial primary, all the top Kennedy staff members were involved. The headquarters at the Kanawha Hotel had been a placid backwater in March, but on April 10 Bobby arrived. So did Larry O'Brien, Ken O'Donnell, and Lem Billings. They spent the next month in Charleston. Ted Sorensen and Ralph Dungan were frequent visitors. Kennedy's brother-in-law, Sargent Shriver, went to Huntington. His close friends, Bill Walton and Charles Spaulding, went to Blue-field and Clarksburg. Bobby's classmate from Milton Academy, Dave Hackett, went to Parkersburg.

For that month West Virginia seemed to be the center of the political universe. David Brinkley was interviewing voters on the streets of downtown Charleston. Reporters from the major papers and the wire services were crowding local hotels. West Virginia was on the network news almost every night.

Kennedy was so skilled at handling reporters that most of the press coverage was favorable. But there were some hostile stories, most of them on the possibility that the Kennedys were buying the election. I don't believe they did. My best estimate is that they spent around $200,000 in West Virginia, less than half the amount usually spent on gubernatorial primaries at that time. I'm sure that some of this money did go to buy votes, for some went to local political organizations that were not known for excessive ethical zeal. But most went to buy television time and to pay campaign workers. The latter was customary in the politics of southern Appalachia. In the cities, one might find a few members of the League of Women Voters who sought no compensation for their work on election day—in our campaign, their ranks were swollen by the Callahans and Gallaghers, who also worked for free. But if you lived in the hollows, you expected to be paid. Your feelings would be hurt if you weren't, because it would mean that they didn't really value your efforts. Often the work, for which the going rate in 1960 was twenty-five dollars a day, consisted of driving voters to the polls. During the ride, the driver was to extol the virtues of the candidate or slate of candidates he was working for. Occasionally, when the driver did nothing but take his own family to the polls, this custom came perilously close to vote-buying. But most of the time it was reasonably legal, if not quite in the pristine spirit of a Vermont town meeting.

Humphrey spent almost as much in Kanawha County as Kennedy did—$10,000 as against $12,000. Most of his money came from Lyndon Johnson, who was trying to keep Kennedy from locking up the nomination before the convention. If we had an advantage, it was that we got our money out early. As other successful presidential candidates have since discovered, it helps to be the first to solicit support. By moving early, we were able to line up the dominant faction in the key counties. In Kanawha County, that faction was headed by a man named Burl Sawyer.

I, too, was supported by Sawyer's organization. And as election day drew near, I began to worry about how to make sure that the Sawyer forces were going all out for Jack Kennedy at the same time I was trying to make sure that they were firmly committed to Charlie Peters for House of Delegates. One day I drove Kennedy to Dunbar, a suburb of Charleston, where he called on the mayor, who was a member of the Sawyer group. Kennedy emerged from the mayor's office, got in the car, and said, "He's not sure about me, but he's definitely for you!"

Kennedy was amused by the incident, but I knew someone had to tell the mayor in forceful terms that as a Sawyer man, he was supposed to be working for Kennedy. I wasn't sure I could be tough enough in cases like this, where I would be risking the loss of my own support. I told Larry O'Brien about my concern, and he deputized Dick Donahue, a lawyer from Massachusetts, to ride herd on the Sawyer organization. I concentrated on working with the unpaid Catholic volunteers. In the two weeks before the election, they distributed more than 80,000 pieces of campaign literature, including 40,000 copies of a *Reader's Digest* article about Kennedy's exploits in the Pacific during World War II. Because a lot of other West Virginians shared my regard for battlefield valor—the state was always at the top of the list in percentages of volunteers and of casualties—this was the most effective vote-getter of all. The volunteers also canvassed voters in the precincts where the Sawyer forces were weak or nonexistent, identifying Kennedy supporters and making sure that each of those discerning citizens got to the polls on election day.

I am seldom quick to admit that I am wrong, but there was one episode in the 1960 campaign in which my error was obvious even to me. I decided that Jacqueline Kennedy would seem phony to West Virginians compared to the natural, down-to-earth Muriel Humphrey. So one April morning, at breakfast with the Kennedy staff at the Kanawha Hotel, I recommended that Mrs. Kennedy be discouraged from campaigning in the state. I was over-ruled unanimously and was fortunate not to be banished from the campaign. Jackie came to West Virginia, where to my surprise she was seen as a princess who added glamour and excitement to the primary.

I spent a lot of time with John Kennedy during the campaign. Usually I was too busy briefing him about the people he would be meeting at our next stop and intro-ducing him to them when we arrived to engage him in serious conversation or even to form a coherent impres-sion of what was happening. But a few incidents were etched in my memory.

One afternoon in late April, when I picked Kennedy up at the airport, he was accompanied by James Reston of the *New York Times*, who sat in the back seat with him during the drive downtown. Listening to their conversation, it was obvious that Kennedy was planting a story in Reston's mind. You have to bear in mind that at that time Reston was widely regarded as the most brilliant journalist in Washington to understand my reaction when I read his column the next day: it was the story Kennedy wanted him to write, practically word for word.

A few days later, when we met with the congregation of the local Unitarian Church, Kennedy had a sore throat, and his doctor told him not to speak. So Ted Sorensen came along to do the talking. The intellectual of the Kennedy staff, Sorensen reportedly was the real author of *Profiles in Courage*, the book that had won Kennedy a Pulitzer Prize. As Sorensen was answering questions about the Kennedys' Catholicism, the most controversial issue in the campaign, I could see Kennedy becoming restive. Finally, he rose, interrupted Sorensen, and in a croaking voice, took over answering the questions. From the way Kennedy phrased his replies, you knew he thought some subtleties had eluded Sorensen. And he was right. I realized then that Kennedy was smarter than the man who was supposed to be his brain.

Another time, as Kennedy and I were working a crowd outside a department store in downtown Charleston, he whispered, "Let's move toward that blonde over there."

"Senator," I said, "that's my wife."

He laughed.

The Kennedy headquarters was the hardest-working I have ever seen. Robert Kennedy was the driving force. Although in later years I came to admire him immensely, he was a pain in the ass then. He was much too conservative for me. At Hickory Hill in 1960, the only nonfamily photographs displayed on the first floor were of Herbert Hoover and Pope Pius XII. He could also be rude and arrogant. One Sunday night, Beth and I picked him up at the airport to take him to my family's home, where he was to meet with political leaders and then spend the night. I had to pass on some bad news about the campaign—this was when our fortunes still were low—and he proceeded to berate me in front of Beth. I have long since forgiven him, having responded with similar gracelessness myself to unhappy tidings from subordinates. But there is a rudeness and arrogance about some of the Kennedys—I never saw it in Jack—that can be extremely unattractive. One of Bobby's children once told me that her mother had been terribly unpleasant to a person who later became a great friend. "She thought he was just a driver," was the explanation, delivered with no sense of its irony.

Another campaign story I must tell is on myself. One evening, around dinner time, Lem Billings called. Kennedy had lost his voice again. Could I accompany him on an all-day tour tomorrow, making eight speeches and concluding with a television appearance? Kennedy would sit there while I did the talking. I thought about it for a minute, entertaining Walter Mitty fantasies of Kennedy turning to me at the end of the day and saying, "Well, Charlie, you were great. I want you on my White House staff."

I said no. My excuse was that, having arranged six of the eight speaking engagements, I felt responsible for making sure everything went smoothly when we got there. My real reason, which I didn't tell Lem, was that I was afraid my hands would shake and spoil everything.

From my earliest memory, I have been afflicted with shaking hands. Both my parents had slight hand tremors, and their genes apparently combined to give me a more severe form of the malady, which was most severe when I had to speak in public. I took great care to keep my hands in my pockets or to have a rostrum to grip, and, after a few harrowing experiences, I never handled loose papers that might flutter in my trembling grasp.

During my first important case in federal court, I was arguing a crucial issue in the judge's chambers and had never been in better form. As I was triumphantly surveying the downcast face of opposing counsel, I reached for a cup of coffee that a court attendant had placed at my side. The cup was in a saucer with a spoon beside it. As I picked up the cup and saucer, the spoon began to rattle loudly, and before the cup reached my mouth, half its contents had spilled into the saucer and the rest was on the floor. It was fear of a similar embarrassing episode that led me to turn down Lem's offer.

As I did more speaking, I got better at controlling the tremor. One thing that helped was a lesson I remembered from my experience in the theater. It was based—very loosely—on the theory of acting developed by the great Russian director, Stanislavski. The idea was to "focus on your object." In other words, don't worry about how you look; concentrate on grabbing your audience by the lapels and convincing them of the great point you are making. Think about your point, not about yourself. This helped me overcome self-consciousness. It can help people overcome self-centeredness, too. When you're thinking about the point you're making, you aren't thinking about yourself. Short of moral regeneration, which, of course, is a more complex enterprise, it's the best way I know to escape preoccupation with oneself, at least temporarily.

Kennedy soon recovered his voice, and as FDR Jr.'s support became widely known, our crowds began to grow. In early April, the only way we could be sure of a crowd was to talk principals into letting kids out of school. By the end of the month, though, Kennedy was mobbed wherever he appeared. We were gaining on Humphrey, but we hadn't overtaken him. The final ten days of the campaign were going to demand an all-out effort. Kennedy responded by becoming a dramatically better speaker than he had ever been. In two memorable television appearances, he convinced many voters that his Catholicism would not affect his presidency and that he really cared about the poverty in West Virginia.

On election morning, I woke up feeling that Kennedy had a chance to win. Dick Donahue and I spent the morning driving around the precincts. From the optimistic reports of the Sawyer people and our own volunteers, we were confident that we would carry Kanawha County, and we suspected that we might take the rest of the state as well. By afternoon there was nothing more I could do, so I took a nap. I got up around 7:00 P.M. and walked to the county courthouse, where the returns would be posted on a blackboard as the votes were counted. It soon was obvious that Kennedy was going to win. My own prospects were less clear at first, but by 9:30 the nomination was mine. I happily walked to Kennedy headquarters and stood at the door to await his arrival from Washington, which was supposed to happen momentarily. It turned out that I had to stand there for two hours. He had gone to a movie in Washington, and he didn't arrive in Charleston until midnight. Toward the end of my wait, Humphrey and his sister passed me on their way into the hotel to congratulate Kennedy. There were tears in their eyes.

A few minutes later, Kennedy drove up. When I shook his hand, his only comment was, "Did you win, too?"

In West Virginia, nomination on the Democratic ticket is often equivalent to election. I was confident that this would be the case for both Kennedy and me, so after the primary I no longer really worried about the ultimate result.

In July, Beth and I went to the Democratic National

Convention in Los Angeles. I was an alternate delegate and got to sit on the convention floor. The most memorable moment of the convention came when Adlai Stevenson entered the hall around 6:00 P.M. on Tuesday. Instead of appearing on the podium, he walked onto the floor, mingling with the delegates. As they became aware of him, a demonstration started and gradually spread through the arena. Most of us had worked hard for Stevenson in 1952 and 1956. He had a strong claim on our loyalty and affection, and as these feelings began to reassert themselves, the roar of the crowd grew louder.

I saw Ken O'Donnell and Larry O'Brien looking worried. An awful lot of delegates who were supposed to be for Kennedy were cheering their heads off for Stevenson, including me. I thought, "This could get out of hand." Then Stevenson was escorted to the podium, and the crowd finally quieted down. He proceeded to deliver what has to have been one of the lamest speeches ever made. It was over in five minutes, and so was the Stevenson boom.

Kennedy and I did both win in November, but the going was considerably harder for Kennedy. When I called Hyannisport on election night with reports on my area, I heard growing anxiety in the voices at the other end of the line as the evening went on and Kennedy's early lead dwindled. Finally, he eked out the narrowest of victories. But the margin didn't really matter. He was on his way to the White House. And I was on my way to the state legislature.

× × ×

I served in the House of Delegates during the 1961 and 1962 sessions. I had been supported by the AFL-CIO and the United Mine Workers, and I was still pretty much a conventional liberal. In fact, my best effort as an orator was in labor's cause.

111

The occasion was the defeat of a workman's compensation bill engineered by lobbyists from the state chamber of commerce. A few days after the vote, I learned that chamber lobbyists had misrepresented the effect of the bill's key provisions. I moved to reconsider, but for some reason—I think it was that I hadn't made my motion soon enough after the orginal vote—I had to persuade four-fifths of the 100 delegates, most of whom, remember, had voted against the bill, to vote to bring it up again. As I began to speak, I wasn't nervous—or at least this time I didn't show it—and I became more eloquent as I went along. When I finished, the gallery erupted with loud and sustained applause (the only time that happened in my legislative career). As we pushed our buttons to vote— green for aye, red for nay—the machine on the wall behind the speaker lit up mostly green. We had more than a majority, but would we get four-fifths? When the speaker announced the total—seventy-nine yeas, twenty-one nays—we had fallen one vote short. At least I had the satisfaction of knowing that I had made the chamber of commerce nervous.

The bills that I sponsored in the legislature were consistent with the conventional liberalism of the day. The one that I worked hardest on—as author, sponsor, and floor manager—was the civil service bill. At that time, West Virginia had no merit system for state employees beyond what Congress required for federal programs that were administered by the state. Even in these programs, employees could be fired without cause by the governor. My bill gave civil service protection to 3,000 of the state's 13,000 employees, covering such people as engineers and accountants, who were in jobs in which political philosophy was irrelevant to the technical competence required.

Civil service bills had been defeated in one legislative

session after another in the fifties. I began lobbying for this one on the first day of the 1961 session, and it passed by a substantial margin.

I also sponsored a bill establishing a state human rights commission. *Brown v. Board of Education* had ended segregation in the state's schools, but there were still too many white people whose attitudes were not much more enlightened than those of the police chief I had encountered on Student's Day. This bill also passed.

My toughest fight was for a bill to prohibit billboards near interstate highways. The billboard lobby worked night and day to defeat it, and the bill's fate was still in doubt when it came to the floor. Amendment after amendment was offered. Some reflected a bona fide desire to improve the bill, but most were designed to kill it. As the debate proceeded, I rushed back and forth from the House floor to a phone in the speaker's office to call a lawyer in the Bureau of Public Roads in Washington who was advising me on how to keep the bill in compliance with federal requirements. He got more involved as the afternoon progressed, and when I called to say we had won, I think he was as excited as I was.

My main ally in these legislative battles was the League of Women Voters, the only public interest lobby in West Virginia. Because most members were house-wives, they had flexible schedules that made it possible for them to prowl the halls of the legislature, buttonholing senators and delegates and presenting the case in person, which is the most effective way. Their husbands, chained to the office during the day, could not do this.

The day after the billboard legislation passed, another of my bills came to the floor. It was to outlaw eyesores within view of the public highways. Anyone who had traveled by car through West Virginia understood the problem. But this didn't mean that I lacked opposition.

113

There was plenty—from egregious offenders like the coal companies and junkyard operators to constitutional lawyers who had problems with defining an eyesore.

It was clear that we were in for another all-day session. I didn't want to appear to be hogging the floor two days in a row; I was afraid of getting a reputation for being a grandstander and thereby losing my effectiveness. So I caved, accepting an amendment that took the teeth out of the bill. Some of my colleagues reproached me for quitting on them: "We wanted to go on fighting." I was miserable. There is no feeling worse than the realization that you have let down the troops who were ready to fight the good fight.

My main regret about my days in the legislature is that I did not try to revive my father's air pollution bill. The possibility never occurred to me. I was still enough of a prisoner of the fifties mentality that I would have deemed the bill too radical to have a chance to pass. My regret may explain my disdain today for the incrementalist, who avoids taking a radical stand, even when it is right, because he thinks it isn't realistic. On air pollution, I was one of them, and I was wrong.

My father, Charles G. Peters, Sr.,
Captain in the U.S. Army, 1918

My mother, Esther Peters, 1940

*The house on Brooks Street in Charleston, West Virginia, where I grew up*

*Geared up for football in the backyard, 1935*

*Meeting the governor's wife, 1933*

**At the circus in Charleston, 1934**

*Military school, 1941*

*The photo of FDR that I purchased at the West Virginia State Fair, 1933*

*Age 19 at Columbia College, 1946*

*With Senator John Kennedy during the 1960 campaign in West Virginia*

**With Sargent Shriver at the Peace Corps,**
**June 1961**

*With Peace Corps volunteers and Thais in
Chiengmai, Thailand, 1962*

*First cover of* The Washington Monthly, *February 1969*

*Editor Taylor Branch, 1971*

*Editor John Rothchild, 1971*

*The staff of* The Washington Monthly, *1973:*
*Polly Toynbee, Walter Shapiro, Charlie Peters,*
*James Fallows, and Suzannah Lessard*

*With James Fallows at the Monthly offices,*
*1973*

*With former editors Nicholas Lemann and*
*Walter Shapiro, 1980*

*Editors Gregg Easterbrook and Jonathan Alter,*
*1981 (Photo by Diana Walker)*

*My wife Beth and I walking near our home in*
*Washington, 1981 (Photo by Diana Walker)*

*With Allen Ginsberg, 1986, forty years after
we first met*

*My son, Chris, 1968 (Photo by Phyllis Crowley)*

*The thirty-fifth reunion of the "eight" from Charleston High School Class of 1944*

*(Photo by Michael Evans)*

# CHAPTER 7

# The Golden
# Spotted Mamba

**A**S my first session in the legislature ended in March 1961, I began to think about going to Washington. Not permanently—my ambition was to be governor of West Virginia—but I also wanted to play a part in the birth of the New Frontier. I asked my friends in the administration to be on the lookout for a job I could fill for three months or so with some possibility of doing some good but without doing any harm.

As we discussed the various agencies, it became clear that my preference was the Peace Corps, which was just getting started. Like many other people of that era, I had been impressed by the case made in the book *The Ugly American* for sending people overseas who knew the language and customs of the country in which they worked. I believed in appealing to the idealism of the young because I remembered how we had responded in World War II. And I believed in what the young could do because of my experience with the summer theater.

Unfortunately, although I knew some powerful people in the administration, I didn't know Sargent Shriver, the director of the Peace Corps. He had worked in the West Virginia campaign, but in another county. And he had been promised immunity from patronage demands in his new job. So when the White House told him I was coming, his reaction was not unrestrained enthusiasm. I was given the title "consultant to the general counsel," which certainly suggested that I would do no harm but did not glow with promise, either.

× × ×

I reported for work on April 27, 1961. Fortunately, the general counsel, Morris Abram, was not offended by my being a legacy of the campaign. Nor were my colleagues Robert Hellawell and Roger Kuhn. They made sure that I got my share of interesting work, and I was soon up to my ears in it.

One assignment changed my life. It was to negotiate an agreement with the Commonwealth of Puerto Rico to establish a training facility near the town of Arecibo. This involved going to Puerto Rico several times, working directly with Shriver and one of his principal assistants, William Haddad, and cutting through considerable red tape. Because volunteers would be ready for training soon, it had to be done quickly. I did it with apparent ease, although the ease was only apparent—I was usually figuring out my next step just seconds before I had to take it.

While I was going back and forth to Puerto Rico, Shriver and Haddad were plotting an organizational revolution. Unlike most Washington officials before and since, they were aware of the bureaucracy's tendency to tell the official at the top only what it wants him to hear. To meet this problem, they decided to send their own man to visit Peace Corps groups in training and overseas to provide them with a report independent of the chain of command. They had just sent me someplace to do

116

something that had required getting around the bureaucracy. I had done it satisfactorily, so before I knew what was happening, I was on a plane to the University of California at Berkeley to report on our first training program. I was called an evaluator.

At Berkeley I found a mostly happy situation, with good volunteers and a good training program. One of the few problems was language. The volunteers, who were going to serve in Ghana, were learning Twi. The trouble was that Twi is the language of only one of Ghana's several tribes. What's more, they were being taught Twi only a couple of hours a week, which was grossly inadequate for those who needed it and a waste of time for those who didn't.

Next I went to Texas Western College in El Paso, where we were training a group of surveyors to serve in Tanganyika, the country now known as Tanzania. Here I encountered a classic failure of communication between the various parts of the Peace Corps bureaucracy. Tanganyika's request to our programming office for surveyors had been translated by our recruiting and selection division into a request for anyone who had ever had any connection with surveying. So most of the volunteers at El Paso were not trained surveyors but rod and chain men, the fellows who stand there holding the stick while the surveyor looks through his gizmo.

The advantage of the evaluation process began to emerge. I was reporting problems that Shriver had not heard through the regular chain of command. This was good for Shriver, but it did not bring instant delight to the chain of command. The bureaucrats, who were not aware of the problems I was reporting or, if they were, had chosen to conceal them, counterattacked, guns blazing, accusing me of being a spy and being competely unqualified to evaluate what they were doing.

My instinct was to fight back, but my three months

117

were up. I had promised my law firm that I would return by August 1, so Beth and I packed our bags and drove back to Charleston.

I was immediately immersed in writing a brief on a key legal issue in a case Bill Mohler was trying. During the evenings, we caught up with old friends and were reminded of how much we liked them and Charleston. And when the governor called and asked me to be his special counsel, a job that would put me in a good position to campaign to be his successor, it seemed certain that we would stay in Charleston.

But then Bill Haddad called to ask me to visit some more training programs. I found that I couldn't say no. I thought evaluation was a good idea and I enjoyed doing the work—and I could not bear having seemed to run away from my critics.

Between August 20 and September 10, I managed to squeeze in trips to Iowa State, Notre Dame, Penn State, and Harvard. (Shriver was spreading training contracts around the way the Pentagon does, and for the same reason—to establish a broad constituency.) I returned to Charleston long enough to finish Bill Mohler's brief. Then, the governor having said he could wait a few months for me to decide about his job offer, I agreed to work for the Peace Corps until the thirty-day session of the legislature began in January.

That fall, I made my first visit to a Peace Corps project overseas. It was in St. Lucia, the Caribbean island that is most like Tahiti and is becoming a major resort. In 1961, however, it was still undeveloped. My first night there, after a hard day driving around the island to visit volunteers at their sites, I went to bed at the small hotel where I was staying, looking forward to a good night's sleep. As I was nodding off, I heard a fluttering sound above me. I looked up. Scores of small black shapes were huddled against the ceiling. Bats! Don't get excited, I told myself, bats don't attack human beings. The only kind you have to worry about are vampire bats, and they're only in the West Indies. . . . Wait a minute! I'm in the West Indies!

(As I did more traveling, I learned how much the volunteers loved to see this kind of thing happen to the visitor from Washington. They constantly tested you with snake stories. You know about the golden spotted mamba, don't you, Charlie? Its venom kills in just five seconds. There are quite a few around here. Oh, the john is a hundred feet or so through that thick grass in back of the house. Sorry it's so dark out there. Wish I could give you a flashlight, but ours is on the blink. Watch your step.)

There were some serious problems in our St. Lucia program and even more serious ones in the next project I visited, in the Philippines, where we had tried to place too many people too fast in the ill-defined role of "teacher's aide." And in the training programs I evaluated that fall at Michigan, Colorado State, UCLA, and Michigan State, I found weakness in the language, cultural, and technical instruction.

My reports of these problems continued to irritate and often anger the bureaucrats in the chain of command. It was clear that, as far as they were concerned, the less evaluation, the better. But Haddad persuaded Shriver that more was better, and plans were drawn up for an evaluation division. While I was home for the legislative session in January, I was asked to return to Washington in February as the division's chief.

I was torn. Because evaluation was unpopular with powerful people in the organization, I thought there was a very good chance that this would turn out to be another job from which I would be fired. And then there was the job the governor had offered me that promised to be a good launching pad for my political future. Finally, there was the guilt factor. How could I leave West Virginia when it needed just as much help as many of the Third World countries that the Peace Corps was serving?

On the other hand, there was the appeal of the people at the Peace Corps and of Washington under John Kennedy. In my life, I had met many people I liked but comparatively few who shared my feelings and values. At the Peace Corps, it seemed as if I found someone like that every day. When I was overseas, I could usually count on the volunteer who lived at the end of a long, dusty jeep ride over some bumpy trace of a Third World road inviting me into his house, fixing me dinner, and turning out to be so thoroughly engaging that by the end of the evening, I knew a lasting friendship was possible.

It was exciting to work for the United States government in the early sixties. We walked to the office each morning alive with the sense that we had important business to attend to, serving a country and a president we believed in. Our attitudes toward pay reflected those feelings. When I arrived in Washington, I thought I was owed something. After all, I had been for Kennedy when practically no one else in West Virginia had any interest in him. I asked for the top salary possible for an employee like me—seventy-five dollars a day. A month or so later, I was told that, because my earnings had been so modest at the law firm, I would receive only forty dollars a day plus twelve dollars for expenses. By that time I had become so immersed in my work and so exhilarated by John F. Kennedy's Washington that I grabbed the forty dollars and thought I was lucky to have it.

What tipped the balance in favor of the Peace Corps was my growing realization that, in evaluation, I had finally found work that fit me like a glove. For the first time in my life I felt both completely competent at a job and completely interested in it. As a lawyer, I had learned how to interview and investigate and put the resulting evidence together. Now I could do that and at the same time serve a cause that I believed in completely.

× × ×

SINCE I was going to have to guide the work of other evaluators, I knew that I needed to get a broad picture of the Peace Corps' problems—as it spread out over Africa, Asia, and Latin America—so that I could distinguish between those that were across-the-board and those that were unique to particular projects. For the next four months, I was on the road almost constantly, adding Ghana, Pakistan, Nigeria, Thailand, Malaya, and El Salvador to the list of projects that I had seen first-hand.

None, except for Pakistan, was in really bad shape, but each had its troubles, including many that resulted from those deficiencies that I had seen during training in the United States—too little language instruction, inadequate technical training, and not enough preparation for the customs of the host country. Also, there were volunteers who had been assigned to jobs that turned out not to exist or not to fit their talents. This problem was worst in Pakistan. I wrote from Karachi, "Only fifteen of the fifty-nine volunteers have real jobs." It was painful to see the idealism of the volunteers squandered as they sat there with nothing to do.

One of the guilty parties was Sargent Shriver. When he started the Peace Corps, he wanted to get volunteers overseas and into action fast and was determined not to let the organization become mired in feasibility studies. Staff members were dispatched to Third World countries with firm instructions to return with "a program in your pocket"—in other words, to get the countries to request volunteers and to do so right away, not after feasibility studies of their own. The scrutiny to which these requests were subjected by the Peace Corps staff in Washington did not err on the nitpicking side. As a result, a

121

good many turned out to be, as in Pakistan, requests for jobs that didn't exist. These fictitious requests were sometimes motivated by the country official's desire to please the brother-in-law of the president of the United States. But more often, the reason was the official's ignorance of what was going on in his own bureaucracy. The minister of agriculture in Nairobi might have no idea of the personnel needs of the experiment station at Kisumu, but instead of admitting his ignorance, he would say, "We need three agronomists and one expert on the eradication of the Albanian fruit fly."

If Pakistan was the most depressing program, Malaya (now Malaysia) was the most heartening. I will never forget two nurses named Sadie Stout and Mary Ianzetti. They worked in a hospital about twenty miles from Kuala Lumpur. As they took me through the leper ward, the patients smiled gratefully at them or even hugged them. If a leper had hugged me, my reaction would have been instant panic. Sadie and Mary hugged back. The patients smiled because Sadie and Mary cared about them. The personal concern that Peace Corps nurses showed for all their patients was unusual in the Third World, where caring tends not to cross the boundaries of family, tribe, or religious group.

There was only one problem with our nurses: most had not been trained to do certain tasks that the local nurses commonly did, such as drawing blood, administering intravenous infusions, and practicing midwifery. The American Medical Association did not want nurses treading on physicians' turf by performing such functions, and we had to fight, not always successfully, to get that training for subsequent nursing programs.

We had similar fights with the schools of education over the generalized methodology they were trying to palm off on us. This was important because more than half of our volunteers were teachers. What we needed to

122

know was: Can the volunteer teach, and does he know his subject? Yet we had to press the schools to provide practice teaching and to appraise the subject knowledge of our teachers before we sent them overseas. If there was to be instruction in methodology, we wanted it to be related to the subject—how to teach science or how to teach math.

The teachers' colleges were offended that we did not want their boring general methodology courses and that we did not require education degrees for volunteers who were going to teach. But our disdain for these things enabled us, like the good private schools, to make teachers out of bright graduates from the best colleges who wouldn't have taken an education course if they had been paid to.

The teachers were generally more successful than the community development workers, the next largest group of volunteers. Almost all assigned to Latin America, the community development workers tried to organize the local people to carry out self-help projects. The possibilities were revolutionary. The volunteers could empower the powerless and array the heretofore helpless campesino against the oligarchs who were oppressing him. The catch was that actually accomplishing all this required a volunteer who was a combination of Jesus Christ and John Kennedy, with a little bit of Tip O'Neill thrown in. So the community development volunteers, with a few heroic exceptions, accomplished little. The concept was so vague that few of them had a clear sense of what to do when they got out of bed in the morning.

By contrast, the teachers—most were in Africa—had structured jobs with a clear set of tasks to perform. Most of them were happy in their work. And they made an important contribution. The greatest weakness in African education was rote learning. Thinking was not encouraged, nor was creativity. In the former French and British colonies, the schools had been designed as training grounds for clerks to man the colonial bureaucracies and trading organizations. Our young American volunteers came from an education system that, though sometimes deficient in imparting knowledge, did encourage questioning and a healthy irreverence for authority.

Their main failing was that they fit in a bit too comfortably with the elitist colonial and African members of the faculty, who stayed in the school compound— most African schools are self-contained units—and did not associate with the villagers. If the colonials, and the African teachers who tended to emulate them, did not have downright contempt for the villagers, there was a line between town and gown that the volunteers were discouraged from crossing—and few did.

As these truths about the Peace Corps began to emerge in my mind, I found myself both excited by the sense that I knew what was wrong and angered by the Peace Corps bureaucracy's unwillingness to admit that there were any problems.

The attacks on evaluation had continued, and I knew I was still in danger of being fired. Finally, I decided that I had to get Shriver to compare what I was telling him with what the chain of command was telling him in a situation where he would be able to judge which side was right. So just before he left on a trip to Africa in the fall of 1962, I sent him a summary of the evaluation reports on the projects he was planning to visit and asked him to decide for himself whether we were right or wrong. Several weeks later, a cable arrived from Shriver, who was winding up his African tour: "Tell Peters his reports are right." The cable was widely circulated within the Peace Corps, and its effect on my critics was immediate and—from my standpoint, if not theirs—salutary. Evaluation would be subjected to attack again, but never with the sustained bitterness of the past year. And I would not be fired, which for a man with my history was very good news indeed.

Of course, Shriver could not always side with the evaluation division. After all, he had to demonstrate some faith in his operations people if he was going to retain their loyalty and enthusiasm. So we still had to convince the rest of the agency that what they had been doing was wrong. In their case, the natural human reluctance to concede error was often compounded by the ideological commitment that underlay the mistake. This commitment involved their basic sense of what the Peace Corps was about. It was difficult for the people who wanted to change the corrupt social order in Latin America to accept our reports that a lovely idea like community development simply wasn't working. And for those who saw the Peace Corps as a provider of skilled manpower to the Third World, the evaluators' concern about the lack of contact between our teachers and African villagers seemed irrelevant.

The Peace Corps was deeply divided on the question of its purpose. On one side were the technical assistance advocates. For them, what was important was for the volunteers to assist in the economic development of the host country. On the other side were those who believed that people-to-people relationships were most important. This group was divided into two factions, one emphasizing what the volunteers would learn from the people of their countries—how they would be the advance guard of a wiser and more understanding foreign policy when they returned to America—and the other emphasizing the volunteers' impact on the host country people, either as revolutionaries or as junior diplomats who would win friends for America.

This debate was not academic. It affected the kind

of people we selected as volunteers, how they were trained, where they were placed, and what sort of jobs they were in.

In the early days, for example, staff members who believed in the junior diplomat role designed training programs devoted largely to courses in American studies, world affairs, and communism, which left little time for training in technical skills, language, and the local culture. The idea of volunteers engaging leftist natives in ideological debate that would rescue them from the lures of Marxism may have sounded good back home, but in the field such discussions were rare.

On the other hand, a volunteer who was selected only because he was a good technician might lack the skills in language and human relations that he needed to communicate technical knowledge. If he didn't understand the local culture, he might know the right seed to plant but not why custom affected the time or place of the planting.

The largest and most influential people-to-people faction was the one that emphasized the learning experience of the volunteer. What the volunteer *did* made little difference.

The learning experience was important. It freed volunteers from the grip of clichés about the Third World, whether liberal or conservative, and exposed them to positive forces in other cultures, such as the strong family values that were increasingly missing in our own. It led them to pick up facts of life about the countries in which they served that were frequently unknown by senior American officials—for example, that the average Iranian hated the Shah. But the learning experience advocates often placed volunteers in jobs of marginal value—such as teacher's aide—or in no job at all. This created a volunteer who was demoralized because he knew his work wasn't important and who was not respected by his hosts because they, too, knew it wasn't.

In Washington, the debate over these issues raged back and forth for several years. Gradually, as reality began to penetrate, first through the evaluation reports and then through the return of former volunteers to staff jobs in Washington, most of the staff came to realize that the volunteer's job and his people-to-people efforts were inextricably related, that success in one depended on success in the other.

This taught me something about theories in general: any theory is likely to be wrong unless it is based on experience and constantly reconsidered in the light of new experience. This is the most obvious kind of common sense. Yet most people, once they have adopted a theory, have a tenacious aversion to facts that don't fit.

What evaluators had been doing for the Peace Corps was to show how the ideas behind it had fared in the test of reality. This kind of analysis had to come from within because no one outside the organization was interested in doing it. The press was extremely kind to the Peace Corps in the early years. The average reporter was a liberal, and the Peace Corps was a liberal idea, an idealistic expression of the spirit of the New Frontier. This predisposition to kindness was nurtured by the skill of the people the Peace Corps assigned to handle journalists— people like Bill Moyers, Tom Mathews, Ed Bayley, Bill Haddad, Don McClure, and Tim Adams. All of them were masters at subtly directing a reporter's attention toward the good news and away from the bad.

Their job was made easier by the typical reporter's approach to government agencies. He usually got his information from the public affairs office, which served as a filter between him and the people on the firing line who knew what the agency was actually doing. If he got interviews with these people, the public affairs office had arranged them and, by judiciously selecting the interviewees, had determined what the reporter would hear.

Reporters often put even more distance between themselves and the story by demanding interviews with the big shots. (Self-important columnists are notorious for this.) What they didn't seem to realize is that one of the ways the top bureaucrats at an agency get where they are is through their ability to handle the press without excessive candor.

If the reporters took the trouble to go to the field—and some did visit the countries where the Peace Corps was working—they usually confined themselves to the capital city and its immediate environs, where the hotels were more likely to be comfortable. Our shrewder country directors soon learned to have a few showcase operations handy to convince visiting journalists that the Peace Corps was a great success.

The top officials would read the glowing accounts in the press and want to believe that they were true. When I reported less happy news, many of them just didn't want to face it, preferring to remain undisturbed in their warm cocoon of self-congratulation, conning themselves with the stories they had conned the reporters into writing.

One example of a failure to get the real story was the press's coverage of older volunteers. When the Corps was about a year old, an article about older volunteers appeared in the *New York Times Magazine*. Ghosted by one of our PR people, it ran under Shriver's by-line and proclaimed the great success of the organization's senior citizens. The article was misleading. Many old people did not do well overseas. They had trouble learning the language and adjusting to the new culture. They were appalled by the filth and frightened by the lizards in their beds and the bats hanging from their ceilings. Even those in their thirties, like me, had problems. The Peace Corps was mostly for the young. They had the flexibility to learn and to adjust. They weren't upset by primitive living conditions. I understood this from my own life. When I was a student at Columbia, I could live in tenements and think it was a lark. But by my mid-thirties, when I was visiting volunteers overseas, I sometimes had to grit my teeth to live the way they did for even a few days.

This was not always the case; in some projects the volunteers lived well and had jobs much like those back home. Secondary school teaching was an example. Here the older people could succeed. And, of course, there were a few of them who were just as flexible and adaptable as any of the twenty-one-year-olds, if not more so. But on the whole, the Peace Corps clearly was not a good place for the senior citizen.

Yet the *New York Times* published an article saying the exact opposite. I have been fascinated over the years to see the press quoting each new head of the Peace Corps on what a great job the old folks are doing, usually in an article accompanied by touching pictures of gray-haired Americans embracing smiling brown children, with palm trees and thatched roofs in the background. It makes a good, heart-warming story, one that appeals to readers and therefore to editors. It makes both the Peace Corps and its director sound good. So who cares that it isn't true?

Congress was no better than the press in finding out the truth about the Peace Corps. In committee hearings, the members almost never asked the right questions. Of course, one reason for that was that we were (in fact, I was) less than forthcoming in providing the General Accounting Office with unflattering information. The General Accounting Office is the investigative arm of Congress. It is supposed to determine how well public money has been spent—in other words, how effectively the executive branch is doing its job.

Since the GAO's role is, in theory at least, similar to the role my evaluation division performed for the Peace Corps, it would seem that I would have been favorably disposed to the GAO investigators who were assigned to cover the Peace Corps. But I saw them as the enemy. Although I took immense pride in telling the truth about the Peace Corps within the organization, I thought it was sinful even to consider helping outside critics find out what was wrong. After all, it might be used as ammunition against us in the press or on Capitol Hill.

The typical civil servant or member of the military feels the same way. That's why he has such low regard for whistleblowers. Sure, they may be telling the truth, but, he reasons, why not keep the bad news in-house, fix things ourselves, and avoid the risk of budget cuts and similar calamities that might result from bad publicity?

This is why civil servants and military officers tend to overclassify documents and conceal and obfuscate when dealing with the press or with congressional investigators. Sometimes they even lie, which is why all congressional testimony should be under oath, as 90 percent is not today.

It is also why outside investigators who want to find out the truth about government agencies should not rely on career personnel. They should seek out such people as Peace Corps volunteers and soldiers and sailors who are in for a short term and do not have time to develop the sense of organizational interest that would make them want to gild the lily.

To help the truth get out, we also need more short-term people in the middle ranks of the military and civilian bureaucracies. The only time in recent history there have been many such people in government was during World War II. It is no coincidence that that is when we had the most responsive government in our history. Fighters that were sitting ducks for the Japanese and the Germans were quickly replaced by planes like the P51, which were really good, all because noncareer pilots were willing to complain to their congressmen and to anyone else who would listen.

The Peace Corps was full of short-term people. I worked there for seven years, but most of the staff served for shorter periods—the average was probably four years—and by 1965 we had made five years the legal limit. This meant that we got people who had enough confidence in themselves to believe that they could get another job in a few years. Although they did make some mistakes and try to cover things up, they were much more candid than the average civil servant. I have since learned that the bureaucratic tendencies I observed at the Peace Corps are much worse in other agencies.

All in all, they were a remarkable group of people, among whom I found many lifelong friends, including my colleagues in the general counsel's office that first spring, Roger Kuhn and Bob Hellawell. During the fall of 1961, I became close to Pat Kennedy, Al Meisel, Tim Adams, and Sally Bowles. They played a crucial role in my life because they made a determined effort to persuade me to stay in Washington instead of returning to West Virginia to run for governor.

There were other people who were not close friends but who had great influence on me during the Peace Corps years. One was Sally's father, Chester Bowles, who had been named undersecretary of state at the beginning of the Kennedy administration. As a result, in my first year in Washington I saw the Kennedy administration not only at its best, in the Peace Corps, but also at its worst, in its treatment of Chester Bowles. Bowles had angered Bobby Kennedy by opposing the Bay of Pigs invasion. Bowles was right and Bobby was wrong. But Bobby had the ear of the king, and it happens that the king wasn't too favorably disposed toward Bowles in the first place. Jack Kennedy favored terseness in his aides, and Chet could be long-winded; his conversation sounded like a public reading from *Foreign Affairs*. If he had any small talk in him, I never heard it. Beth and I stayed in his house for six weeks while he and his wife, Steb, were abroad. At night I scanned the rows of books that lined the shelves throughout his house. I could not find one sexy novel or detective story—and my search was diligent. Every book had a title like *The World Economy Today*.

Although Chet was short on light conversation, his foreign policy judgments were the best in the Kennedy administration. If he had had his way, there would have been no Bay of Pigs and no Vietnam, either. His opinions, alas, did not prevail. The Kennedy brothers exiled him, first to a meaningless special assistantship and then to India as ambassador.

The Kennedys were the center of Washington during my first years there. I saw them much less frequently than I did in West Virginia. I was a smaller fish now. On one occasion, while waiting in the East Room of the White House for Kennedy to speak to the Colombia and St. Lucia volunteers, I stood next to the prettiest woman in the group. When Kennedy entered the room, he glanced around briefly and then appeared to head directly for his old friend, Charlie Peters. My friends were impressed, because they didn't know what I had guessed from Kennedy's expression of interest in Beth outside the department store in Charleston.

Actually, except for his affair with Judith Campbell Exner, which exposed him to blackmail, Kennedy's womanizing never offended me the way it did others. He had no macho desire to dominate. He did not put women down. I suspect that he had the almost insatiable sexual curiosity—"What a great looking woman. I wonder what it would be like with her."—that was common among men of my generation. It may have been rooted in some moral and personal deficiencies, including an insensitivity to his wife's feelings and a mechanistic view of sex, but it had nothing to do with the most dangerous form of machismo, the need to win at any cost.

That Kennedy did not have this kind of machismo became clear during the Cuban missile crisis. He repeatedly resisted the urgent advice of such influential hawks as Dean Acheson that he bomb Cuba. He got the Russian missiles out of Cuba without bloodshed. And, to do it, he made the very unmacho move of sending Bobby to assure Anatoly Dobrynin, the Soviet ambassador to Washington, that we would remove our missiles from Turkey. Jack Kennedy took great pains to conceal this fact—he even misled his friends Stewart Alsop and Charles Bartlett, who wrote an article for the *Saturday Evening Post* portraying Adlai Stevenson as a sissy for suggesting removing the missiles in Turkey. Kennedy was concerned about appearing tough. But his real behavior was not that of a dangerous tough guy but that of a thoroughly reasonable man determined to handle the conflict effectively, without killing people.

I hope that Kennedy's legacy will be the unmacho rationality he brought to the missile crisis and the nuclear test ban treaty and the spirit of service he called forth with "Ask not what your country can do for you, ask what you can do for your country." But what I fear is that his main legacy will be the nation of snobs that it seems we are becoming. He took over a White House that had been occupied in the previous decade by Harry and Bess Truman and Ike and Mamie Eisenhower and a country that watched television shows like "I Love Lucy" and "The Honeymooners"—a country that identified with the average man. John and Jacqueline Kennedy gave it, instead, a prince and princess to emulate. Jack's closest friend had this to say about his motivation for marrying

Jackie: "I knew right away that Jackie was different from all the other girls Jack had been dating. . . . Her mother's second marriage to Hugh Auchincloss carried the family into the social register, which gave Jackie a certain classiness that's hard to describe."

Because they were upwardly mobile themselves, the Kennedys understood the upward mobility of others—and how to take advantage of it. The famous campaign "teas" were consciously designed to appeal to the social aspirations of the women who attended. Similar aspirations were behind the public's use of the Kennedys as behavior models. By the early sixties, men stopped wearing hats because Jack didn't wear one, and women were having their hair done like Jackie's and buying clothes that imitated her designer dresses. They found out what was the right thing to do by watching the first family. As one writer observed, "Everyone wanted to be in high society with the Kennedys."

Certainly much of this was harmless—indeed, the general level of taste may have improved as a result—and certainly snobbery has always been with us, but it does seem to me that since the Kennedys came to power, the tendency to identify with the elite and the need to feel superior to others have been much more evident in the American character.

I was, however, largely unaware of all this at the time I worked under Kennedy. To me, he was an inspiring leader, and I was proud to serve him. I felt the same about his brother-in-law, Sargent Shriver. Shriver had the kind of charisma that makes men charge the barricades. He inspired enormous effort on the part of those of us who worked at the Peace Corps. Sometimes, however, he came across as a Boy Scout, and the Kennedys, especially Bobby and sometimes even Shriver's wife, Eunice, could treat him with condescension. He actually was very smart. He could discuss Catholic theology with insight and wit.

And he was a brilliant talent scout, who taught me that anyone who runs an organization should give the highest priority to searching for the right people to man it.

Shriver's most serious fault was also his greatest virtue. He set goals that goaded the organization to action, but the pressure to meet those goals sometimes caused his subordinates to err. It is to his great credit that he saw the need for people like the evaluators, who would make sure that he was confronted with the errors before it was too late to correct them.

Jack Vaughn, who followed Shriver as director of the Peace Corps, had been in charge of our Latin American programs from 1961 to 1964. After that he was ambassador to Panama and assistant secretary of state for Latin American affairs. Jack was not the exciting leader that Sarge had been. He would not have been nearly as successful in getting the organization started, when it needed inspiration to help it do the impossible. But for the period in the organization's life when he was director, Jack was the best for the job. He was more concerned than Sarge had been with making the basic reforms that were needed in programming and training. To give just one example, he doubled the number of hours devoted to language training.

In 1966 Jack asked me to chair a committee whose purpose was to figure out how to reduce the number of employees in the Peace Corps Washington headquarters. "There must be some people sitting around doing nothing," he said. "Or if they are doing something, maybe it doesn't need doing."

It turned out that there was only a handful of such people. Almost everyone was spending at least part of the day doing something worthwhile. If a job was eliminated, something wouldn't get done that needed doing. This is the stubborn, inconvenient fact that most efforts to "cut the fat" out of bureaucracies run into. It's why most fat-cutters shrug their shoulders and give up. The solution, the committee discovered, was to look not for jobs that could be abolished but for jobs that could be consolidated. Suppose you have three employees, each of whom performs real, necessary work for about a third of the day. If you combine the three jobs into one, you can eliminate two positions and still get all the work done. But if you abolish two jobs, two-thirds of the work will not get done, and the remaining employee will still be working only a third of the day.

Even when employees appear to be busy all day, they may be keeping busy dealing with one another. At the Peace Corps, we had three jobs that provided support for overseas operations: desk officer, training officer, and volunteer services officer. Many of these people worked themselves to the point of exhaustion each day, but much of their work consisted simply of communicating with each other by telephone, in meetings, and by memo. If the need for communication were eliminated by consolidating the jobs, one person could do the work of three. Needless to say, this idea did not spread joy through the corridors, and it was not adopted. But it is a key to the kind of reform that could dramatically reduce the government payroll without impairing essential functions.

Jack expanded my small bureaucratic empire by placing the Research Division under me. While the Evaluation Division had been concerned with appraising programs in a way that produced rapid feedback, at the risk of erring on the side of impressionistic journalism, the Research Division was supposed to support more thorough, systematic, and academically respectable inquiry. Most of the evaluation work was done by full-time employees of the Peace Corps; research was carried out under contract by universities and other institutions.

When I took over the Research Division, it was asking for a budget of $1.4 million for the next fiscal year.

The division staff was convinced that this was the minimum it needed to carry out its mission and that any cutback should be resisted vigorously.

Although I knew little about the division's work, I wanted to win the regard of my new subordinates, and I didn't want to begin our relationship by telling them that I didn't trust their judgment. Better to start out as their knight in shining armor. So I enthusiastically embraced their cause and fought and won the first round of the budget battle within our agency. I've forgotten how I got it past the Budget Bureau, which is what the Office of Management and Budget was called at that time, but I did. Then I testified before the House Foreign Affairs Committee. They authorized only $500,000. I was devastated and proceeded to tour the offices of the members of the Senate Foreign Relations Committee in an effort to get the money restored. I failed.

Over the next four months, however, I learned what was really going on in Research. We had solid plans for spending only about $200,000. Even with monumental effort, which included setting up a research unit at Harvard headed by David McClelland and David Reisman, we were able to spend only $400,000 by the end of the fiscal year. This sort of thing goes on in every agency. Bureaucrats ask for more money than they can spend, because they are fearful that their request will be cut somewhere along the long road it must travel through the agency, then the OMB, and finally Congress. When that process fails to wring out all the excess in the budget—and it almost always does fail—the bureaucratic unit will frantically try to dispose of the money so that its original request will not be exposed as inflated. This effort reaches its peak in the "September spending spree," when all the agencies in government compete to shovel money out the door before the fiscal year ends on September 30.

One reason we were able to spend so little on Peace Corps research was the stunning dullness of most of the proposals we received from social scientists (McClelland and Reisman excluded). They seemed to scorn insight and observation and to value only the quantifiable. Their prose was obscure and laden with pretentious academic jargon.

On the whole, it was clear that the evaluators were a lot better than the social scientists at helping the Peace Corps learn from its experience. Most of the evaluators were journalists, from such places as CBS News, the *New York Herald Tribune*, the Associated Press, and the *Miami Herald*. They were skilled observers who could report what they had seen in prose that was readable. They prized their independence and the independence of our division. They were willing to place the blame where it belonged, even when that meant taking on the most powerful people in the organization. There should be people like them in every agency. Regrettably, there is no similar group anywhere in the government today.

Even though the evaluators never gave me reason to doubt their integrity, I went to great lengths to make sure that they would resist any temptation to soften their criticism. I hired several part-time evaluators who were not dependent on the Peace Corps financially and who were not around long enough to form the friendships with other Peace Corps employees that might affect their willingness to call a spade a spade. I reasoned that if a full-time evaluator knew his evaluation might be followed up by a part-timer's, he would be more likely to identify that spade accurately himself.

One of the part-time evaluators was Richard Rovere. There was no journalist I admired more. His "Letters from Washington" in the *New Yorker* were models of lucidity, and he stood out as both thoughtful and courageous during the McCarthy era. He was one of my heroes.

I asked him if he would be interested in doing an evaluation, and he said yes. He went to Kenya, wrote an incisive report, and thoroughly enjoyed the experience. Soon he began sending me young writers from the *New Yorker*, such as John McPhee, Renata Adler, Robert Rice, and Calvin Trillin. Unfortunately, I was able to use only Rice and Trillin before I left the Peace Corps.

A few years earlier, I had met another person at the Peace Corps who, like Rovere, came to play an important role in my future. Early in the summer of 1962, a tall, lanky fellow stuck his head in my office and said, "I'm Jay Rockefeller." I had already heard he was coming to work at Peace Corps headquarters. At twenty-four, he had been the youngest member appointed by Shriver to our national advisory council. The appointment was inspired by a long article in *Life* about the modest, getting-to-know-the-people life that Jay had lived in Japan a few years earlier. I was prepared to dislike him because the *Life* article had made him sound almost prissily perfect, and I had a deep suspicion of *Life*'s sycophantic treatment of the Rockefeller family.

Jay turned out to be a nice guy—so likable, in fact, that we talked for an hour or so and agreed to meet for lunch the next day. He shared my passion for football and baseball and had a good sense of humor, including an ability to laugh at himself. An added attraction was that he sought my advice about his relationships with young women, which were many and fascinating, and gave a married man like me a chance to explore forbidden territory vicariously. We soon were good friends, having lunch every week and seeing each other or talking on the phone every day.

In the summer of 1963, Jay moved to the State Department, but we remained in close touch. By the beginning of 1964—the year the Johnson administration's War on Poverty began—he had begun to catch the concern for the problem of domestic poverty that was sweeping Washington. He felt he had spent too much of his life in foreign affairs and not enough learning about this country and its problems.

I said, "Why not go to West Virginia. If you want to find out about poverty, you'll see it there." As we talked about this possibility, I became more and more determined to persuade him to go. I'm sure I wanted to give him good advice, but I was also motivated by guilt for having left West Virginia when it was in such bad shape. I felt that if I could just get Jay down there, he would become involved enough to do something about the state's problems. My task was made easier by the intercession of Bobby Kennedy, who offered Jay a job in Kanawha County with Action for Appalachian Youth, a pilot poverty project that was under Bobby's jurisdiction.

So Jay went to West Virginia. Soon he was immersed in his poverty project in the little town of Emmons, about thirty miles from Charleston. People liked him. They built a community building while he was there and named it Rockefeller Center. And Jay liked the people so much that he decided to make West Virginia his home. In 1966 he ran for the House of Delegates from Kanawha County and was elected that November.

I had made a difference in Jay's life. Now it was his turn to make a difference in mine.

# CHAPTER 8

# The New
# Political
# Journalism

**F**OR many of my friends who had come to Washington with John Kennedy, his assassination was the end of the magic. For me, this was not so. I grieved along with everyone else—I remember suddenly bursting into tears in a restaurant on that gray Saturday after Dallas. But I still had a lot to accomplish at the Peace Corps, and I wasn't hostile to Lyndon Johnson, as many Kennedy loyalists were. For that matter, I thought Johnson was better on civil rights than Kennedy had been. So I stayed on.

But by the spring of 1967, the main problems Evaluation had been reporting were being attended to. And working in the government was no longer exciting. Vietnam had taken care of that. I wasn't proud of what Johnson was doing there—I was ashamed and depressed. I was ready to leave the Peace Corps and try something else.

Two thoughts came together in my mind, neither of them modest. One was that I knew something about organizational behavior that American journalism seemed unaware of; no one person had had the opportunity that I had for six years at the Peace Corps to examine the operation of a government agency from top to bottom—not just to uncover fraud and abuse (the job of the inspectors general in other agencies) but to determine why programs succeeded or failed. My other thought was of Henry Luce, who had just died. Luce had proved, first with *Time* and then with *Life*, that one man could change journalism. The conclusion seemed obvious: I, too, should start a magazine and change the way journalism covered government.

In late April, I told Jack Vaughn I would be leaving the Peace Corps in one year. I also told him about the magazine. I knew I had to trap myself by publicly proclaiming my intentions, because I realized that as I found out what I was getting into, there would be times when I would want to back out.

The case for backing out did not take long to emerge. As I let friends know about my plans, they asked me whether I had any magazine experience. I didn't. I hadn't even worked on a school paper since junior high. This, they pointed out, might not be reassuring to potential writers, not to mention investors.

After several months of listening to these doubts, I called Richard Rovere and arranged to meet him for lunch the next time he came to Washington. I told him people were wondering how I could run a magazine without ever having had anything to do with one. They might feel more comfortable if I had an experienced advisor. He agreed.

As we talked, I tried to work up the courage to ask him to do it. I knew he would endow the project with instant credibility, but I thought that he might not want to risk his reputation on a venture with prospects as uncertain as this one. Finally, I put the question. His answer, to my relief, was yes.

The other matter my friends kept bringing up was that I had no money. Those who knew something about publishing estimated that I would need half a million dollars or more. They also said that in approaching prospective investors, I should have some money already in hand, to show that this was a serious proposition. So I asked Jay Rockefeller if he could put up $20,000. He, too, said yes. If either Dick or Jay had turned me down, my nerve probably would have failed, but now I felt ready to go forth and sell my project to the world.

It quickly became obvious that most of the potential investors I talked to weren't concerned about making a lot of money from the magazine. I had little exposure to the purely greedy, because few of them would even see me. On the other hand, even the nongreedy didn't want to just give their money away—or, if there were going to be losses, they hoped there would be some kind of tax break to ease the pain. What they seemed most interested in was how the magazine would be different. What would it do that other magazines weren't doing? There was an answer, but it was not going to be easy to explain to people who, unlike Dick and Jay, knew nothing about the Peace Corps Evaluation Division.

What I wanted the magazine to do was to cover the rest of the world in the same way that Evaluation covered the Peace Corps—with an emphasis on understanding the institutional imperatives that govern what organizations and the individuals who work for them do. I wanted to look at Washington the way that an anthropologist looks at a South Sea island.

It was hard to avoid thinking anthropologically at the Peace Corps. As we watched American volunteers interact with the people of other countries, we realized how much culture affects human behavior. It didn't take much of an intellectual leap to begin to examine the bureaucratic culture of the Peace Corps in the same way. It was clear, for example, that the pressure to produce results led our staff in the field, who were eager to prove themselves, to rush to propose programs to Washington that were very close to fictitious. The same pressures led them to be less than candid with their superiors about what was going wrong with these programs as they went from the drawing board to reality overseas. Finally, some of the officials in Washington didn't want to know what was wrong, because they didn't want to be held accountable.

These were not the kinds of problems that you read about in the newspapers and magazines of the sixties. Books such as David Halberstam's *The Best and the Brightest*, Bob Woodward's *The Brethren*, and Timothy Crouse's *The Boys on the Bus* were yet to be written. The existence of a culture of bureaucracy on the banks of the Potomac was simply not recognized by journalists of that era. Social scientists wrote about the organization man, but they focused on the organization's effect on the man, not on how the interaction of the two affected the organization's behavior.

It was this story of the whys of organizational behavior that interested me, and, in going after it, I wanted to avoid relying on the big shots and their close associates, who were the main sources for conventional reporters. During World War II, Ernie Pyle and Bill Mauldin showed journalists that the worm's-eye view is often more interesting and candid than the view from the top. But outside the realm of war reporting, their lesson was largely ignored. I had seen its truth proved again by the contrast between the stories evaluators got from Peace Corps volunteers and the stories other journalists were getting from high Peace Corps officials, so I was confident that Pyle and Mauldin had the right idea.

Another movement in journalism of which I wanted to be a part had also begun in the World War II era. It was the novelistic approach to reporting that John Hersey used in *Hiroshima*. It continued with Lillian Ross's account in the *New Yorker* in the fifties of the filming of John Huston's *The Red Badge of Courage*, and it came to considerable prominence through the journalism of Theodore White, Truman Capote, and Tom Wolfe in the sixties. In these works, facts were reported, not stripped of their flesh, as in traditional journalism, but enriched by a novelist's feel for the telling detail, for characterization and plot, and for the emotional context of ideas and events.

I also had some ideas about journalism that I had developed over my years of reading newspapers and magazines. I did not believe in the traditional distinction between journalist and intellectual, which, to put it baldly, held that a reporter should essentially be a stenographer and should not think about the meaning of his story, while the intellectual need not immerse himself in experiences that would test his ideas. The intellectual pondered in his study while the reporter was out doing interviews, never the twain to meet.

I believed that journalism should have a point of view. An emasculating objectivity had dominated reporting throughout most of this century. Even first-rate journalists had been taught to keep their opinions—in fact, all signs of life—out of their stories. Peter Lisagor of the *Chicago Sun-Times*, one of the deans of the Washington press corps and a member of our editorial board, was a perfect case in point—you became aware of Lisagor's brilliance only through conversation with him, not by reading his stories.

Everyone has prejudices that affect his writing. It's better to bring them out into the open. The best protection against prejudice is to acknowledge it to your readers and to lean over backwards to face the facts that don't fit your case, realizing that they may mean that you should change your mind.

I admired Henry Luce for the way he used his magazines to tell the truth as he saw it. Unfortunately, Luce let his prejudices—his love of Chiang Kai-shek, for example—blind him to the facts that didn't fit his case. Other opinionated journalists I admired, I.F. Stone and George Seldes, had the same fault from the opposite political perspective. I wanted to be as fearless as they were in saying what I thought, but I hoped also to be fearless in facing facts inconvenient to my prejudices.

There were already some early stirrings of the kind of Washington journalism I wanted. In 1967, Elizabeth Drew had become Washington editor of the *Atlantic*. She was married to a lawyer who worked in the Agency for International Development and knew a lot of people in government; she already had written several articles for the *Atlantic* emphasizing the hows and whys of Washington. Bob Manning, the *Atlantic*'s editor, had become interested in the bureaucratic process while serving as an assistant secretary of state under Kennedy.

Still missing, however, was the flavor and feel of the inside. That appeared at last in April 1968, when Manning published an article by James C. Thomson, Jr., who had served on the National Security Council under McGeorge Bundy and was then teaching at Harvard. Though it appeared in the *Atlantic*, I have always thought of it as the first *Washington Monthly* article. It explained America's continuing errors in Vietnam by examining the interaction of the culture of the higher levels of government with the character of the men who worked on national security affairs. Thomson used concepts like "the domestication of dissenters" and "the effectiveness trap" that at last shed light on why good men in the government who were privately opposed to the war had not spoken out publicly. Although the article annoyed me because it was just what I had hoped to be the first to do, it also delighted me because at last I had a sample of what I had in mind to show to potential writers and backers. But it hadn't appeared when I started raising money in the fall of 1967. And the Peace Corps evaluation reports were still classified, so I couldn't use them as examples. Instead, I came up with a brief statement of purpose to give to potential investors and writers:

> *The Washington Monthly* is a new magazine with a new purpose—to help you understand our system of politics and government, where it breaks down, why it breaks down, and what can be done to make it work.
>
> The American system is in trouble. It's not responding well enough or fast enough to our crucial national problems.
>
> *The Washington Monthly* intends to illumine that system with disciplined fact-finding and analysis that will help you discover what needs changing and what needs support. It also intends to enjoy the show.

That last thought was especially important. Political magazines in the sixties were drab in content and in appearance. I told investors that humor was going to be an essential ingredient of the *Monthly* and that I would use glossy paper and color to communicate to the reader that it would be fun to read. But to communicate that I was also serious about substance, I chose the 7-by-10-inch size that was customary for scholarly publications.

In the fall of 1967, I began to take a few days off each month to go to New York in search of money, talent, and advice. Of these, money was the hardest to come by. I must have approached a significant proportion of the nation's rich, but almost all of them turned me down.

In August, after Jay invested, my parents also put in $20,000, which was more than they could comfortably spare. I then entered a financial desert that lasted for months. There were many nights when I came home feeling like Willy Loman. Then my luck turned. First, two old Charleston friends pledged a total of $3,500, and Joseph Crowley, the husband of Beth's roommate at Vassar, promised $4,000. A few days later I met Alfred Clark, one of the heirs to the Singer sewing machine fortune, for lunch in the Oak Bar at the Plaza Hotel. He was late, and I was nervously worrying that I would get stuck with the check. I had given him a prospectus when we met but had no idea what he thought about it. Finally, Alfred arrived. As he sat down, he said, "I'm in for $20,000."

For that one week, fundraising seemed absurdly easy, but it soon settled back into the old demoralizing routine. One possible investor, mentioned by almost everyone I talked to, was Katharine Graham, the principal owner of the *Washington Post* and *Newsweek*. Here was someone who seemed worth a major campaign. James Reston had told me that McGeorge Bundy, then the president of the Ford Foundation, was the person Graham trusted the most. I didn't know Bundy but Jack Vaughn did, and he wrote a letter of introduction in my behalf. When I saw Bundy, I asked for two things—money from Ford and an introduction to Graham. He said he would have to think about the first—he later decided no—but would definitely take care of the second. While I was in his office, he called Graham and described the *Monthly* in enthusiastic terms as a project worthy of her support. She agreed to see me. Bill Moyers and Jay also wrote urging her to invest. It looked promising, but my memory of my one previous meeting with Graham kept my hopes from getting too high.

The occasion had been a large dinner party at her home in 1964. It was the first big-time Washington social event that Beth and I had been to, and we arrived early. At the door, a servant handed each of us a small, triangular, folded card that looked like a miniature elongated tepee. His manner indicated that of course we knew what it was. As we cast uncertain glances at one another, he led us into a large room decorated in red brocade where our hostess was seated talking to two people who seemed to be the only other guests to have arrived. The servant introduced us and withdrew. Instead of rising to greet us or asking us to join her group, Graham merely nodded and continued her conversation, leaving us standing alone in the center of the room with only our tepees to comfort us. I gingerly stuck mine in my inside coat pocket and Beth tucked hers in her handbag, both of us carefully trying to avoid flattening the card, as we awkwardly tried to make conversation with each other. An hour or so later, when dinner was announced, I asked someone, "How do we know where to sit?" and finally learned what the cards were for.

So although I seemed to have impressive support, I was apprehensive as I entered Katharine Graham's office, and I was right to be. As I was sitting down in the chair in front of her desk, she said: "Mr. Peters, I should have called you and told you not to come. We're just not interested." Perhaps moved by the stricken look on my face, she added, "But tell me about it anyway."

So I presented my case. As I listed the reasons why the *Monthly* was certain to play a historic role in American journalism, she listened attentively, and I felt my confidence growing. Finally, she said, "Well, maybe we should take a good look." My spirits soared, but only for a second. Her next words were: "I'm going to ask Mel Elfin to evaluate this for me."

As with Graham, I had met Elfin, then the Washington bureau chief of *Newsweek*, only once, at a dinner party, and it had had an outcome even less auspicious than Graham's. At the dinner table, the issue of the bombing of North Vietnam came up. I was against it. Mel was for it. This was the kind of discussion that produced an "Oh my God, here we go again!" look on the faces of Washington hostesses during the late sixties, because the debate was almost certain to be long and acrimonious, as it was that evening.

My sense that Elfin would not be an enthusiastic advocate of *The Washington Monthly* proved accurate. There was no investment by Mrs. Graham.

Jack Vaughn had another idea: Elizabeth Greenfield. I had met her briefly when she was a member of the Peace Corps National Advisory Council, and I liked her. Jack was even more enthusiastic: "She's very simpatico—and she's loaded. Her husband just died and he was one of the richest men in Philadelphia."

Armed with a letter from Jack, I took the train to Philadelphia. Mrs. Greenfield was not at her downtown office, so two train changes and two cab rides later (the first driver couldn't find the house), I arrived at her door in Chestnut Hill. After a very pleasant chat, during which she was totally charming, she explained that her husband's estate would probably take years to settle, and she wasn't sure what she could do for me when it was. She then drove me back to the North Philadelphia station, where I waited for the train to Washington.

Although Elizabeth, Kay, and Mel all later became my friends, they were not exactly bringing joy to my life at this time. Furthermore, the North Philadelphia station is not a good place to contemplate defeat. The night was dark, there was a freezing wind, and the crumbling platform symbolized what was happening to my hopes. If you know North Philadelphia, you know how I felt.

The next week I went to New York to see John Spencer. John was then married to Jay's sister, Hope, and I assumed that he must have some money. He was an Africanist who had done some part-time evaluating for the Peace Corps and therefore had firsthand knowledge of how the magazine would be different. In fact, it was a conversation with him in March 1967—during which he had argued that I had done all I could at the Peace Corps and would become stagnant if I stayed—that triggered the thinking that led to my decision to leave and start the magazine.

So I said, "You got me into this, how about helping me?" He didn't pull out his checkbook as I had hoped, but he did say he had a friend who might be interested, Louis Marx, Jr.: "He's the son of the toy man and he's made a bundle on his own. He's a great guy." He said he'd call Marx first thing in the morning.

The next day I waited in my hotel room for John's report. No call came, so at checkout time I left for La-Guardia to catch the shuttle back to Washington. At the airport I decided to check one last time with the hotel. There was a message—from a Mr. Marx.

Marx could see me at 5:00 at his office in midtown Manhattan. It was now about 3:30. As I headed for the cab line, I looked in my billfold. I didn't have enough for cab fare! I didn't even have enough for the bus to the East Side airline terminal. But from my days working at LaGuardia for American Airlines, I remembered another way to get to midtown. It involved a combination of city bus, subway, and shoe leather, but it cost less than a dollar and got me to Marx's office at 4:55.

He heard my story and said, "You can count me in for $10,000." Thinking that it might not be confidence-inspiring to then ask if he could lend me the cab fare to get back to the airport, I walked to Alfred Clark's apartment and borrowed the fare from him.

There was no more investment activity until June, when Fiona Rust, the daughter of Marshall Field—who had once published *PM*, the paper to which I had been addicted in the forties—put in $10,000. Then in August came the big breakthrough. Alfred Clark increased his pledge to $50,000, and Joe Crowley increased his to

$75,000. This meant that we had enough money—if only barely enough—to begin publication.

The advice side went well from the beginning. Whitney Ellsworth, the publisher of the *New York Review of Books*, to whom my college friend Jason Epstein introduced me, was a great help on business matters, having spent the past four years learning the same ropes I needed to know.

Through Alfred I met Fred Papert, head of what was then one of New York's hottest advertising agencies—Papert, Koenig and Lois, the firm that had been working for Robert F. Kennedy's presidential campaign. When Kennedy was assassinated in June 1968, the staff that had been assembled for his campaign had nothing to do, and Papert put them to work creating promotional material for *The Washington Monthly*. Instead of demanding money for their services, he accepted payment in the form of stock.

The editorial advisory board was probably the most impressive thing about the magazine. After Rovere had agreed to become the first member, I asked him to recommend others. He suggested Russell Baker, Murray Kempton, and Peter Lisagor. His advice was easy to follow. Baker was, I thought, the best writer in Washington. I had become a fan of Kempton's when he began writing a column for the *New York Post* while I was in graduate school at Columbia. Of all the members of the White House press corps, Lisagor was the most highly regarded by his peers. He also happened to be in person, if not in print, the funniest man in town. Lisagor recommended Hugh Sidey, who was then with *Life* magazine and was doing the best job in Washington of covering Lyndon Johnson. To complete the editorial board I chose Edgar Cahn, who had written an influential article in the *Yale Law Journal* that made him the father of the poverty law movement, and James Thomson, the author of that first

"Washington Monthly" article in the *Atlantic*, whom I had met through Chester Bowles in the early days of the Kennedy administration.

Rovere and Baker were the most active board members. From the planning stage through the first year of publication, Rovere and I met for lunch at least once a month. He was valuable in guiding me to good writers and in helping me learn how to deal with the inferior ones or with bad pieces written by good authors. At first, I spent too much time trying to save articles that simply didn't have it, especially when I had commissioned a story and felt guilty about the time the author had invested. Rovere taught me that if you're going to put out a good magazine, guilt about the losers must yield to concentration on the potential winners.

Baker and I also had lunch at least once a month from 1968 until 1973, when he and his wife moved to New York. Before becoming a columnist, he covered both the Senate and the White House for the *New York Times*, so he knew Washington well. And as Mary McGrory once remarked, "He looks like Huck Finn and writes like Mark Twain." The humor he brought to several articles he edited for us in our early years was crucial in establishing the tone I wanted the magazine to have.

Another group that helped get the magazine under way was the White House Fellows. The Fellows were young people, mostly between the ages of twenty-five and thirty-five, who came from all over the country to work for a year at the White House or as assistants to cabinet members and other heads of agencies. A good many seemed dedicated mainly to building a better resume, but they were almost all quite bright and they were in positions that gave them an inside view of government that was available to few others. In March 1968, while I was still with the Peace Corps, I was invited to speak to the current crop. The evening went well, and by the end of my talk I was feeling comfortable enough to confide to them my plans to start *The Washington Monthly*. Several came up to me as I was leaving and said that they were interested in participating in some way. This led to a series of meetings, first at my home, then at the magazine's office, which opened on May 1, 1968.

The office was in a once-elegant nineteenth-century apartment building on Connecticut Avenue that had been converted into offices. It was a bit shabby but still had the original fireplaces, bay windows, high ceilings, French doors, and a marble staircase. It was a comfortable, relaxing setting for the meetings, which we held once or twice a week in the early evening throughout the summer and fall.

The Fellows who attended the first meeting—Doris Kearns, Joe Freitas, Tim Wirth, and Barbara Currier—suggested friends who might also be interested. These friends suggested other friends, and so on, until ultimately more than fifty people came to one or more of the meetings. Most of them were in the government at the special assistant level, where they worked with both the political appointees at the top and the civil servants below. They were a rich source of ideas. In fact, five years later we were still doing articles they had suggested. They also brought along talented but unknown young journalists like Seymour Hersh and Robert Kuttner, who would be among our first writers.

The easiest part of getting ready to publish the *Monthly* was assembling the staff. Its original members—Timothy Adams, Peggy Anderson, Carole Lee Smith, Carol Trueblood, and Cheryl Strange—had all worked with me at the Peace Corps. Tim had been a newspaperman in San Francisco and had come to the Peace Corps public information office in 1961. In 1962 I persuaded him to be deputy director of Evaluation. Peggy Anderson had been a volunteer in Togo and had joined

Evaluation in 1965. Both Carole Lee and Carol had served at different times as my secretary, and Cheryl had been an office assistant.

The one non–Peace Corps person on the staff was Joe Crowley, the early investor whose wife had gone to college with Beth. As I discusssed the magazine with him during the winter and spring of 1967 and 1968, Joe became increasingly interested, and I came to respect his good sense and sound judgment. He had one kind of experience I didn't have—running a successful business. That summer he agreed to be the publisher.

By October 1968, all of us were busy preparing to publish the first issue. The reception room overflowed with aspiring writers and salesmen for all the services a magazine needs. It was an exciting time, but it was an anxious time as well. None of us had put out a magazine, and although we had advisors who were experienced, finally we had to make the decisions, and our self-doubt was acute. Our insecurities showed in our behavior toward one another. Tim Adams and I, who had never had a moment of discord at the Peace Corps, fought constantly, as did Joe Crowley and I. Joe, who later became a close friend, and I discovered that we had different approaches to management. He was a delegator; I was hands-on all the way. Besides, he didn't like living in Washington and wanted to move back home to New Haven. Peggy Anderson had been a truly outstanding evaluator at the Peace Corps, but it turned out that she knew very little about politics and government, which were, of course, the main subjects of the magazine. Cheryl Strange must have thought we had reinstituted slavery, as we burdened her with an impossible work load. Within the next eighteen months, they were all to leave—first Joe, then Peggy and Cheryl, and finally, Tim.

The lowest point was in late November 1968, when Tim and I met with Baker and Rovere to go over the manuscripts we had in hand for our first issue. Dick and Russ agreed—they were dogs, real dogs. In our hearts, Tim and I knew this, but out of desperation we had deluded ourselves into thinking we could save them. Now we had to face reality, and we had to face it fast. There were only six weeks before the first issue was scheduled to go to press.

I thought about the kind of magazine I wanted, not one that published a variety of interesting articles without regard to whether the editor thought they were right or not, but one that would tell the truth as best I knew it—articles that could be verified by my own experience or that of people I trusted. So I decided to concentrate on writers who had been there, who had actually done what they were writing about.

A friend told me that David Broder, who was rapidly establishing himself as one of the best political reporters in Washington, might be willing to write frankly about the role of the press in presidential elections, which was unexplored territory in those days. I immediately called Broder. Two weeks later, he delivered an article that, in its freshness and candor, anticipated *The Boys on the Bus*, published four years later.

I renewed earlier efforts to persuade Bill Moyers (who I discovered was an excellent writer while working with him at the Peace Corps and who subsequently was Lyndon Johnson's top aide) to examine the rivalry between the White House staff and the cabinet and to get Arthur Ross, the outgoing commissioner of labor statistics, to describe the way the government uses numbers to con itself and the rest of us—a practice, in the form of McNamara's body counts, that was having disastrous consequences in Vietnam at the time. Like Broder, Ross came through quickly, with an article we called "The Data Game."

Moyers was another story. He had developed a severe

case of writer's block. Richard Nixon was already saying that he would not let his White House staff get between him and his cabinet. I was eager to get the Moyers article into the first issue to show why Nixon's effort would fail. After giving Bill several futile pep talks on the phone, I knew a more dramatic approach was necessary.

I appealed to Hugh Sidey, the White House correspondent Moyers respected the most, to go to New York and get the story out of Bill in the form of an interview. Sidey was frantically busy, having just taken over as Washington bureau chief for *Time*, but he agreed. We proceeded to give him the wrong directions about where to meet Bill, so he wasted an afternoon lost in a cab on Long Island. But they finally got together, and Hugh returned to Washington with an interview that was full of such nuggets as the first account of the March 1968 reversal of the Wise Men's position on Vietnam, which was probably the main impetus behind Johnson's decision not to escalate further.

I had an idea for an article about how the young special assistants in government (whom I had gotten to know at the Peace Corps and through the White House Fellows) tended to adopt and cling to certain roles, often for the good or ill (mostly the ill) of their bosses and the Republic. I was anxious to do the piece because I wanted to use it to inaugurate a section of the magazine called "The Culture of Bureaucracy" that would give special emphasis to the anthropological approach to Washington that I thought was going to be a unique aspect of the *Monthly*. But I had sketched out only the roughest first draft. I called Russell Baker to ask for help. He agreed to take a look. I rushed to his office in the *New York Times*'s Washington bureau and sat apprehensively as he read the draft. Then he turned wordlessly to his typewriter and began to hit the keys with the steady rhythm of a man who knows what he is doing. As he finished each page, he handed it to me. I had called the first kind of special assistant Iago, but the name was just about as far as I had gotten. Here's how Baker began his description:

(1) *Iago*. Chronic paranoia is the common affliction of government executives. They live in constant fear that the man down the hall or over in the next agency has plots afoot to steal their program, or their jobs, or to make them look incompetent before their superiors. The reason the man down the hall or over in the next agency has plots afoot is that he has been persuaded by the special assistant who is his own Iago that other men down the halls and over in other agencies have plots afoot against him.

Interestingly, Iagos rarely recognize their true roles on the staff. It is not uncommon to find a group of them, having spent the morning exacerbating their bosses' panics, lunching together and mutually deploring the petty bureaucratic tendencies of their superiors.

As I walked back to the office, clutching this copy in my hand and happily contemplating the by-line—by Russell Baker and Charles Peters—I began to sense that we were going to pull it off after all, that a really good first issue was now within reach.

The next day I arranged to have lunch with James Boyd, who recently had ended his career as an aide on Capitol Hill by exposing corruption by his boss, Senator Thomas Dodd of Connecticut. I talked with him about when I'd testified before a congressional committee for the Peace Corps and the members had seemed unprepared. Occasionally, they stumbled onto the right question, but they seldom followed up. I asked him if he could write an article describing the problem and said we needed it in two weeks. He delivered on time. The article, describing how a typical day on Capitol Hill leaves members of Congress ill-equipped to deal with their most important duties, began with an account of what happens when the voting bell rings and senators begin to converge on the chamber:

> Possessed of the prima donna's disdain for peers, compelled by their profession to fight one another on issues, they have often measured each other as enemies. But they are conscious, too, that they are brothers, that ambition makes them endure the same indignities, wage the same lonely struggle for career survival. And so they compensate for the mutual hostility inherent in their situation with the kind of exaggerated cordiality that is evident as they enter doorways together.
>
> But as the senators approach their desks the cordial glow is fleetingly interrupted by a look of perplexity—what the hell is the vote about this time? Some have aides who now come forward to whisper a 30-second summary of the three-hour debate. Some just follow their party leader, who has minions stationed about the floor to pass the word "aye" or "nay" to the faithful. Some, who are not faithful, follow the lead of their particular Senate guru. Some, particularly those who are committee chairmen or near-chairmen, automatically support the position of the chairman who has jurisdiction over the measure—for they expect the same hierarchical support when they are piloting their own bills through the Senate.
>
> On occasion, there is a concluding element of burlesque. Announcement of the vote is delayed, for the chair has learned that a colleague, recently disembarked at National Airport, is somewhere in the corridors of the Capitol rushing toward the floor. Breathless and unbriefed, the tardy solon enters, all eyes fixed amusedly on him. The clerk calls his name. "Aye," he says, hopefully, and looks to his nearest deskmates for

confirmation. But they shake their heads in disagreement. "Nay," he corrects himself, to a burst of understanding laughter. The result is officially announced. A new law is on the books. The world's greatest deliberative body has completed another deliberation.


Boyd was writing about Congress as, to the best of my knowledge, no journalist ever had before—with a novelist's flair for conveying tone and feeling, and with empathy. This last quality was crucial—empathy is the key to understanding motivation, which in turn is key to understanding the behavior of the public figures journalists cover.

Allen Drury tried to do this in his novels but never in his reporting. Tom Wolfe didn't cover politics at all. Theodore White did, but he stuck to presidential elections—government was boring. James Thomson's great article was about government, but only the most glamorous part, the White House. Now Boyd was showing that the ordinary everyday events of government could be made to come alive on the printed page. His article showed that he had been there, that he could describe what he had seen, that he could understand what the people he was writing about were feeling, and that he could think about what it all meant.

Later, some other good articles—from Jane Stein, Murray Kempton, Stephen Hess, and Calvin Trillin—came in time for the first issue, but it was Boyd's that gave us the sense that we were going to have a magazine that would be different.

× × ×

IN November 1968 we bought an ad in the *New York Times*. The copy, written by Fred Papert, began:

> Announcing—one year too late—
> *The Washington Monthly*, a bold
> experiment in political journalism.
>
> What a year 1968 has been for
> democracy! From a spring of assassination
> and riot to a November that brought us
> within a hair's breadth of constitutional
> crisis, 1968 has been the year we all
> found out what some of us had long
> suspected—that our system of government
> is in trouble. And so are we.

The ad hit a nerve, producing the most remarkable response that I have ever heard of for a magazine like ours: more than $18,000 in subscription revenues for an investment of less than $3,000. Fred had an instinct that we should tap the national mood in mid-November, which, particularly among the thoughtful liberals who were our most likely subscribers, was one of bleak depression.

1968 had been a year of calamitous events. It had started with the Tet offensive in Vietnam. Then came the assassination of Martin Luther King, Jr., followed by the riots in Washington. Two months later, Robert Kennedy was murdered. Next, the Russians invaded Czechoslovakia. The student riots at the Democratic National Convention were followed by Humphrey's loss to Richard Nixon, a man who definitely did not bring joy to liberal hearts, in an election that, because of its closeness and the presence of a strong third-party candidate in George Wallace, could have produced a disastrous electoral deadlock. There was a pervasive feeling that the nation had lost its way—and had lost the leaders who could help us find our way again. I remember standing at my office window, watching the black clouds of smoke rise over Washington the day after King's murder. I remember walking to Robert Kennedy's headquarters the day after he was shot to ask if there was any hope that he would recover. When Tom Mathews shook his head, I left to walk the streets aimlessly, overwhelmed by the realization that the three greatest leaders of the decade were gone. Despite their faults, I thought (and still think) that John Kennedy, Robert Kennedy, and Martin Luther King, Jr., were great men and that, given history's batting average in producing people of such caliber, we probably would not see their like again for a very long time.

But I didn't think we should give up. If there was a shortage of great leaders, the rest of us had to take up the slack. We had to figure out things for ourselves. What had gone wrong with the country? Why? How could we get on the right track again? I thought I knew some of the answers, and I felt a sense of urgency about communicating them and about figuring out the answers I didn't know.

The continuing horror of 1968 was the daily news of death in Vietnam. Why we were mired in this tragedy was the central question facing the nation as we began publishing *The Washington Monthly* in January 1969. And the war dominated our table of contents for the next several years.

One theme that soon emerged from our Vietnam articles was the importance of speaking up and listening down. Subordinates in government must speak up, to confront their superiors with bad news, and the people in charge must listen down, to encourage subordinates to make them face unhappy truths. People of ability and character often think it is their duty to handle difficulties themselves without bothering the boss. If the subordinate is of lesser quality, this sense of duty is heightened by an awareness of the fate that often befalls bearers of bad news. If the subordinate also fears that he might be caught having covered up, he includes the bad news in his report but buries it in language calculated to be overlooked.

Now, suppose the subordinate's boss is a general in Vietnam who is scheduled to return to the States in six months to be superintendent at West Point and in line for the next appointment as the army's chief of staff. The general definitely does not want to hear facts that might blot his record, anger his superiors, and threaten his anticipated promotion.

So when he gets a long report containing some vague words on page 32 about civilian casualties at a village called My Lai, the general, in all probability, will not investigate—as the man who actually got that report, Lt. Gen. Bernard Kosters, did not. Indeed, the man who finally did uncover the whole truth about My Lai, Lt. Gen. William Peers, found his once-promising career stopped dead in its tracks and had to retire.

Sometimes people are willing to speak up within their agency but not outside, which is the way I was at the Peace Corps. What changed my mind was Vietnam. I knew that a large part of the Washington foreign affairs bureaucracy opposed the war. But there was not the slightest hint of it in the press. In part, this was because reporters weren't very diligent. But the main reason was that the bureaucrats weren't saying what they really thought. When they did speak up, they put it off the record at those charming Washington dinner parties that almost always seduce the journalists in attendance.

I was convinced that the government needed more people who were psychologically ready to resign—who, when vital issues were at stake, would stand up to their superiors and fight to the point of losing their jobs. Of all the wrong decisions I had seen made in government, wrong ideas and information had played no greater role than the failure of the people with the right ideas and information to press their case courageously.

Another reason for our continuing involvement in the war, I believed, was the machismo of the American male—his need to prove his manhood, his need to win, and his deep reluctance to admit having been wrong. I wanted to push the cause of liberating men from their prison of masculinity, to show them that every encounter was not a battle from which they had to emerge victorious.

Lyndon Johnson and Richard Nixon provided striking case studies of how the need to prove masculinity could distort national policy. John Kennedy, too, felt that he had to appear harder and tougher than he really was. (Recall how he ridiculed Adlai Stevenson for suggesting the very policy Kennedy had secretly followed during the Cuban missile crisis.)

The *Monthly*'s concern with the macho element in the male character led us to early involvement in the feminist revolution. A month before the August 1970 march down Fifth Avenue that marked the emergence of the women's movement as a major force in American life, we published an article called "Violence and the Masculine Mystique," which was an exploration of what was wrong with the American cult of masculinity. Unlike some feminists, we saw the male as someone to be pitied, not imitated. Our concern was more the liberation of males than that of women or gays, because the liberated male would no longer need to beat up on other people, either psychologically or literally.

We were not welcomed by those in the women's movement whose goal was to play male roles in the same way that men have traditionally performed them. They wanted to imitate men, when in many ways we thought men should imitate women. Volunteerism was an example. Many women had come to scorn volunteering as a form of being a sucker. Why should they work without pay? But I recalled my experience as a legislator in West Virginia, where the only lobbyists for the public interest were the members of the League of Women Voters. They were free to do this important work because they did not have to worry about making money. Was the triumph of their daughters' revolution going to mean donning dress-for-success suits and being paid to lobby for the special interests? Women who valued work only in terms of how much they were paid for it frequently ended up doing dull, largely meaningless work simply because it offered high financial rewards and prestige.

I wanted women—and men—to free themselves from slavery to money. If you have enough income to live in reasonable comfort, do you really need that Mercedes? Why not do work that is worthwhile (including caring for children), without concern for how much it pays beyond what you really need to live on.

What I had admired, back in New York, about homosexuals or bisexuals like Allen Ginsberg and Jack Kerouac was the way they were different from the conventional strivers among the heterosexual males of the time; they didn't need to dominate and win. What I liked about the women of the forties and fifties was something similar. They were much more inclined toward peace and nonviolence and had fewer chips on their shoulders than the average male. Removing those chips from men's shoulders, not making women more like men, should be the goal of the feminist revolution.

But in 1969, the problem was not macho women. It was still the traditional male trying to prove his masculinity. One tough guy, Lyndon Johnson, had just been replaced by another—our first issue came out two days after the inauguration of Richard Nixon—and the war went on. In October we published an editorial that said,

"Richard Nixon has dreams of a peace that will justify the lost American lives." Then it continued:

> One can understand him—as one can
> understand all the American presidents who
> have sent men to die in Vietnam—you can't
> tell the families they died for nothing. But
> to save other men from dying, we have to admit
> that those who have died have not died for
> nothing, but to bring America to its senses.
> It's time to get out, not with fantasies of
> victory, but with practical plans for the
> survival of our troops and of the South Vietnamese who
> have been led to rely on us—not
> with a saving of face, but with saving of life
> for their people and for ours.

Although they had six more years to make those plans, the Nixon-Ford-Kissinger administrations failed to do so, and that horrible 1975 photograph of an American kicking South Vietnamese away from the door of an escaping plane remains their legacy.

The *Monthly*'s approach to the war differed from that of the conventional left in that we did not assume that the South Vietnamese were all closet Viet Cong, eagerly awaiting the victory of the North. Many of them did not want to live under the communists—as was later made clear by the mass exodus of boat people. And we believed that the United States, having encouraged them to fight and to rely on our support, had an obligation to help them escape.

We also differed from the conventional left in that we tried to state our dissent with civility and with an understanding of the motivation of those who supported the war. Many of our allies in the peace movement seemed more intent on being outrageous than on ending the war. Remember the photograph of the bearded young demonstrator, arms stretched in the air, naked except for the miniature American flag attached to his penis?

We wanted these people to realize they were damaging their own cause. We learned that Sam Brown, the most respected of the young leaders of the peace movement, felt the same way. Taylor Branch, who was then one of the *Monthly*'s editors and a friend of Brown, talked him into writing an article. He said what we had hoped, that "only a movement which reaches Nixon's constituency" could stop the war.

To reach Nixon's constituency, we had to credit them with at least the possibility of some nonmalevolent motive, rather than call them war criminals or worse. I knew some of the people who had gotten us involved in Vietnam, and I knew many others who silently, if unenthusiastically, had gone along with them. They were not monsters. Understanding why they had gone wrong required empathy, not accusation.

In an article about Mary McCarthy, another of our editors, James Fallows, tried to explain the value of empathy. McCarthy had emerged in the beginning of the seventies as a prominent critic of the war and as one who generally took the hard-line, war-criminal position. Why, if she felt so strongly, hadn't she gotten on the case earlier? For example, in 1966, when she was invited to go to North Vietnam by Robert Silvers, the editor of the *New York Review of Books*, she said no. The reason was that McCarthy's husband, James West, was then an official in the State Department, and as she revealed several years later in *The Seventeenth Degree*:

> If I went, he said he would have to hand in his resignation. "Are you sure?" I said. "Yes." He had three children to support, as well as alimony payments to make and had spent most of his life in the Air Force

and later with government agencies. "Well, then, I can't go." I did not feel he was constraining me, only presenting me with an ineluctable fact. There it was. I could not invest his life in my desire to go to Vietnam.

What McCarthy should have understood, Fallows argued, was that far more important than the war criminal in the tragedy in Vietnam was the failure of decent men like her husband to put their careers on the line for the sake of their beliefs.

Another subject liberals didn't want to face was draft evasion by the upper class. This not only left the poor to die in Vietnam but helped to lengthen the war. If the sons of the rich had gone, opposition to the war from their influential parents would have brought it quickly to a halt.

Try as I might, I could not find a young man willing to write this piece. Finally, in April 1972, Suzannah Lessard agreed to do it. But as she began writing, an office rebellion developed. Taylor Branch and John Rothchild, another editor, argued that any criticism of draft evaders could damage the antiwar movement. After many heated discussions, Taylor and John finally saw the light enough to concede that Lessard and I had a point worth publishing. The article appeared under the title "Let Those Hillbillies Go Get Shot," which was a remark Beth had overheard a college student make in a bookstore.

Unfortunately, the article didn't receive much attention. Then, a few months later, James Fallows joined the *Monthly*'s staff. Jim told me he had evaded the draft by starving himself to get his weight below the minimum army requirement for his height and that most of his Harvard classmates had used similar tactics. At the same time, he saw young men from the lower-middle-class neighborhood of Chelsea go through the induction center without trying any tricks, and a high proportion of them went on to risk their lives in Vietnam.

As Jim and I discussed this issue over the next couple of years, he became increasingly obsessed with the belief that he had to face what he had done. So even though we had already published one article on it—a consideration that, in any event, has never weighed heavily in editorial planning at the *Monthly*—he decided to try again. The result was "What Did You Do in the Class War, Daddy?".

This article had impact; it was widely reprinted and quoted. I think there were several reasons that it was more successful than the Lessard piece. For one, the draft was still going on when Lessard's article appeared. The truth she was telling was one that could have landed the evaders in jail. And the guilt for many of them must have been too terrible to face, because the blacks, the hillbillies, and the boys from Chelsea were still dying in Vietnam. Also, Fallows was writing in the first person, and it's always easier to accept moral guidance from a fellow sinner.

But the most important reason for the impact of the Fallows article was that by 1975, when it appeared, thoughtful people were becoming concerned about the social fragmentation of America, a process in which the undemocratic Vietnam draft had played a significant role. Affluent Americans had chosen to let the lower classes do the dying, and the cost of their choice now had to be confronted. The cost was most obvious in the embitterment of the Vietnam veterans. But beyond that, serious damage had been done to the idea of democratic community, which was at the heart of the American dream.

Like many themes that were to dominate the magazine, this commitment to democracy and community emerged from our articles on Vietnam. So did our belief in civility and empathy and an advocacy of risking one's career on behalf of principle.

CHAPTER **9**

# Taking the Risk

**W**HEN it came to risk-taking, *The Washington Monthly* was practicing what it preached. When we started publication, we had enough money to put out exactly three issues. I didn't think we needed any more money because I was convinced that the first issue would make or break us.

This idea, which I later realized was quite bizarre, came from my earlier careers. The opening night reviews in the theater, the returns on election night in politics, the jury's verdict in the law—all told you whether you were a winner or a loser in a matter of hours. But the *Monthly* didn't get any opening-night reviews or anything resembling an election-night result or a jury verdict. The first article about us in *Time* appeared two years after we started, the first appraisal by the *Columbia Journalism Review* was in our fourteenth year, and the first article in *Newsweek* came on our fifteenth birthday. Although all were quite favorable, none of them did us much good in 1969.

We were saved at the time by Fred Papert's advertising and direct mail materials and by word of mouth from our readers. Together, these got our circulation up to 20,000 by our third issue and produced enough money to guarantee our survival to the fall.

By September, though, we were running out of funds, having gone through close to $300,000. I went to Philip Stern, an investigative reporter who had been one of our part-time evaluators at the Peace Corps and who, I subsequently discovered, had money. Phil liked to use his philanthropies—and obviously he regarded the *Monthly* as a charity, not a business—to stimulate other contributors. He made a pledge of $12,500, conditioned on our raising a total of $150,000. Jay Rockefeller and Louis Marx got us to $100,000 with additional pledges. Then Jay introduced me to Warren Buffett.

Warren, who is now a legend as one of the nation's most successful investors, controlled a financial empire from a quiet base in Omaha, Nebraska. In October he flew into Washington with two friends, Joseph Rosenfield, from Des Moines, Iowa, and Fred Stanback, a North Carolinian who was heir to a headache remedy fortune. Together, they agreed to put up the remaining $50,000.

We took all that money and blew it. Instead of using the proven direct mail material that Fred Papert had produced, we decided we were smarter, created our own, and mailed it without even bothering to test it. The new material was spectacularly ineffective. The previous mailing had produced returns of 3 to 4 percent, which is very good for direct mail. This one brought in exactly one-half of one percent, which is terrible.

During the many bleak fiscal periods that the magazine has since endured, I never once have feared what I feared then—that we were finished. I remember driving home one December night and saying to Carol Trueblood when I dropped her off at her apartment, "I think we've had it." I did not see how the investors could have faith in me again. I had taken their money and practically thrown it away.

At this point, a short note arrived from Theodore White: "You're putting out a hell of a good magazine. Keep it up." If ever a letter arrived at precisely the right moment, this was it. Because White was a pioneer in the kind of journalism we were trying to practice, his words gave me new heart. I resolved to try to hang in.

One day loomed ominously before us: January 12, when we had scheduled, before the direct mail disaster, a joint meeting with our editorial board and our leading investors. Why had I been so insane as to plan such an event? What could we tell them that wasn't totally depressing? The only good news was our renewal rate. People who were reading the magazine liked it enough to extend their subscriptions. Our recent mailing, however, suggested that we had lost our ability to get them to subscribe in the first place. So we decided to try a test mailing with the old Papert materials to see if they would still work. By this time, the meeting was only three weeks away. We put in a rush order for the envelopes, letters, brochures, and cards, and the staff celebrated New Year's Eve staying up all night stuffing envelopes. By January 12 we had enough returns to show that the Papert materials were still effective.

I would like to be able to recount that the meeting was a triumph. But while the evening wasn't as funereal as I had anticipated, it was clear that the investors were now wary.

We made it through the next few months only because of some unexpected success with advertising—we got ads from AT&T, Polaroid, and Eastern and American airlines, as well as from several book publishers—and because of renewals. Patient creditors also helped. But some weren't so patient. One morning I was escorting a potential investor to the office after breakfast at a nearby hotel. As we walked down the hall, we noticed a strange contraption on the office door—the landlord had locked us out. I of course feigned indignation ("Miss Trueblood must have forgotten to pay the rent"), but my humiliation was so great that I have erased the name of the potential investor from my memory. Needless to say, he must have thanked providence for this timely sign that he might more prudently invest his funds elsewhere.

Not long after the January meeting, Jay and Warren Buffett went to New York to ask James Kobak, a prominent magazine consultant, if there was any hope for the *Monthly*. Kobak convened a meeting of successful publishers to discuss our problems. Among them was Gilbert Kaplan of *Institutional Investor*, who said that his best guess was that we did have a chance. He also indicated that he might be interested in helping with the magazine's management. Warren was impressed by Kaplan's success with *Institutional Investor* and said that he might be willing to put up another $50,000 if Kaplan took over the direction of the *Monthly*'s business affairs long enough to get us straightened out.

Jay held several meetings that summer in his room at Columbia Presbyterian Hospital (where he was recovering from back surgery), at which first Kaplan and then Buffett were importuned to change their "mights" into "woulds." Kaplan agreed. Warren was torn. Part of him was rooting for the magazine to make it, but his shrewd investor side kept saying, "How did I get into this and how can I get out?" Jay and I labored mightily to persuade him at the hospital meetings, and shortly thereafter in a phone call, during which Jay told him that he and Louis Marx would put up another $25,000, Warren seemed close to saying yes.

But in early September came a fifty-minute phone conversation with me in which it was clear that Warren's two sides were still at war. I was grateful for what he had already done for us and could understand his suspicion that the magazine was at best doomed to a life on the fiscal margin. So I wasn't angry when, at times during the conversation, he tried to withdraw from further involvement. But if I wasn't angry, I was desperate, because I knew I had to hold him in if the magazine was to survive. The conversation went back and forth: Warren would come within an inch of pulling out, and I would slowly try to pull him back. Then the dance would be repeated. Warren, who did not get to be a billionaire by being slow-witted, kept finding new escape routes, each of which had enough instant plausibility to put me into a state of near panic. My mind went into its highest gear as I tried to block the exits.

Finally, he agreed to stay in. I have never been more keyed up than at that moment. I spent the next hour walking it off, recounting the details to Taylor Branch, who came with me, and heaving huge sighs of relief every five minutes or so. All was well. Warren's sympathetic side had won out over the hard-boiled investor. The deal was on.

Kaplan immediately reduced our expenses by 25 percent simply by switching us to a printer in Vermont. We discovered that it took the copy only an hour longer to get there by plane than it had taken to drive it from downtown Washington to our previous printer in suburban Maryland.

On our own, before Kaplan became involved, we had cut our payroll dramatically. I had reduced my beginning salary of $24,000 to $20,000. Then two employees who were also making $20,000 left, and we replaced them with people whom we paid half that. Applying the lesson of my experience with the summer theater and at the Peace Corps—have faith in the young if you use care in selecting them—we began the practice of hiring bright

175

young writers who would stay for two years of low pay and hard work. The advantage for them was that by the time they left, their articles in the *Monthly* would have attracted the attention of future employers.

Kaplan's year expired the summer of 1971. He left us in good shape, with just one exception: our circulation was shrinking. Gil thought we could fall to a solid base of 12,000, which would not require expensive promotion mailings to maintain and would still be attractive to advertisers because the readers were so obviously influential. Instead, the advertising shrank because of the recession in late 1970, so for the magazine to survive, we had to increase our circulation.

Just about that time, I.F. Stone called to tell me that he was closing down his newsletter, *I.F. Stone's Weekly*, and would sell us his mailing list for $40,000. We were excited. All of us admired Stone and were flattered that he would want us to carry on for him. We went to work raising the money, and by late September we had it. I called Stone to tell him, "You've got a deal." He said, "Wonderful." Our lawyer talked to Stone's lawyer and confirmed the verbal agreement.

A week later, Stone backed out. He sold his list to the *New York Review of Books*. He had been associated with the *Review* for years and had had no connection with the *Monthly*, so in that sense what he'd done was understandable. Still, we thought we had an agreement, and so did our lawyer. He called Stone's lawyer to complain. The result was that the *New York Review* got ownership of the list, but we were permitted to use it twice for subscription mailings at no cost. Since we had already raised the $40,000, we could afford the materials and postage for the mailings to the Stone list and to others as well. So although the loss of the list was one of the major disappointments in the *Monthly*'s history—it put the *New York Review* into the black, and I think it would have done even more for us—our circulation did double as a result of the mailings.

We completed the mailings in the spring of 1972. As summer approached, we seemed to be in reasonably good shape. There was still a fly in the ointment, however—or, to be more precise, three flies. We had about forty creditors with whom, during Kaplan's reign, we had begun a program of small but regular monthly payments. No one creditor was preferred; we were trying to be fair to all. But now, in the summer of 1972, three of them said they wanted more. One sued, and the other two were threatening to sue. If we gave in to them, the other creditors, feeling cheated, might close in on us for their fair share. There was only one alternative: Chapter XI.

Chapter XI is a provision of federal law that permits struggling companies to avoid bankruptcy by stretching out payments to creditors to a point where they are manageable—in other words, by doing exactly what we had been doing, but this time with the backing of a federal court to restrain those creditors who were tempted to seek more than their share.

The danger was that one of the local newspapers would learn of our situation and come out with a headline: "Washington Monthly Bankrupt." At that time, the average journalist's ignorance of both business and the law was almost absolute. Newspapers invariably described Chapter XI proceedings as bankruptcies, even though the whole point of Chapter XI is to keep the business in operation.

We worried that if the papers incorrectly reported that we were bankrupt, advertisers would stop advertising and—an even more dangerous possibility—readers would stop subscribing and renewing. During this period, I went to great lengths to stay out of the sight of reporters, slinking in and out of the courthouse with all the furtiveness of a mafioso trying to avoid photographers.

To win approval for Chapter XI, we needed to convince the judge that we had a sound financial plan and that we had the support of a majority of our creditors. Since all but three had been going along with our informal payment plan, we were confident about our creditors. The judge was another matter. In balance sheet terms, *The Washington Monthly* did not exactly throb with viability. It had been many a moon since our bank balance had exceeded four figures. Every day was an adventure as we opened the mail, hoping for enough checks from subscribers and advertisers to cover our bills. One week we might have closed down except for a $5,000 bookkeeping error by Carol Trueblood that showed we had $1,000 in the bank when in fact we were $4,000 in the hole. Thanks to the "float"—the period from when a check is written to when it's cashed and cleared—we had received enough other income to cover the $4,000 by the time it had actually departed from our bank account.

We could not help suspecting that the more the judge learned about the real state of our fiscal affairs, the less confidence he would have in our future. There was only one solution: raise more money. Unfortunately, with most of our investors, the well had gone dry. Warren made it clear that he had taken the never-again pledge, and Jay was totally immersed in his first try for the West Virginia governorship. The rest always seemed to be on another line when I called. But Alfred Clark did come through with $15,000, as did a new investor, J.T. Smith, a Washington lawyer who was then one of Elliot Richardson's aides at the Pentagon.

But our lawyers felt we needed at least $50,000 to impress the judge, and the last $20,000 simply wasn't in sight. In desperation, I asked Beth if she would consent to a second mortgage on our home in that amount. She agreed, and we lent the proceeds to the *Monthly*. Unfortunately, I forgot to ask the *Monthly* for interest, though

Beth and I still had to pay interest to the bank. This was the subject in our domestic life of what the State Department calls "a frank exchange of views" until the oversight was corrected when we made a second loan to the magazine in 1977.

In any event, we had the $50,000, the court approved our plan—and, equally important, no reporters found out about it. Once more we had dodged the bullet.

It must be clear by now that the business side of the magazine, though not lacking in excitement, did not bring me unqualified pleasure. The time I spent on it was the price I paid for the freedom to express my ideas without having to compromise with an employer. But because I've had to devote roughly a third of my time to it over the years, the business side has been a constant reminder to me of the plight of people who are doing work they don't like or don't feel they can do well.

At best, I've become like the grizzled old skipper of a rustbucket in the South China Sea who, if definitely not destined to become the captain of a great ocean liner, has nonetheless developed a sixth sense about where disaster lies: "Bosun, check that bolt in Number 4 hold. I have a feeling it's about to come loose again." Also, though I have little aptitude for maximizing profits, I do seem to have a talent for minimizing expense. I'm not sure when or how I acquired it, but it was evident by the time I organized that sixty-five-dollar trip to New York when I was sixteen. And of course, it was also the secret of the summer theater's survival.

In those experiences, as with the magazine, I was motivated, in part at least, by the sheer delight of doing something that others said could not be done. In this regard, stubbornness helps a lot. If the landlord says he's going to raise the rent, you have to reply that you'll be moving next month. If the printer says he's going to increase his prices, you immediately seek bids from other printers. Many suppliers count on your being too lazy to make a change and gradually increase their prices on the assumption that you will not go to the trouble of taking your business elsewhere. It is important to let them know they're wrong.

If there is one secret to survival—please note that I'm saying survival, not success—in business and in every other profession with which I am familiar, it is tenacity. If you have some minimal talent, bathe with reasonable regularity, and aren't certifiably insane, you can survive in any field of endeavor if you simply are determined to hold on. I was astonished to discover in the theater, where I thought talent alone counted, that although some talent was necessary, the fellow who lived, slept, and ate the theater, wanting to be part of it above all else, might not become a star but was certain to endure. With the *Monthly*, I realized that this was it for me and that I had to hold on.

Thus, it has been determination more than skill that has enabled me to keep the magazine alive and in the general vicinity of the break-even point. We have never made a profit, at least not one that creditors did not have first claim on. So I have only the most modest regard for my abilities as a captain of industry.

But I have developed intense admiration for the entrepreneur. I know how hard it is to start a business, to convince the people who can finance it that you have a good idea and can pull it off, and to muster the grit to hold your course during the inevitable bouts of bad weather.

× × ×

BY the time we had survived the Chapter XI proceeding in 1972, entrepreneurship was practically a religion with me. I saw it as the key to overcoming the economic stagnation that threatened the country, and I was deeply troubled that liberals tended to scorn it.

At that time, liberals thought of the businessman as a Babbitt at best and a cruel exploiter at worst. I wanted to convince them that without the businessman who created jobs and wealth, we would never be able to get the revenue to finance the social programs we believed in, and our society would become more class-bound and restricted in the opportunities it offered.

I tried to persuade journalists to pursue this theme, but most of them shared the liberal's prejudice against businessmen. Some were even embarrassed when I described my own business experiences. They seemed to feel that an editor should not have to soil his hands with the grime of commerce; he should be above such things.

I think the opposite. Anyone who works for an organization shares responsibility for everything the organization does. The more ability he has, the more his organization needs him. The greater his power to influence it, the greater his responsibility to exercise that power. Most journalists like to think of themselves as completely separate from the advertising department of their paper or magazine. Indeed, they prize the separation as evidence of their integrity. But what if the advertising department solicits ads that make smoking seem glamorous—the kinds of ads that lure the young into trying their first cigarette and thus into an addiction that for many is extremely difficult to overcome? Does the writer have a responsibility to oppose those ads? I think he does. I don't think he can say, "I'm just a writer; it's not my affair." He should not feel superior to his boss because the boss gets his hands dirty engaging in business. But he should be embarrassed, he should protest, and maybe he should resign if the boss conducts the business in a dishonorable or socially harmful way.

Most of the liberal writers I knew lumped all businessmen together. They failed to see the crucial difference between the entrepreneurial businessman and the one who was a trader, advisor, or manager. (This failure, by the way, was just as common among the conservatives of the seventies as it was among the liberals.) The distinction is important, because the entrepreneur who starts new businesses and expands old ones creates jobs. The trader who merely rearranges pieces of the existing economic pie, the lawyer or consultant who gives corporations advice, and the manager who runs the plants that are already in place may be needed, but it is the entrepreneur who enlarges the pie, making a better life possible for everyone.

Once you make this distinction, you begin to see the importance of policies designed specifically to help the entrepreneur. My own experience at the *Monthly* made me an advocate of several. First is the need to give a tax incentive to new investment. The promise of return from a new business is seldom so certain as to make it as attractive as other investment opportunities. There are always existing companies whose records inspire an assurance of capital appreciation and dividend income that new enterprises can only rarely provide.

I ran into this reality again and again as I tried to raise money for the *Monthly*. By the end of the first few months of fundraising, I knew we were not going to be able to come up with anything like the money we really needed. I sought the help of a tax lawyer, John B. Jones, Jr., who had been an assistant for tax policy in Robert Kennedy's Justice Department. He devised a way for wealthy investors to buy, in effect, a one-dollar share in the *Monthly* for only fifty cents. Even the modest fundraising success we had would never have happened without this incentive.

The problem with most of the tax incentives the

country has tried is that they have not been targeted on investment in new plants and new businesses. The capital gains tax break, for example, applied to the proceeds from the sale of existing issues of stock as well as new issues. The mortgage interest deduction is still available for the purchase of old houses as well as new ones, even though the sale of an existing house involves only a few extra hours' work for a real estate broker and the employees of a lending institution. The new house, on the other hand, provides work not only for them but also for plumbers, electricians, glaziers, carpenters, and masons. The solution isn't no tax breaks at all but breaks confined specifically to investment that will produce jobs and growth. By increasing the supply of new homes, such a policy would bring down the prices of all housing and deprive the yuppies of one of the few legitimate reasons for their focus on making money.

I doubt very much if I would understand the importance of encouraging new investment had I not been an entrepreneur faced with the need to raise money. There were two other facts of business life that I would not know had I not learned them through experience. They concern gross receipts taxes and "going public."

The gross receipts tax—a tax you have to pay whether you're making money or not—is levied by some state and local governments. At the federal level, there's one heavy tax that you have to pay regardless of whether you have a profit—Social Security. At the *Monthly*, it has become a steadily crueler burden, having risen from $4,000 in 1969 to $14,000 in 1987. In most of the intervening years, we have operated in a profit and loss (mostly the latter) range of plus or minus $20,000.

Obviously, it would be much better for us and for other struggling businesses if the Social Security tax were paid as a percentage of profit, as the corporate income tax is. Profitable businesses would have to pay more than they pay now in order to provide for employees of unprofitable ones. But they can afford to pay more; struggling businesses can't afford to pay anything.

Going public means registering your stock with the SEC and selling it to the general public instead of restricting the sale to members of your family or to a small number of friends, as we did with the *Monthly*. If you go public, you incur a legal obligation to your shareholders to maximize profits. To see why that's bad, let's go back to cigarette ads. I have never solicited or published a cigarette ad that made smoking seem glamorous. But Katharine Graham does not have the same freedom. In the early seventies, she changed her company from family to public ownership. Now if she decides to turn down cigarette advertising, stockholders can sue, saying that she's depriving them of income.

"Going public" sounds so much better than "going private" that most liberal intellectuals, whose understanding of business matters is modest in the extreme, don't have any idea of the harm that is done "in the best interests" of the public stockholders. The duty to maximize profits in their behalf means, to most managers, spending the least that is required by law on worker health and safety, on cleaning up smoke and waste, or on any other act of corporate good citizenship that is not clearly justifiable as good public relations. The private-business owner, so long as he is at least breaking even, can spend all he wants on these things. The moral neutrality of the market economy is the reason we have to have regulation to protect health and safety. But the private owner is free to do good without being required to. He can also put enough money into research to be able, five years from now, to seize the market from his Japanese competition, which will mean that he will be hiring new employees and thus contributing to the general prosperity. Of course, he can be just as wrong as the manager of

184

the publicly owned company. But he is much freer to do the right thing.

By 1974, my arguments in favor of entrepreneurship had persuaded our editors enough for them to help me write "Putting Yourself on the Line":

> General Motors and the Post Office each have 700,000 employees. One turns out lemons. The other loses packages. Managers and workers are more concerned with preserving their positions and expanding their benefits than with doing their work. The old organizations—public or private—simply aren't doing the job. They require regeneration or replacement. This means we need people who like to start new enterprises and make old ones come alive again. What we need, in short, is a rebirth of entrepreneurship.

We went on to argue that the adventure of creating a new enterprise, which had once stirred the American soul, had been forgotten as our attitudes were molded by a conservatism dedicated to the defense of established big business and by a liberalism too closely allied to big government and big labor, with branch offices in the foundations and the universities, where profit was a bad word. We were determined to change those attitudes. We wanted liberal idealists to see how ridiculous it was to automatically regard the entrepreneur as a robber baron. Sometimes he is a robber baron. But he can also be something else—a creator, just as deserving of praise or blame as the creative artists for whom liberal idealists have such high regard.

Throughout the seventies, we were alone among liberal magazines in these concerns. It is amazing to look back and see how rarely the word entrepreneur appeared outside our pages.

As we were becoming convinced of the importance

185

of risk-taking, both in government and in business, we began to think about why so many people are reluctant to take risks. One reason is the desire for job security. By the seventies, tenure had become firmly established among white-collar workers, not only in the civil service but (by custom, if not by law) in universities, foundations, and many large corporations. Unfortunately, tenure can entrap. Once people have it, they cannot face risking its loss, even when they are offered the chance to do something more stimulating and worthwhile.

Another part of the fear of losing one's job is the fear of losing the identity badge it provides. In small-town America, everyone knew who you were, and you didn't have to impress people with your title or your organization. But America has become a highly mobile nation—each year, one in three of us moves. If you grew up in a small town, you probably don't live there any more. But you still want people to know who you are. If you can say "I'm with IBM," it establishes your place in the world. At a more sophisticated level, let's say you're at a New York cocktail party, where you're lucky if you know one person in ten. When that beautiful girl turns to you, you feel you have to flash your identity badges fast, and you want them to be instantly recognizable and impressive—"I'm with the *New Yorker*" or "I'm with Morgan, Stanley."

The most familiar excuse for not taking career risks is "I've got to get the kids through college." The excuse is a good one, since it can cost more than $250,000 to finance college and a professional education for two children. Therefore, the *Monthly* has urged a national program of higher education loans to the student, not the parents, that would be repayable over his or her lifetime as an addition to annual income tax payments. This not only would free the parents from fearing risk, it also just might make college students take their education more seriously. It would be their own money they'd be wasting if they slept through class or chose courses that were the educational equivalent of junk food. Because the student would pay, this plan would ultimately cost the government practically nothing. The relative efficiency of the income tax collection system could assure that bad debts would be few.

Another way to deal with the high cost of higher education is to attack the wasteful practices that have become customary at American universities. From 1981 to 1985, administrative expenses at West Virginia University rose at four times the rate of inflation. Generous salaries often are wasted on professors who don't teach. I recall those years at Columbia when the Trillings and Barzuns taught ten to fifteen hours and wonder why prestigious professors today often get away with teaching five hours or less.

Even without cost-lowering reforms, parents can save by sending their children to one of the good state universities, where the fees are roughly half those of the Ivy League schools. Are parents really showing the highest confidence in their children when they tell them it will be a disaster if they don't go to Harvard—implying that they really don't have the stuff to make it without the leg-up that a degree from the most prominent university can give? (Sometimes the kids are sent to Harvard for the sake of mom's and dad's egos. Not long ago, I came across a woman's resume that included the fact that her son and daughter were attending Brown and Princeton, respectively. That was the *mother's* resume.)

Whatever the expense of college may be, it may be either unnecessary or deferrable. College does not make sense for everyone. And it definitely does not make sense for all eighteen-year-olds to be dispatched automatically to institutions of higher learning upon graduation from secondary school. Many of them simply aren't ready for serious learning and would profit, as did so many World War II veterans I knew, from delaying the experience until they're ready for it.

I dwell on these ways of dealing with education expenses to expose the fact that a lot of people use the kids as an excuse. In other words, they chain themselves to money-making jobs not for the sake of Junior's tuition but for a BMW or a house in the Hamptons. Sometimes they buy these things just to show that they have money. More often, and this has been increasingly true since the Kennedy influence began to take hold in the sixties, they buy the BMW or the house in the Hamptons because they want to be perceived as people of taste, to establish their identity as members of a superior class. And demonstrating taste in everything from summer residences to motor cars to the paintings on your wall can cost a lot of money. These people could free themselves from bondage to money if they simply stopped caring about proving that they're part of the upper crust.

I don't contend that money is unnecessary, but I do believe that most affluent Americans need far less than they think they do. My salary is $24,000 a year, which is what it was when *The Washington Monthly* opened its doors in 1968. Had I stayed in the government at the same rank as when I left, I would now be making more than $70,000. If I had returned to private law practice, the figure could be considerably higher.

Not only did my salary not increase in dollars, it steadily decreased in buying power because of inflation. But the resulting downward mobility was not nearly as unbearable as the mere possibility of it seems to many people, involving little more than a succession of cheaper cars and cheaper wines and living in the same house for more than twenty-five years instead of making the series of upward residential changes that is customary in modern America. Especially since 1976, when Beth went to work for a private school, adding a second, if equally modest, salary to our income, we have been able to lead a comfortable life, accompanied only rarely by any sense of hardship or sacrifice. You don't have to be rich to be happy. You do have to do work that you respect.

× × ×

ONE reason the *Monthly* has survived is that most of the people who have worked at the magazine have shared the attitude Beth and I have toward money. When they need more, they leave; they seldom complain about the *Monthly*'s salaries while they're with us. Our offices have never been fancy—we have often been surrounded by sleek new buildings, but we've never been in one. Each room's a crowded, chaotic jumble of people, machines, boxes of magazines, stacks of books sent by publishers for review, and manuscripts we haven't gotten around to reading.

We always seem to be behind. At one point, when Taylor Branch and John Rothchild were managing editors, the copy was so late coming in that they had to stay up all night to get the issue out. They were so exhausted that it was several days before they started to work on the next issue, putting us behind schedule again, which meant another all-nighter to make it to press on time. This cycle, broken briefly on occasion by our efforts to pull ourselves together, has continued to this day. Editors have coped with these long deadline nights in assorted ways. Taylor and John chose bourbon. I would not recommend this to everyone, but for them it seemed to stimulate the wit that the rest of us like to think alcohol inspires, until we hear quoted back to us what we've said under its influence.

During this period, the young man who designed the layout and made up the pages for the printer did his share toward emptying the bourbon bottle. The mornings after those all-nighters, he was usually draped across a small sofa in the front room of the office, snoring loudly. This was somewhat unsettling to guests who had to share the reception area with him—not to mention its effect on our receptionist, who was a refined lady of mature years.

Another man, a writer, slept in the office with some regularity. Years later, someone found his toilet articles still neatly packed into the back of the circulation director's left-hand drawer.

Beth was filling in for the circulation director at the time that the writer was residing at the *Monthly*, but no one had told her about him. One night she decided to stay late to clear up some work, and she thought she was alone in the office. Around midnight, she heard a ringing sound and then some ominous shuffling in the next room. Suddenly, a man appeared at her office door. It was the writer, looking for his toothbrush. Beth, thinking he might have something else in mind, was about to let out a terrified scream. But he explained he had set his alarm so that he could get up and write, which he liked to do in the middle of the night.

In this atmosphere, it was hard to take oneself too seriously. Irreverence was the guiding spirit of the office. Taylor and John, in particular, loved to make good-natured fun of everything and everybody, including me. They were never gloomy. Even in moments of the most dismaying difficulty (editorial or financial), or of grinding fatigue, their attitude was light and playful.

Taylor, a reddish-blond, blue-eyed Georgian, had gone to the University of North Carolina and then to the Woodrow Wilson School at Princeton for graduate study. He was active in the national antiwar movement and visited Washington often to work with Sam Brown and David Mixner and the other planners of the 1969 Moratorium. On one of these trips, he dropped by our office to propose an article on desegregation in rural Georgia.

He was bright and engaging, so we urged him to go ahead. When the article came in a few months later, it was good—very, very good. So I offered him a job and he began work in June 1970. He had just turned twenty-two.

John, after graduating from Yale, where he was managing editor of the *Yale Daily News*, joined the Peace Corps and served in Ecuador for two years. He came to the *Monthly* in September 1970 at the age of twenty-four. He was a trifle chubby and usually slightly disheveled, which, together with his brown beard and twinkling eyes, gave him the aspect of a friendly bear.

The third new member of the editorial staff came aboard in September, too. Suzannah Lessard, nicknamed Suki, was a wide-eyed twenty-five-year-old New Yorker with an Orphan Annie hairdo who had been trying to make it as a writer without much success. A job as secretary at Random House was as close as she had gotten to being published. I liked the writing sample she sent us so much that I took the train to New York to have dinner with her. There was instantaneous rapport, and I ended the evening by offering her a job.

Suki was the most intellectually daring of the three. She was willing to advocate then-unfashionable causes such as entrepreneurship, to take on sacred cows like tenure in academia and the civil service, and to criticize the *New York Review of Books*, when it was the reigning intellectual power. She wrote that first article on the dark side of the antiwar movement, "Let Those Hillbillies Go Get Shot," at a time when most of her friends were part of the movement.

John is the author of one of my favorite lines from the *Monthly*. It was in a 1971 article, "The Senate's Lame Doves," which dealt with the failure of the antiwar senators to take the potentially most effective step open to them, which was to vote against the appropriations that paid for U.S. forces in Vietnam. They feared that they would be accused of taking the guns out of our boys' hands, or, as John put it:

> There is that vision of a battlefield with a few brave young Americans surrounded by a closing knot of North Vietnamese, while a credit adjustor slips through the enemy lines to repossess our guns and declare, "Senator X wouldn't pay for these."

(Taylor and John, by the way, deserve the credit for recruiting as a *Monthly* author Michael Kinsley, then a student at Harvard, who was to excell at writing such lines.)

Taylor and John were the originators of the outrageous headlines that became a *Monthly* tradition. A classic was the cover of the May 1972 issue: "Abolish Social Security"/"Cancel the National Debt." The purpose of these headlines was to shock people into paying attention to the accompanying articles pointing out that Social Security was now serving the affluent elderly more than the needy and that most of the national debt was owed to bankers and the rich. The portion of the debt that was held by the average person was in the form of savings bonds that paid only half the interest the rich were getting. Millions of people had bought these bonds—usually through payroll deduction plans—trusting their government to give them a fair deal. Instead, they were being cheated.

Taylor wrote the national debt article as a leaked Treasury Department document that proposed cancellation of all the debt except for savings bonds, so that the average person would be protected and the banks and the rich would be left holding the bag. Taylor so perfectly captured the flavor of official Washington prose that some of our wealthier readers thought the document was genuine and made anxious calls to their bankers.

Taylor, John, and Suki had become so essential to the *Monthly* that I considered them irreplaceable. So I was depressed when, in the summer of 1972, I had to face the fact that they would all leave soon. Taylor first went to Texas to manage George McGovern's campaign and then joined *Harper's* as its Washington editor. Suki moved back to New York and became a staff writer for the *New Yorker*. John took off on a trip around America to visit communes, which led to a book he wrote with his wife, Susan.

That summer was also when we went into Chapter XI. It was a bad time; I woke up in a panic almost every night and lost my temper almost every day. I felt like I was on the *Titanic* and the band was about to play "Nearer My God to Thee." Something good had to happen. And it did, one morning in August, when a young man walked into the office to apply for a writing job. He looked like the adolescent Skeezix of the "Gasoline Alley" comic strip of the thirties—tall, skinny, with a shock of blond hair over his forehead, and somewhere between fourteen and fifteen years old. But when he started talking, I knew I had struck gold. His mind worked with the speed of a computer and with a clarity that was remarkable.

This was James Fallows. He had just turned twenty-two and had been working for Ralph Nader that summer, having spent two years at Oxford on a Rhodes scholarship. He had published a condescendingly dismissive review of the *Monthly*'s first issue when he was president of the *Harvard Crimson*, but he had subsequently changed his mind.

He was so obviously a talent of the highest order that I was careful in our conversation not to give excessive emphasis to our financial plight lest it frighten him away. But the office was small enough that he could not help knowing that we were in trouble, and I was grateful that he decided to join us anyway.

In November, another applicant walked in the door— a just-defeated, twenty-five-year-old congressional candidate named Walter Shapiro. He had run as a liberal Democrat in a Republican district in Michigan the year the Democratic ticket was headed by George McGovern—not a promising combination, as the election result confirmed. We asked Walter to do a trial article. He wrote it quickly (Walter, we learned, either wrote quickly or dragged on forever), and it was wonderful. The title was "How Walter Shapiro Sank, Riding the Wave of Popular Support for Acid, Amnesty, and Abortion." As soon as I read it, I called and offered him a job.

A month later, Suki tipped me to a promising young English writer, Polly Toynbee. Polly was in Washington because her husband, Peter Jenkins, was the American correspondent for the *Manchester Guardian*. Suki gave me a book Polly had written called *A Working Life*. It described (several years before Studs Terkel's *Working*, by the way) what life at work was like for typical people in England, and it did so with a purity of style and humanity of insight that were so impressive that I knew I wanted her to write for the *Monthly*.

I had worried needlessly about replacing Suki and Taylor and John. Now we had Jim and Walter and Polly. Over the years, we've managed to come up with a good many others like them, but I've never stopped worrying that the well might run dry. I always have my eye out for talented writers. What I look for first is the courage to be different and to take on the powerful; then I look for intelligence, humor, curiosity, and a feel for the language.

A case can be made that any particular form of academic preparation is irrelevant to journalistic success. Mickey Kaus, who joined the *Monthly* in the late seventies, spent his entire college career immersed in the works of Karl Marx and survived not only without brain damage but with perhaps the best pure-analytical mind of all the writers who have worked at the *Monthly*. But usually I prefer to hire someone who has a solid background in history and literature. There is no doubt in my mind that Cervantes, Twain, Shakespeare, and Dickens, and a through grounding in the American past, are more help to a writer than anything that can be learned in journalism school. A good law school sharpens the thinking process enough to be valuable, but one year is all that is needed, not the three that Kinsley, Kaus, and I endured. Also useful is practical experience in politics or government, which I had in West Virginia and at the Peace Corps, Shapiro had in Michigan, Kaus had at the Federal Trade Commission, and Jonathan Rowe, an editor who joined us in the eighties, had as a member of the staff of Rep. Byron Dorgan. This kind of experience gives a journalist an insider's feel for the world he will cover.

Another way to acquire experience is doing in-depth journalism. That is why we look for past work that shows a writer's inclination and ability to delve deeply into a subject. The quality of the writing samples is the most important factor in the hiring decision. I don't care whether the sample has been published—or not, as was the case with Suki's. Next is references from people I respect. This may help explain why we have had so many *Harvard Crimson* alumni on our staff. Once Fallows and Kinsley established a beachhead, the reference chain naturally tended to favor former *Crimson* writers. Fallows recommended David Ignatius, who recommended Kaus, who recommended Jonathan Alter, and so on. But a Harvard education is definitely not a prerequisite to employment at the *Monthly*. We have taken people from all over the academic map, including Johns Hopkins, Northwestern, Pomona, Michigan, Manhattanville, Hobart, Colorado College, Augustana, and my own alma mater, Columbia.

I have given careful attention to hiring writers because they have more influence over the *Monthly*'s content than any other group—including our investors. At many publications, the people who put up the money call the shots. This has not been the case at the *Monthly* for two reasons. First, although I have had to give away most of the equity to keep the magazine afloat, I have managed to retain 51 percent of the voting rights. And second, we have been blessed with investors who have gotten involved because they like me or like the magazine, not because they want to dictate its content. In 1970, we published an article that was quite critical of Nelson Rockefeller's embrace of Latin American dictators like Papa Doc Duvalier. I awaited an indignant call from Jay, but it never came. Louis Marx once asked me to review a book a friend of his had written. It turned out that we had just gone to press with a review that was less than kind. When I called to tell Louis, he laughed good-naturedly, continued to support us, and over the years has become the *Monthly*'s major backer.

Another time, Warren Buffett called me with a tip about a scandal at Boys Town, which was located near Warren's home in Nebraska. I passed it on to Taylor and John. This time they may have been guilty of too much irreverence. They decided not to pursue the story, largely, I suspect, on the grounds that an investor's article idea had to be suspect. Warren then gave the story to an Omaha newspaper, which won a Pulitzer for it.

These episodes comprise the sum total of our investors' efforts to influence our editorial content. Sometimes they have asked me for advice or for some favor unrelated to the magazine, but these requests have been uniformly innocent. Warren, for example, asked me to introduce him to Kay Graham, which I did, and it turned out to be a very good thing for both of them. He became her principal financial advisor and the leading minority holder of *Washington Post* stock. They have made each other a lot richer than either was before they met. I should have asked for ten percent.

In our first years, the *Monthly*'s editorial board did have editorial influence by setting high standards of quality, but it never tried to dictate content. I can think of only one bad experience I had with a board member. Unfortunately, it was with the one to whom I owed the most, Richard Rovere. In the early seventies, he went through several periods of mental illness during which he would ask me to run pieces he had written that were sadly beneath his customary level. I had to refuse, which, because of my great debt to him, has to rank among the most painful experiences of my life. His spells mercifully ended in the mid-seventies, and our relationship during the last five years of his life was again warm.

If the investors and editorial board have rightly avoided trying to influence me on matters of content, the writers on our staff—equally rightly, I think—have had no compunction about telling me what they think. They have often changed my mind. For example, in 1980, Gregg Easterbrook, who had just visited the natural gas fields in Canada and the American West, persuaded me to publish an article saying that the energy crisis was over, which turned out to be right and was a year ahead of our competition.

They also edit my writing—so vigorously that I usually end up having to rewrite half the items in my column, "Tilting at Windmills." Actually, "Tilting" was their idea, or, to be precise, it was Nicholas Lemann's. I suspect that Nick, who has been especially generous in advising me over the years, was not entirely selfless in this proposal. I had long been in the habit of trying to get our writers to shoehorn into their articles whatever happened to be my enthusiasm of the moment, often without what they felt was due regard for its relevance to their subject. The author of an article on income maintenance might find himself importuned to conclude with a denunciation of aircraft carriers. "Tilting" gave a home to such points, and life became distinctly more bearable for our writers.

Although most of the time the influence of our writers has played a salutary role in my life, on one occasion it led me to an action that I regretted. I had decided to give our political book award for 1972 to three books: Daniel Ellsberg's *Papers on the War*, Frances FitzGerald's *Fire in the Lake*, and David Halberstam's *The Best and the Brightest*, a book that mirrored my own perceptions about the people who had been in charge of our disastrous Vietnam policy. We had commissioned a drawing of the three authors by Vint Lawrence. Then two of our editors who disliked the Halberstam book talked me into excluding it. We didn't have time to change the illustration, so it ran, to the bewilderment of our readers. I was ashamed, and as a result, at least once a year a ringing endorsement of *The Best and the Brightest* appears in our pages.

As these young writers were influencing me, I was influencing them. Having lived two or three decades longer than they had, I knew some things they didn't. Often the brightest young people can encompass in their imagination all the possibilities, one of which is the truth. But they are short on the experience that can help them smell out which one is the truth. I try to add to their store of experience by imparting to them what life has taught me. I do this by arguing with them. I edit by argument.

This approach was not common in the magazine and

newspaper world of 1969. There was style editing and fact-checking—the *New Yorker* excelled in both—but there was very little examining of manuscripts for intellectual loopholes or for facts that were either missing or there but irrelevant. This is what I have tried to do at the *Monthly*.

I was trained as a lawyer, not as a journalist. A lesson you learn very early in practicing law is how important it is for your partners to find the flaws in your case in the privacy of the office before opposing counsel has a chance to reveal them in the courtroom. When I was editing evaluation reports at the Peace Corps, this lesson impressed itself on me once more—it was crucial that I avoid mistakes that could provide ammunition to my bureaucratic enemies.

Established writers resisted my argue editing, regarding it as a threat to their dignity or their freedom of expression—and their dislike of being questioned was heightened by the way I'd go about it. In the course of the discussion, I can become so excited that I jump up and down, shout, and wave my hands to be sure my point is getting across. Taylor and John called it the "rain dance." It tends to dismay the faint of heart, but fortunately most of the writers at the *Monthly* have not been faint of heart. On the whole, they have liked the argument approach and have continued to use it—or a more civilized version—in their later work for other publications.

The arguments are almost always spirited and sometimes approach ferocity. And they can go on and on and on. I remember early one day when Taylor, Suki, John, and I began debating tenure—Suki and I were against it, and Taylor and John were for it. We argued through the morning and then over burgers and fries at a nearby fast-food restaurant. As we proceeded back down Connecticut Avenue to the office, the heated discussion went on, accompanied by enough shouting and gesticulation to give the impression that we were about to start a street fight. As we entered the office, Taylor was saying, ". . . and furthermore . . .," and the argument continued the rest of the afternoon.

The arguments—and this will shock most journalists—often preceded the reporting of the story. Most reporters believe that a journalist shouldn't approach a story with prejudices of any kind. I disagree. A writer has to have at least some beginning assumption, suspicion, or hunch to guide his research. The danger is that he will look so hard for confirmation of his preconceptions that, in the manner of Henry Luce and his writers, he will ignore evidence to the contrary.

At the *Monthly*, we had an insurance policy against letting our theories triumph over the evidence. It was that the writers and I usually disagreed about what our articles should say. My position was a synthesis of conservative, liberal, and even radical left, while the young writers, although they were all too original to fit neatly into any category, shared certain conventional liberal prejudices that my life had made me question. These prejudices could be summarized as Don't Say Anything Good About the Bad Guys. For liberals of that time, the bad guys were businessmen, the military, the police, and—with the exception of a social activist element—the clergy and religion in general. The corollary was Don't Say Anything Bad About the Good Guys, who included blacks, Hispanics, American Indians, teachers, union members, civil servants, and liberal public officials.

It was wrong, in other words, to give your friends a hard time or your enemies aid and comfort. Unfortunately, in the seventies, this meant ignoring some of the most serious problems of the decade, such as the decline in the quality of teaching in the public schools and the higher wages labor was winning without increasing productivity, both of which were hurting the people at the bottom in particular.

Incompetent teachers made it less likely that poor black children would get the kind of education that would enable them to escape the ghetto. Wage increases without productivity increases raised the prices of products such as automobiles and steel to a level where they were no longer competitive with foreign products. This, in turn, meant fewer jobs for the unemployed. The unions were pulling up the ladder. Every wage increase they got without a productivity increase made things worse, because there was less money left to hire the people who were trying to grab the bottom rung. In the eighties, the unions found a new way to screw the fellows at the bottom. It was the two-tier wage agreement, which permitted the older employees to keep their high pay while the new guys took the cuts.

In government, the pull-up-the-ladder syndrome not only decreases jobs but also reduces service to the public. During the seventies, the city of Los Angeles eliminated 7,000 jobs while radically reducing its street repaving and its library hours. At the same time, it increased to 75 percent the proportion of its budget devoted to salaries and fringe benefits. Liberal journalists were less than dogged in uncovering this sort of thing, because they felt that the civil servant was underpaid and did not want the world to find out that his pay raise was resulting in less service to the public and fewer or no job openings for people who wanted to become librarians or highway maintenance workers.

*The Washington Monthly* was alone in reporting a similar phenomenon in the federal government. As the pay of federal employees steadily rose until that of the *average* civil servant in Washington reached $32,000 in 1987, the number of chiefs increased and the number of

Indians dwindled, so that there were a lot of supervisors at the IRS but not enough working-level employees to answer the phone and help taxpayers with their problems. In many agencies needed employees weren't being hired because personnel budgets were being eaten up by raises for those already on board.

The liberals were following the Don't Say Anything Bad About the Good Guys rule and refusing to criticize their friends in the unions and civil service who were pulling up the ladder. Liberalism was becoming a movement of those who had arrived, who cared more about preserving and expanding their own gains than about helping those in need or serving the public.

In the *Monthly*'s early days, it was difficult to get articles that criticized the good guys. It was equally hard to find writers who would say a kind word about the bad guy. Among the toughest nuts to crack at that time were the prejudices against the police and the military. The police, after all, were using clubs to break up the left's demonstrations against the war—a war that was being prosecuted by the military. This made it hard to persuade young writers to see that such real crimes as murder and robbery did require effective police as part of an effective criminal justice system. And similarly, even though Vietnam may have been a war we shouldn't have fought, there might be unavoidable wars in the future for which we should be prepared.

I am scarcely a sentimentalist about either the police or the military. I remember well my first sergeants and that chief in Charleston. But I have also known decent cops; and my father and I had been in the army, one of my closest friends from high school spent his life in the navy, and Beth's family had a tradition of service in the army and the navy. As a result, I could not think of the military solely as a harbor for stupid, brutish war criminals, which was the view of much of the left at the time I started the *Monthly*.

In the magazine, this conflict between our writers' preconceptions and the lessons I thought I had learned from life produced a critique of liberalism in which the central issue was how liberal ideas stood the test of experience. One way of doing this was to compare liberal belief with liberal practice, in other words, to explore the differences between the ideas liberals professed and the way they behaved in their daily lives. In 1970–71 alone we published four such articles, each dealing with the hypocrisy of the liberal Washington establishment—the people who got misty-eyed singing "We Shall Overcome" and "I'm Working for the Union" at the same time they were pocketing fees from some of the slimiest clients in the country.

Our first assault was called "Moral Blindness on the Distinguished Bank Board." It described how such respectable liberals as Clark Clifford and Patricia Roberts Harris—as board members of the National Bank of Washington, which was owned by the corrupt United Mine Workers—were fronting for a scheme in which the miners' pension fund paid for the salaries and limousines of union officials, including the infamous Tony Boyle, who was at that very time plotting the murder of Jock Yablonski, the leader of a UMW reform movement.

The scheme worked this way: The union deposited the pension fund money in a non-interest-bearing account in the bank. The bank then lent the money to other customers, who paid interest to the bank. The interest income was turned into dividends that the bank paid to the union to provide the good life for Boyle and his associates. The bank's directors got their fees, not to mention the money and influence that a seat on the board of a large metropolitan bank provides. Only the pension fund was left out, receiving absolutely no income from its deposits.

A few days after the article appeared, my phone rang. I picked it up to hear a courtly voice say: "Mr. Peters, this is Clark Clifford. I read every issue of your magazine from cover to cover and I want you to know that I am deeply troubled by what you have written about the National Bank of Washington. You may be sure I will examine the situation carefully."

I had admired Clifford when he worked in the White House under Harry Truman, so I waited for him to resign with a public repudiation of Boyle and his entourage. But the repudiation never came. Clifford quietly left the bank board more than a year later. The other members stayed on. Harris resigned several years later, not on principle, but to accept a seat on the board of Chase Manhattan.

In another article, we caught the staunchly liberal and proenvironment *Washington Post* polluting Canadian waters with discharges from its paper plant. Fourteen years later, when we were writing about the *Post* again, I suggested that the author check on the plant. It had stopped the discharge, but now it was spreading a poisonous pesticide that was prohibited in the United States.

During the Kennedy and Johnson administrations, I had encountered another example of liberal hypocrisy— at the White House mess and the Department of Transportation dining room. At both, Kennedy and Johnson liberals were waited on by white-coated Filipinos. The general atmosphere was that of a colonial plantation. So I asked a writer named Timothy Ingram to look into the practice. He found that the navy and the coast guard, which staffed these dining rooms, recruited Filipinos as waiters and as servants for high-ranking officers but didn't let them do anything else; other jobs in the navy and coast guard were closed to them. The Filipinos still wait on tables, but our article did prompt Admiral Elmo Zumwalt to open up other navy jobs to them.

In the fall of 1971, when Daniel Ellsberg was being hailed as a hero for giving copies of the Pentagon Papers to senators and to newspapers, we pointed out another inconsistency: the same liberals who were praising Ellsberg had, during the Kennedy administration, condemned a conservative government employee, Otto Otepka, for giving confidential executive branch reports to the Congress. It wasn't that we didn't admire Ellsberg. We did, but we also liked to try shoes on the other foot.

By coincidence, the day before the article was to appear, Ellsberg brought Senator and Mrs. Ernest Gruening to my house for tea. Gruening, one of the few senators who consistently opposed U.S. involvement in Vietnam, was a great hero of the antiwar movement. I knew that Taylor and John would like to meet him, so I invited them, too. As we were chatting in the living room, Taylor suddenly looked ill. I saw his eyes directed toward the coffee table, where an advance copy of the issue with the Ellsberg–Otepka article, which Taylor had written, was clearly visible. The article wasn't really an attack on Ellsberg; but by pointing humorously to some of the similarities between the Otepka case and his own, it slightly dulled the high moral glow of his position. I knew Ellsberg loved that glow, and I did not want to ruin his afternoon. So with a quick motion that would have done a riverboat gambler proud, I shuffled the *Monthly* under a copy of *Newsweek*.

As other articles criticizing liberals and liberalism continued to appear in the *Monthly* throughout the seventies, some people began to identify us as part of the neoconservative movement. They included the author of a long article about the *Monthly* that appeared in the *Washington Post* on the morning of our tenth anniversary in 1979.

The neoconservatives *had* sprung from similar roots. Both Norman Podhoretz and I had been students of Lionel Trilling in the late forties and had been influenced by his critique of the mushy Marxism that ruled many liberal minds of that era. The neoconservative publication the *Public Interest*, founded in 1965, had used social science research to test liberal assumptions; a few years later, the *Monthly* came along to use journalism for the same purpose.

But I felt that there was a fundamental difference between neoconservatives and those of us who had worked at the *Monthly*. They were liberals who had taken a critical look at liberalism and decided to become conservatives. We were liberals who took a similar critical look, decided to reject the automatic prejudices of conventional liberalism, but continued to adhere to the old liberal goals of freedom and justice and a fair chance for all, of mercy for the afflicted and help for the down and out.

On the domestic front, their coldness toward the down and out often bordered on disdain when the poor were black. They and we found fault with government programs, but we did so from the standpoint of believing that government should act and wanting that action to work. They seemed content merely to prove that the programs weren't working. In foreign affairs, communism—which to us was only one of the threats to peace and freedom—had become an obsession with the neoconservatives, blinding them to other dangers, such as those presented by tribal, religious, and racial hatreds, not to mention right-wing dictatorships.

All these thoughts were whirring through my head when, after more than a few glasses of wine at our anniversary dinner, I got up and said, "We're not neoconservatives, we're neoliberals."

# CHAPTER 10

# Sharing the Burden

**T**HE word caught on, and over the next few years, one began to see both journalists and politicians described as neoliberals. The more I thought about it, however, the more I wished I had come up with something better. It seemed to invite misunderstanding, and there was a pretentious quality about it that irritated people. I certainly would never have used it when I was campaigning in the hollows of West Virginia. In that sense, it violated the *Monthly*'s editorial code, which insists on accessible prose—our writers try to deal with complexity without adding to it by using words the average reader cannot understand. But I've reluctantly come to the conclusion that we're stuck with neoliberal. By 1982, it was enough of a part of the political landscape for *Esquire* to devote a cover story to "the neoliberals." The article, by Randall Rothenberg (he later turned it into a book, published in 1984), was in part a lively and accurate account of the *Monthly*'s ideas. But in making his tent large enough to include people like Bill Bradley, Richard Gephardt, Gary Hart, Robert Reich, and Lester Thurow, Rothenberg ascribed to all neoliberals some views—including a faith in high technology and an unswerving middle-of-the-road-ism—that some of us do not share.

Unfortunately, this high-tech middle-of-the-roadism became the average journalist's notion of neoliberalism. Many people also confuse neoconservatism and neoliberalism and assume that we are considerably further to the right than we really are. They think of us not as the practical idealists we consider ourselves to be but as cynical sellouts who are trying to win votes by imitating Ronald Reagan. So one of my aims in writing this book is to make clear just what *The Washington Monthly* version of neoliberalism is, because I of course think it is the one true faith. And it is what I will be referring to when I use the terms neoliberal or neoliberalism hereafter.

We differ from conventional liberals both in our ideas and in our approach. Let me deal with the approach first. It involves a willingness to test liberal ideas by regularly exposing them to the facts—to say something bad about the good guys if that is what the evidence calls for.

This is not easy. Most people tend to seek and remember information that reinforces their prejudices and to avoid or forget information that challenges them. Many of these prejudices are rooted in emotional loyalties developed long ago, often during childhood. A simple example is my love of trains when I was a boy, which has made me a good deal readier to find flaws in the arguments against Amtrak than in the arguments for it. Similarly, as I grew up, it was hard for me to concede that Lee had made a terrible mistake when he ordered Pickett's charge and that FDR had sinned badly when he kept Americans of Japanese descent in relocation camps. Even *risking* the discovery that our gods have feet of clay is difficult. I remember once asking a granddaughter of FDR what kind of person he really was. I was suddenly afraid that the reply might be, "Well, if you must know, he was a terrible man," and I was relieved to hear her say, instead, that he was warm and kind.

So all of us have heroes and causes that we are reluctant to abandon. But neoliberals believe in keeping their political absolutes to a minimum. For me, that minimum consists of allegiance to the Declaration of Independence, the First Amendment, and the Golden Rule. They are the secret of America's potential greatness and the rudder that gives direction to my life. What they mean to me are human concern and practical help for those who have fallen on hard times, and freedom and justice—not for one privileged class, race, or religion, but for everyone.

But even these basic beliefs are subject to qualifications. Like many other people, I don't think free speech should include reckless libel or shouting "let's lynch a nigger." The Declaration of Independence can't mean that we are equal in ability or in luck. In fact, it must mean that those who are blessed with good fortune or unusual talent have a special obligation to help those who aren't similarly blessed. The direct pursuit of happiness has always seemed to me to be a bad idea, more often than not leading to experiences like that night in Atlanta when I was in the army. The Golden Rule should not be applied automatically without considering the Shavian corollary that others' tastes may be different. Thus, even with the ideas we believe in most strongly, neoliberals try to avoid the stubborn adherence to dogma that puts blinders on the intellectuals of the right and left, keeping them from seeing reality when it's not in accord with their theories.

In this respect, neoliberalism is in the tradition of Ben Franklin and Mark Twain. It is the common sense that I admired in Uncle Lloyd, who was willing to examine almost any political argument I would make, only rarely giving me the feeling that he had already come to a final judgment or that he was not prepared to look at all sides of the question. This did not mean that life had not equipped him with an assortment of beliefs and hunches with which he approached new situations. In my own case, as anyone who knows me will testify, this assortment is vast, but I see those beliefs and hunches as lessons of experience that, except for their moral element, can be changed by new experience. They are like traffic signals that flash green and yellow at the same time, meaning that it is probably safe to proceed, but that you should look to your right and left. If you see another car speeding into the intersection, you should be willing to change your mind about going ahead.

Conventional liberals—and conservatives— respond too automatically to the green lights and aren't willing to look to their right or left and see that car barreling down on them. That failure can be costly.

As an example, recall those price increases that were among the reasons for our industrial decline in the seventies. One cause that liberals wouldn't face was the high wages demanded by unions. Similarly, the conservatives didn't want to face the outrageously high salaries of management. The neoliberal approach would have been to face both causes and to propose a solution: lower wages for the worker and lower salaries for management, with each receiving shares of stock in the company instead. Each would take the risk of sacrificing immediate gain for the sake of the company's long-range prosperity and their own. In the past, the worker usually has been asked to be the sucker, to give up higher wages without getting a share of future profits to make up for his loss. On the other hand, greedy managers have become accustomed to receiving excessive salaries *and* stock options. The neoliberal solution means that no one has to be a sucker and that no one is the exploiter. Everyone shares the burden, and everyone shares the reward.

This example illustrates not only the facing-all-the-facts approach but also the two great imperatives of neoliberalism. One, which I've already explained, is to take the risk. The other is to share the burden. Our belief in sharing the burden reflects the commitment to democracy and community that is the idealistic side of neoliberalism. It underlies our views on everything from military service to the public schools.

× × ×

MILITARY service is one area in which the burden is definitely not being shared. The truth the Lessard and Fallows articles told about the Vietnam draft continues to apply to the post-Vietnam volunteer army and to the navy, air force, and marines. The upper middle class and the rich have not shared the burden. They have bribed the poor and the lower middle class to serve for them.

When I was in the army, I was paid $50 a month. Since I got free room, board, and clothing, I didn't need any more. In fact, I could afford to have $18.75 a month deducted from my pay for savings bonds. Twenty years after I entered the service, the beginning pay had risen to only $78 a month because there was still a draft. But today, because the military has to meet its manpower needs solely by attracting volunteers, it has to offer beginning pay of around $600 a month. If a draft were instituted, the pay could be cut in half. The other half represents the bribe that persuades the poor to enlist and permits the affluent to avoid doing their part. The waste and the immorality are so blatant that one wonders how anyone can justify not having a draft that takes both rich and poor.

Nevertheless, people do come up with excuses. The affluent say that they don't want their children drafted to die in another useless war like Vietnam or to be brutalized by the kind of vicious superiors who were depicted in *From Here to Eternity*. They also fear that, if their children go into the military for two years, they might lose the place on the fast track to success that their parents have worked so hard to give them since nursery school. The more thoughtful argue that compulsion is wrong in a free society and that it is most wrong when it is used to force pacifists to become part of the military machine.

But *From Here to Eternity* was about an all-volunteer army with the same class structure as today's, and Vietnam would never have happened if there had been influential parents to object. Indeed, it was fear of just such opposition that kept Lyndon Johnson from drafting the rich. As for losing position in the race for success, if the draft were universal, everybody would be held back equally. The race would be run against others who had been drafted. Besides, it is foolish to think that any form of meaningful success would be denied anyone solely because he is two years older than his competitors.

I wish compulsion weren't necessary. I wish people would volunteer. But the rich and the upper middle class aren't volunteering. It would be nice if people volunteered to pay taxes, but they never have. We need the force of law to make sure that some burdens are shared.

And it will be *law*, not some dictator's whim that creates a draft—a law enacted by representatives we elect. If we don't want it, it won't be passed. The average congressman will not leap to support a measure that has a good chance of angering the mothers and fathers and 18-year-old voters in his district. He's going to vote for a draft only if he is confident that we want it. If we stop wanting it, we can get rid of the law—which is what we have done three times in our history. If people begin to volunteer in droves, it certainly should be repealed. The neoliberals' devotion to the ideal of burden sharing is a constant, but we also believe in changing our views on a specific program when the facts justifying it change and we see a better way of serving the ideal.

As to the argument that pacifists should not be compelled to join the military, neoliberals agree. In fact, we believe that civilian service in such organizations as the Peace Corps, VISTA, and a new version of the Civilian Conservation Corps should be an option open to everyone, not just pacifists. (The term of service should be longer to make sure that the civilian option is not taken as a way of evading military service, and civilian service should not be open to nonpacifists during a war.)

There is plenty of work for civilian draftees, work that the country needs done but can't afford to pay prevailing wages for, such as daycare for the children of the working poor, care for the elderly, tutoring of ghetto youth, cleaning up the environment, and rebuilding the roads, bridges, water mains, and sewers that seem to be disintegrating all over the country.

Consider just the case of the elderly. They are now the fastest-growing segment of the population, and of them the fastest growing group is those over eighty-five. Most members of this group require the help of someone else to get through the day, but who is to do the helping—an elderly spouse, who is often pretty frail, or a nursing home, which can easily cost $25,000 a year? The answer is the thousands of young people a national service program could send into homes to provide the care that is needed.

A national service draft should involve every young person—rich and poor, male and female. But in the era of Gramm-Rudman, the cost of including them all—estimated to be around $30 billion a year—may be more than the nation feels it can afford, so a lottery may have to be used. It is crucial that the lottery be fair and that people from all classes be taken. National service should bring people together. When I was growing up, the social classes mixed in both the public schools and the service. Those fifteen crumpled one-dollar bills on my bunk at Fort McLellan left an indelible impression on my mind. The affluent don't have such experiences today, because they scorn military service and avoid the public schools.

× × ×

OUR concern about this avoidance of the public schools is as great as our concern about the scorn of military service. For a neoliberal committed to community and democracy, it is a tragedy that in 1987 in New York City, 90 percent of the non-Hispanic whites were attending private schools—a tragedy that occurred because of what happened to the public schools in the sixties and seventies. Beth and I saw it happen in Washington.

When our son, Chris, was five, in 1968, we enrolled him in kindergarten at Hardy, a public elementary school near our home in Washington. The District of Columbia's schools had been legally desegregated for more than ten years, but because of the residential racial patterns, considerable de facto segregation remained. There was only one black child in Chris's class. But while there were no poor people in the Hardy neighborhood and the very rich sent their children to private schools, Hardy maintained a reasonably democratic mix of lower middle class through upper middle class. The teachers, mostly women in their fifties, were excellent. Through the third grade, Chris's experience at Hardy was good. Several of his friends' parents became our friends. Then the District's public school system implemented a judicial order, known as the Skelly Wright decision, after the judge who was its author.

On its face, the decision was reasonable and just. The problem it addressed was a result of the white flight from the public schools that followed desegregation. A sizable minority of the District's whites had not waited to see how desegregation would work out. They either sent their children to private schools or moved to white suburbs. This meant that the public schools in the white areas of the District were underpopulated compared to the schools in the black areas, but they had retained their old budgets and staffing levels. Judge Wright decreed that the budgets and staffs must be spread out so that there would be equal allotments for all students regardless of where they lived.

The District dealt with Wright's order in two ways: it bused black students to white schools, and it transferred resources from white schools to black ones. It sounds good—but it didn't work.

The veteran teachers at Hardy, threatened with transfer across town, away from the neighborhood and the school they were comfortable with, retired. New teachers were brought in, but, because of the reduced budget, not enough of them. They weren't as good as the veterans had been, either.

The older teachers had gone into teaching when it was one of the few careers open to bright young women. The teaching profession therefore attracted a high proportion of the intelligent female population. Even if these women had been trained at inferior teachers colleges—as was often the case—they had enough natural ability to work wonders in the classroom.

But the young teachers of the early seventies came from a generation of women who had a wide range of career choices. Some of them looked down on teaching as a symbol of the bad old days. Certainly, the best and brightest weren't going to subject themselves to the kind of noneducation that the teachers colleges provided. Even though most of the teachers colleges had awarded themselves fancier names (for example, the District of Columbia Teachers College became the University of the District of Columbia), most were as bad as they had always been, if not worse. The result was that the new teachers coming into the public schools in the early seventies were a clear cut below their predecessors.

With the radical decline in the quality of teaching at Hardy came busing, which was (no pun intended) a mixed blessing. The buses turned Hardy into a black-majority school. Many of the new blacks and the remaining whites got along well, but a few blacks brought knives with them.

The combined threats of inferior education and violence rapidly drove the remaining whites away. By the time Chris was in the sixth grade, he was the only white left of those who had entered Hardy in 1968. The next year he switched to Georgetown Day, a private school nearby. Beth got a job on the school's staff so that we could pay the tuition.

Her work included involvement in the process of hiring teachers. Through this experience, we have learned something else about the education problem. Throwing money at it isn't the solution it's cracked up to be. Georgetown Day, like the other private schools in Washington, pays teachers about 20 percent less than the public schools in the area do, yet its faculty is unquestionably better than the average public school's. The reason is that Georgetown Day hires solely on the basis of teaching ability and knowledge of the subject; it does not require an education degree or a teaching certificate. Thus, it has a whole other world of potential teachers to hire from— liberal arts graduates. Even after the cultural changes that have opened up other jobs to women, many liberal arts graduates are willing to teach if they don't have to waste a lot of time in mind-numbing education courses. What's more, they are, on the whole, better teachers than the people with the education degrees. That's why they, not the graduates of teachers colleges, are hired by the best private schools.

The conclusion Beth and I were drawing about how to improve public schools by improving the quality of their teachers was reinforced by my experience at the Peace Corps and by articles on education that Joseph Nocera, Phillip Keisling, and Susan Ohanian wrote for the *Monthly*. First, hiring on the basis of subject knowledge and aptitude for teaching is crucial. Second, methodology courses for people being trained to teach are not necessarily irrelevant—but methodology is seldom useful unless it is subject-related and is taught in connection with classroom practice under the supervision of a skilled teacher. Third, the conventional liberal solution to the problem of the public schools—higher salaries for all teachers—is not the right answer. In many places, higher beginning salaries *are* needed. But higher salaries for all teachers is the wrong way to go, because bad teachers will then be motivated to stay in teaching. Higher salaries should be paid strictly on the basis of merit. But when they're deserved, they should be generous. So more money *can* help, but it has to be spent to encourage good teaching, not to reward incompetence.

Public school teachers argue that merit pay won't work because fair evaluation of their classroom performance is impossible. Yet these same teachers do not hesitate to evaluate their pupils every day. The grades these teachers would get would probably have the same value as those they give their own students—prejudiced and inaccurate in some cases but on the whole a very good guide to the worst and best performers.

The conservative answer to inferior public schools is to give pupils vouchers so that they can go to private schools. But most private schools tend to segregate children into groups that their parents are most comfortable with because they share either the same religion or the same social class. Not enough offer the diversity of association that it was my good luck to enjoy in the

Charleston public schools. Rich and poor were brought together so that we could get to know one another and acquire a faith in democracy that was not theoretical but grounded in real life. That the bonds formed at Charleston High were real, not merely a sentimental memory, is suggested by the fact the fortieth reunion of my class was attended by a majority of its surviving members, even though most of them no longer lived in Charleston. Eight of us have managed to get together almost every year since we graduated.

× × ×

WHEN you have actually known people from all walks of life, you're not going to believe that any class has a monopoly on virtue or vice. You will not make the error of the liberal who assumes that the poor are all deserving any more than you will make that of the conservative who thinks they are all lazy or dumb. You will not trust any one group, either rich or poor, to make decisions for you. A plutocracy under which the board of directors of the local country club determines the town tax structure is obviously wrong. But equally, if less obviously, wrong are liberal doctrines of community development and participatory democracy when they are used to say, for example, that slum dwellers should make all the decisions affecting their lives. It is a cross section of society that is most likely to come up with the wisest decision. A good example is the jury. In most cases, it represents the entire society, excluding only some of the least responsible, who fail to register to vote, and the most irresponsible of the influential, who have the combination of "pull" and indifference to public duty to get themselves excused. More often than not, this cross section of society will come to the right decision. Indeed, as I learned practicing law in Charleston, it almost always does when the playing field is even and the rules are fairly interpreted—meaning that opposing counsel are roughly equal in ability, that the judge is not incompetent or prejudiced, and that the community as a whole is not biased, as it was in the South when a case involved race.

Juries confirm the lesson of the World War II draft and of public schools like Charleston High. People with common sense can come from all walks of life. The same is true of the people you can count on in the clutch.

During infantry training at Fort McLellan, my friends and I would sometimes speculate about which of the men who were in charge of us we would most want to lead us into battle—which of them would best combine the intelligence, judgment, courage, and dependability we would want in the man who would be responsible for our living or dying. The man most of us chose was not one of the battalion officers. He was a relatively uneducated but superbly competent staff sergeant named Lightfritz, who had served with the 32nd Division in its harrowing struggle across the mountains of New Guinea.

If democracy and community are what I believe in most strongly, it is the antidemocratic forces in society—those that separate us and keep us apart—to which I am most opposed.

Of all the things that separate us, the worst is the snobbery that makes people think they are better than a Sergeant Lightfritz—or a Huck Finn—simply because their ancestry is more distinguished or they have gone to fancier schools or they have more money. I still cringe at the memory of my own snobbery at Columbia, and I am alarmed when I see it in other people, especially in those I otherwise respect. The snobbery that now guarantees liberalism's status as a minority movement is the liberal intellectuals' contempt for religious, patriotic, and family values. Instead of scorning people who value family, country, and church, liberals should be reaching out to the average man, trying to find common ground with his deepest beliefs.

Consider school prayer. Although I can easily understand why the custom of my youth—requiring children to recite the Lord's Prayer at the beginning of school—was not only offensive to many but violated the First Amendment, I can't see any reason to oppose a few minutes of silent meditation that would permit the freedom of choice that was intended by the establishment clause. Those who want to pray can pray, and those who don't want to pray can think about baseball (which I often managed to do at the same time I was reciting the Lord's Prayer) or anything else. If a teacher tries to force students to pray, fire him. But there is absolutely nothing wrong—indeed, there can be great good—in asking young people to think quietly for a few moments about the meaning of it all.

There was an explosion of snobbery in the sixties that continued through the seventies and the eighties. As I have noted, the Kennedys were one of the reasons for this development, but they were working fertile ground. The mobility of postwar Americans meant that people were moving every few years and having to reestablish their identities in new communities. This was easiest to do by using demonstrations of taste as the means of indicating their social class. And the easiest way to demonstrate taste was by buying the right things, from the right tonic water to the right shirt.

A result was the growing prosperity of the *New Yorker* during the late forties and fifties, as it swelled with ads that told people—including me during my snob period—what to buy and with editorial columns that told us what to admire in the arts. But after the Kennedys, the need was more than the *New Yorker* could satisfy. In the sixties, city magazines like *New York* and the *Wash-*

*ingtonian* sprang up all over the country, each dedicated to furnishing even more explicit guidance of what was "in" than the *New Yorker* provided. More and more people became preoccupied with showing that they had better taste than the other fellow. In the seventies and eighties, these magazines were joined by dozens of other publications, like the revived *Vanity Fair* and greatly expanded lifestyle sections in newspapers, all designed to help the upwardly mobile ascend the ladder.

× × ×

CLOSELY related to snobbery is credentialism, another divisive force. It says, "We don't care how able you are, Huck. If you don't have the right degree or the right test scores, we're not going to let you into this school or give you that job. We're going to consign you to an inferior class."

People should be judged on their demonstrated ability to perform, not on credentials that are not related to the job at hand. The ultimate silliness of credentialism was revealed a few years ago when a school denied a former major leaguer, Paul Blair, the chance to coach baseball because he lacked a teaching certificate. Blair finally got the job, but only, I suspect, because sports is one of the few areas of American life in which demonstrated ability is the main test for employment. If he had been looking for a job as an English teacher, a demonstration of superior knowledge of and ability to impart that subject to the young would have gotten him nowhere in most schools without an education degree.

Credentials that accurately reflect ability to do specific tasks such as teaching English—or trying cases—can be valuable in helping society protect itself from inept professionals. But far too many credentials are in many respects irrelevant to the performance of the job for which they are supposed to qualify their holder. Consider this question that, until quite recently, District of Columbia cab drivers were asked on their licensing examination: "All but one of the following words describes a person who displays a low dominance: (1) a follower; (2) agreeable; (3) cooperative; (4) persuasive."

Someone in the District government finally realized that knowing the correct answer was "persuasive" had nothing to do with knowing it takes a left turn from Key Bridge to reach Canal Road. But how did the question get on the test in the first place? And how many others like it are keeping good people from getting jobs in the many fields in which such tests are used? Every time I hear someone brag about their—or more often now, their children's—scores on tests like this I remember that high grade I got on the language aptitude test in the army.

Credentialism threatens our economic prosperity, too. As part of what was, in many ways, America's desirable movement toward meritocracy after World War II, test scores and grades became the main factor in getting a start up the ladder to success. However, since they do not measure the combination of courage and imagination that are needed in business, it seems possible that the corporations have been hiring the wrong people or finding the right ones only by chance.

Law school has been another way in which credentialism has threatened our economic growth. During the seventies, law school enrollments were exceeding 100,000 per year and included many of the ablest young people. If they had chosen productive work, they would have been on the cutting edge of needed economic growth. Instead, they spent three years sitting in some library, trying to focus their eyeballs on one soporific treatise after another. Today we have fifteen times more lawyers per capita than Japan, which, with a population half our own, produces twice as many engineers a year. "Anthropologists of the next century," Michael Kinsley wrote, in another of my favorite lines from the *Monthly*, "will look back in amazement at an arrangement whereby the most ambitious and brightest members of each generation were siphoned off the productive work force, trained to think like a lawyer, and put to work chasing one another round in circles."

As I learned at Virginia, roughly half of the members of a law school class do not really want to become lawyers. They just want the credential the law degree supplies. Unfortunately, in the process of getting the degree, they are trained to believe in another thing that divides us—the adversary system. Adversarial thinking breeds paranoia and suspicion. It has poisoned relations between management and labor. It means that Congress cannot trust the information it gets from the executive branch. In legal cases, including contract disputes, auto accidents, and divorce—in other words in the majority of civil cases—the adversary system can turn a situation in which both parties are to some extent at fault into an insane effort to put all the blame on just one. The case ends with everybody hating everybody else instead of reconciling or at least going forward with mutual acknowledgment of the good side of the other person's case, which in turn makes mutual understanding, affection, or respect more likely.

× × ×

THE most dangerous aspect of the adversarial approach is its chemical reaction with the macho element in men (and in man-imitating females), which turns every transaction in life into a win–lose situation. Nowhere is this danger greater than in the realm of foreign policy, where the adversarial attitudes that both produced and were engendered by the Cold War have again and again kept us from dealing with reality and finding peaceful solutions.

An early example of the harm these attitudes can do occurred in the Korean War, where the catastrophe of Chinese intervention could almost certainly have been prevented if we had stopped our troops well short of the Yalu River and assured the Chinese that we had no intention of invading Manchuria. Instead, we refused even to talk to the Chinese and proceeded to the Yalu for no reason other than to stomp on the North Koreans (we had already captured their capital city) and show them how thoroughly we had beaten them.

Because the adversarial approach led us, during the fifties and sixties, to view the communist world as an evil monolith, we failed to see how Chinese–Russian or Vietnamese–Chinese differences could help us. We finally did something about the former in the early seventies, but we never took advantage of the latter. In fact, we made many bad decisions in Vietnam based on the erroneous assumption that the Chinese were just looking for an excuse to come to the aid of North Vietnam.

Our hysterical focus on communism made us oblivious to other causes of war, such as the tribal, racial, and religious hatreds that have been the basis of many of the recent conflicts in Africa, in the Middle East, and on the Asian subcontinent. Sometimes, as in Afghanistan, Russia *was* the principal villain, but we saw it as the villain everywhere and thus often failed to deal with the real roots of the fighting that occurred in such places as Ceylon, Cyprus, and Nigeria and between such countries as Israel and its neighbors, Iran and Iraq, and India and Pakistan.

By the time of the communist takeover of Czechoslovakia in 1948, I had become part of the anticommunist majority. I was convinced by the evidence at their trials that Hiss and the Rosenbergs were guilty. I supported the Berlin airlift and the effort to repel the North Korean invasion of South Korea. But I disagreed with the majority when it came to McCarthyism and going to the Yalu. The guilt of Hiss and the Rosenbergs did not justify McCarthy's campaign of reckless character assassination, and North Korea's invasion of South Korea did not justify our drive to the Manchurian border. We had stopped the aggression, I thought. Wasn't it now time to stop the killing? What disturbed me most about Vietnam was the massive escalation and search-and-destroy policies followed by Johnson and Westmoreland from 1965 to 1968, which resulted in the unnecessary death of tens of thousands of American draftees and Vietnamese civilians.

My differences with my fellow anticommunists are clearest over this issue of bloodshed. I remember sitting across the table from Irving Kristol at a conference in 1983, when he said, "What the United States needs is a nice little war that we can win and feel good about." To me, there is no "nice little war." There may be a time when we have to stand up for our rights—or for the rights of others—but when that time comes, I want to be sure that we try our best to avoid killing people.

By using the Berlin airlift, we got the Russians to back down and we didn't have to shoot anyone. Nor did we have to resort to killing to get them to back down again during the Cuban missile crisis. The tragedy of the missile crisis was that Kennedy left the public with the impression that he had simply out-toughed Khrushchev, when in fact he had been reasonable and fair, as well as firm. Unfortunately, despite the *Monthly*'s efforts to publicize it, few people knew about Kennedy's offer to pull our missiles out of Turkey until the story was published in the *New York Times* in 1987. Now that it is widely known, I hope it will reduce the machismo factor in our foreign policy.

On the domestic scene, the adversarial approach combined with the ethos of the Me Decade to fragment the nation into interest groups, each of which seemed to be saying, "If we can't win, we don't want to play." It was as if every group had decided to imitate the National Rifle Association and to tell its congressman, "It doesn't matter how good you are in every other respect; if you don't support our special interest, we won't support you." This threat was made real by the explosion of political action committees, which backed it up by giving or withholding campaign contributions. At the beginning of the seventies, there were only a handful of these committees. By the end of the decade—thanks to a legislative goof by liberal congressmen that opened the floodgate and the politics of selfishness that produced the flood—there were thousands.

The campaign contributions of the PACs are so immense that they threaten to destroy democracy. Just as jurors may reach the wrong verdict if one side can afford the best lawyer, the voters may choose the wrong candidate if he can afford the slickest television commercials.

If the field is uneven, congressmen want it to tilt in their favor. They are therefore strongly predisposed not to offend the PAC that can tilt it for them, meaning they seldom are willing to represent the public interest when it differs from whatever the PAC wants.

× × ×

AT the *Monthly*, we felt that the only thing that would turn this situation around was a rebirth of idealism that would lead people to subordinate individual interests to what is best for the country as a whole. This would mean making it clear to our representatives that we are going to vote for them only on the basis of their overall performance, not their subservience to any lobby, even if it's our own. This new idealism would replace the politics of selfishness with a politics of doing our part. We saw this happen during World War II. Uncle Lloyd, a typical common-sense American without a shred of the grandstanding super-patriot in his character, enlisted in the navy even though he was forty-two years old and would not have been drafted.

We don't have to have a war for people to do things like he did. "We Do Our Part" was a New Deal slogan that inspired millions to share the burden of the struggle against the Depression in the thirties. The same spirit could inspire people to serve in the military for a couple of years or give up the government benefits they don't need, which is just as important.

Today, a disgracefully large number of people get money from the government that they don't really need. Even as early as the fifties, when I applied for unemployment compensation in New York, there were women in mink coats ahead of me in line. Now my wealthy Aunt Alice uses her Social Security income to go to Europe. Because of my back injury at Fort McLellan, I have received a veteran's pension since 1946. It never has been much—ranging from $30 to $130 a month—but although there have been occasions when I have needed it, most of the time I could have gotten along without it. On the other hand, many of us have elderly friends whose only income is Social Security. Pud was one of them until she died in 1985. These people are barely able to get by. Their rooms are threadbare, and their diet gets worse each day as the time goes by since their last check arrived. In most states, families on welfare share the same fate.

The answer is to consolidate all income maintenance programs—Social Security, unemployment compensation, veterans' pensions, welfare, worker's compensation—into one program that will insure each of us against need. We will be paid only if we become needy, as in the case of the auto insurance that we collect only if we have an accident. Now there is not only waste in the payments to those who aren't in need but also duplication in that some people receive money from several programs at the same time.

This consolidated program should have a work requirement. Those under sixty-five should be required to accept any job that they can perform. Welfare mothers with infant children should be given work that can be done at home. But they must do some work in return for what society is doing for them. If work is unavailable, the insurance would be paid. And it should be more generous than most of these programs are today, giving the needy a decent life. Money would be available to do this because we wouldn't be wasting any on the affluent or on duplication.

We also should take a hard look at how these programs are paid for. In particular, the way Social Security is financed should be changed. Today, a majority of workers pay less in federal income taxes than they and their employers pay in Social Security taxes. The burden is worst for those who can afford it least. In 1987, a married worker with two children who was earning $8,000 paid $572 in Social Security tax. Stop and think—this worker can't afford to pay *anything*. But by 1990 he will have to pay $612. So will his employer. And if the employer is a marginal business like *The Washington Monthly*, it may have to let the worker go. (Sharing the burden doesn't mean asking people to pay taxes they can't afford to pay. It means asking each of us to do our *fair* share.)

If Social Security were financed through the income tax, neither the low-wage worker nor the marginal employer would have to pay anything. Social Security would be paid for by individuals and companies that can afford to pay for it and would be given only to those who need it.

There are two arguments against the changes I propose. One is that if the rich don't get Social Security, they won't support it. The other is that there will always be a gray area in the middle where it will be difficult to draw a line between those who should and those who should not receive Social Security payments.

Modern bureaucratic liberalism dearly loves such gray areas because they excuse its failure to try to make needed distinctions. But we can certainly tell the difference between giving Social Security she doesn't need to Mrs. John D. Rockefeller and giving too little to a poor widow who has no other income. Why should we countenance the injustice of these extremes just because we're going to be confronted with difficulties when we get to the middle?

A simple example will demonstrate that government *can* make distinctions. It used to be that everyone who traveled for the government was paid the same amount to cover expenses. This usually meant that the fellow who went to Pierre, South Dakota, got too much and the one who went to New York City got too little. But the bureaucrats justified the policy on the ground that it would be too difficult to figure out different amounts for different places. Today that is just what they do. You get two and a half times more if you're going to New York than if you're going to Pierre. This is sensible and fair—and it wasn't so difficult to compute after all.

As for the desirability of bribing the rich by giving them Social Security so that they will support it, I think that is just as wrong as bribing them with a tax cut they don't need so that they will support a tax cut for those who do need it. The rich have always tended toward moral obtuseness, and today's wealthy may be a tad worse than the usual run in this regard. There is nothing wrong with the rest of us—for we are the majority—enacting laws that make sure that they do their duty when their own selfishness blinds them to what it is.

ɪ realize that drafting the rich and taking away their Social Security means radical change, but is it unrealistic? I don't think so, because I've seen so much radical change take place in my lifetime. In the fifties, I smoked cigarettes, and so did practically all of my friends. Today, none of us smokes. The cruel economic depression of the thirties turned into prosperity almost overnight in 1940–41, and that prosperity lasted for more than four decades. The indifference that greeted my father's efforts in the forties to clean up all that filthy smoke in the Kanawha Valley was replaced in the seventies by a vigorous environmental movement, which, although it still has miles to go, has made real progress in dealing with pollution.

The vicious anti-Catholic feeling that I saw in the 1960 Kennedy campaign had almost disappeared by the time of his death three years later. The state of Virginia I knew as a law student in the mid-fifties was dominated by the reactionary Byrd machine. Its intellectual eminence was James J. Kilpatrick, the editor of the *Richmond News-Leader*, who was proclaiming a doctrine called "interposition," under which the states were to resist integration. There was only one black student in the law school. And few Virginians would even look at those Stevenson leaflets I was trying to hand out.

Thirty years later, a moderate liberal was elected governor of Virginia, a black man was elected lieutenant governor, and a woman was elected attorney general. The change that produced this result was gradual. But it never would have occurred if the call to reform had simply been "We ought to be a little bit nicer to the colored folks." Radical change happened because people like Martin Luther King planted a flag out there, in what to many seemed extreme territory, so that we could see where we should be heading—so that even the incrementalists would do their incrementing in the proper direction. This is one reason the *Monthly* is not shy about taking positions that appear to be extreme or at odds with the prevailing wisdom.

The progress made by causes we have advocated over the years has provided additional support for our faith in the possibility of change. Many of our ideas have gone on—if not to triumph—then at least to a point well beyond what most people would have thought possible at the time we proposed them. In the seventies, we were almost alone in praising the entrepreneur. As recently as 1982, we were the only magazine to seek the rights to print an advance excerpt from *In Search of Excellence* by Thomas Peters and Robert Waterman, a book that described successful companies as those that encourage innovation, risk-taking, and experimentation. By early 1983, the book was at the top of the best-seller lists, where it remained for more than a year as a sign of the high regard the country was beginning to have for entrepreneurship. This regard was due far more to the growing concern about the Japanese challenge than to a mass awakening to the wisdom of the *Monthly*. But whatever the cause, students were seeking MBAs instead of law degrees, and Bill Bradley, one of the most widely admired senators, was saying, "Americans have to begin to treat risk as an opportunity, not as a threat." And by 1985, there seemed to be a new television commercial every day that talked about how risk-taking had made this country great.

Still, there is evidence that the idea hasn't quite gotten across in the way that I had hoped. The best and the brightest got the message that they should go into business, but too many of them were getting MBAs to become consultants or to go into mergers and acquisitions on Wall Street instead of to become entrepreneurs who create new jobs.

NATIONAL defense is another area in which the *Monthly*'s approach has enjoyed considerable success. At the time we began publishing in 1969, there was not one liberal Democrat in the Congress who took a truly responsible attitude toward national defense—asking what works and what doesn't work and what the nation really needs. Defense was not a fashionable issue among liberals because of their opposition to the war in Vietnam. In our second issue, we published an article by Robert Benson, who had just left the comptroller's office at the Pentagon, that explained how the Pentagon could save $9 billion without weakening national defense. A year later, we published the first of a long series of attacks on the supercarriers, "The Oldest Established Permanent Floating Anachronism on the Sea." As we criticized the bad weapons, we offered alternatives: more submarines instead of more carriers; a modified A-10 or a propeller plane to provide ground support instead of the too-fast jets that had shot up more of our own troops than the enemy's in Vietnam, or the attack helicopters that we were sure would, like the carriers, be destroyed in the first days of any serious war. By the early eighties our general approach, if not all our specifics, had become that of the majority of liberal Democrats, thanks in considerable part to Gary Hart, who deserves great honor for this if not for Donna Rice. This change in attitude among the politicians was accompanied by a dramatic improvement in the quality of reporting about weapons systems and other defense matters. There is still not enough written about the weapons we need, but there is plenty about those we don't.

On the issue of competitiveness, there was a growing awareness in the eighties that wage demands should be moderated and that executive salaries are often too high.

Unfortunately, the awareness did not lead to enough actual cuts, especially in the bosses' pay. And while some progress has been made on the worker-ownership front, too many workers are still denied a fair share of the profits their work has helped create. (Sometimes, alas, this has been because union leaders have feared that a worker share in ownership would put them out of business.)

The decline in the status of law degrees represented some success for our case against credentialism, which reached a far larger audience when James Fallows took it to the the *Atlantic*, with a readership ten times that of the *Monthly*. The greatest victory against the meaningless credential has been in the public schools, which by the second half of the eighties were beginning to hire teachers who did not have education degrees. This has been happening in New Jersey, Connecticut, Los Angeles, and New York City. And in Arlington County, Virginia, the schools have begun to audition teachers to find out if they have the most essential talent of all, the ability to perform in the classroom, which a paper credential could not possibly prove.

Just as Fallows carried our concern about credentialism to the *Atlantic*, he and Gregg Easterbrook gave the *Atlantic*'s readers our approach to defense. Easterbrook's articles on the Sgt. York anti-aircraft gun actually resulted in the cancellation of a major weapons system. Joseph Nocera, who had edited the 1979 article at the *Monthly* that gave the merger mania its name, went on, in a long piece for the *Texas Monthly* about T. Boone Pickens, to do perhaps the most insightful reporting yet about that depressing phenomenon. David Ignatius took over the "Outlook" section of the *Washington Post* and began publishing articles about the need for sharing the burden and the need for a "we decade." A series of articles on unions in 1981–82 provides another illustration of how our alumni spread the word. The first article, by Phillip Keisling, appeared in the *Monthly*, then came Gregg Easterbrook in the *Atlantic*, and finally Mickey Kaus in *Harper's*. The major points were the same, but each article improved on its predecessor, and each added thousands of readers to the total audience that was exposed to the message.

Anyone who reads the *New Republic* knows that many of its articles are not neoliberal. But there is no question that the work of Michael Kinsley, its editor, often is, and that he has endowed much of the *New Republic*'s content with the kind of lively irreverence that Taylor and John and he and Art Levine—and in our early days, Russell Baker—did so much to impart to the *Monthly*.

Probably the most heartening development of the eighties for me was one that the *Monthly* had little to do with, but for which Kinsley was a leading proponent: the Tax Reform Act of 1986. Although I believe that the bill was wrong in not providing enough encouragement for new enterprise and in cutting the rates for the rich too much, it was nevertheless a great triumph of the national interest over the special interests. A gratifyingly large number of lobbyists had to report sheepishly back to the home office that this time they just hadn't been able to protect that special exemption.

In 1969, when we launched the feature called "The Culture of Bureaucracy," most readers probably assumed that it was going to be about concerts at Constitution Hall and exhibits at the National Gallery. The concept of culture as applied to modern organizations was not widely understood. Today, the term corporate culture appears in the business press several times a week, and though the word culture is used less often in writing about government, we now regularly see articles that show an awareness of it in magazines and newspapers.

On income maintenance, there were small but significant victories when taxes were enacted in 1979 on unemployment compensation and in 1983 on Social Security. These taxes mean that the affluent are able to keep less of what they don't need.

× × ×

ALL these changes have delighted me, and I would love to take credit for each of them. But I can't because so many other factors have been involved, from the Japanese on entrepreneurship to Gary Hart on defense. Anyway, the bragging rights are not important. What *is* important about these changes is that they show that progress *is* possible.

I should note, however, that I am very far from thinking that progress is inevitable. There is that side of me that always feels as if I'm with General Lee, marching toward Appomattox. (In terms of the *Monthly*'s financial situation, there have been several times when I've felt I was almost there.) Certainly, a good case can be made that the world is a chaotic mess, that it more than likely will stay that way, and that one might as well not get out of bed in the morning.

But once you do decide to get out of bed and go outside, you begin to do things that can affect others for good or ill. Action inevitably involves us in responsibility for our fellow human beings, so we have to try to do what is best for the community. It is comforting to know that this effort can result in success. But frustrating failures are also possible, and the *Monthly* certainly has had its share.

Our most depressing failure involved the space shuttle, which we began criticizing in 1972. By 1980, Gregg Easterbrook was questioning the shuttle's safety. Speaking of the crew, he wrote: "Here's the plan. Suppose one of the solid-fuel boosters fails. The plan is you die." But we persuaded no one—or at least no one with any power at NASA. Six years later came the fatal launching of the *Challenger*. Of course, we were proud of having been right, but we had to face one of the most painful of all truths—that there is absolutely no virtue in saying the right thing if you can't get anyone to listen. I also had to face the fact that, although I am infamous for repeating points I deem worthy, I did not repeat this one once after 1980.

Another of our disappointments was Jimmy Carter. The three other men who have served in the White House during the *Monthly*'s lifetime have seldom showed the slightest sign of agreeing with us on anything. But as he campaigned around the country in 1975 and 1976, Carter did seem to be trying very hard to free himself from conventional liberalism and conservatism. I knew that he read the *Monthly* because my old girl friend, Helen Parker Dougherty, and her husband, Bill, who live in Atlanta, had given him a subscription. When Carter chose Jim Fallows as his speechwriter, I began to have visions of the entire *Monthly* program being presented in the first State of the Union address. And when Fallows found that Carter's personal files were full of *Monthly* articles that Carter himself had clipped, I tried to summon an air of calm statesmanship as I awaited what I confidently assumed would be a long series of meetings with Carter and his aides, during which they would earnestly seek my counsel.

As things turned out, all my statesman's mantle did was gather dust in the closet. Those articles had been clipped only to be forgotten. Fallows, finding that—unlike his predecessors as chief speechwriter, such as Ted Sorensen—his responsibilities began and ended with writing speeches, resigned halfway through the administration. Before he left, he tried to create a job that would have been a first step toward opening up Carter's lines of communication with the rest of the government, minimizing the failure to speak up and listen down that had been responsible for Vietnam and so many other disasters. Jim proposed that he rove through the government, serving as an extra set of eyes and ears for Carter, seeking to uncover good ideas that had been cut off by the bureaucracy and to identify problems before they became disasters—much as I had done for Shriver during the early days of the Peace Corps. Carter did not respond, I suspect because he had too much faith in the chain of command to do anything so irregular as to try to get around it. His engineer's mind simply could not see that government seldom works the way the organization charts say it does.

If, for example, instead of relying on assurances about Desert One from the chain of command, Carter had sent Fallows out to check on the operation, he would have discovered that the Delta commandos thought the marine helicopter pilots were incompetent and that there were a lot of other reasons the mission should have been scratched or reorganized. There is no question in my mind that Carter lost the 1980 election the day that picture was published showing the mullah exulting over the charred American bodies that had been abandoned in the Iranian desert.

It is tragic that so few presidents have understood the necessity of going outside the normal channels to get information. John Kennedy did, but only after he had been burned by the Bay of Pigs, which taught him that he could never trust the chain of command to give him bad news. Thereafter, Kennedy became a faithful practitioner of the bureaucratic end run—the call to the desk officer at State that would tell him what the people in the trenches really thought.

The great master of the art was Franklin Roosevelt, who, if confronted with a proposal from Harold Ickes, would immediately call Ickes's number-one bureaucratic enemy, Harry Hopkins, to ask, "What do you think of this idea of Harold's?" Roosevelt also used his wife, Eleanor, to play the eyes-and-ears role. She and Hopkins, in turn, used her friend Lorena Hickock to visit New Deal projects and report back on the problems she found. It is absurd that Hickock lives in history only as a suspected lover of Mrs. Roosevelt, when her reports stand as an example to every White House of the kind of information the president should be getting about the programs for which he is responsible. Someday, a wise president will institutionalize the Hickock role and hire people like Fallows and her to perform it. (If they were known to be able, just a handful of them would be enough to inspire a dramatic improvement in chain-of-command reporting throughout the government. No one would want to be the person who got caught lying.)

There is another way to solve the communications problem—by working from the bottom up as well as from the top down. The need is for subordinates to speak out when they have information that the fellows at the top need to know but either don't want to face or are prevented from knowing by intermediate officials who cut off the flow of information to protect their own careers. Such whistle-blowing requires a person who is courageous and willing to take risks. The problem is that, perversely, the job security the civil service provides to protect the brave actually attracts the cautious. A few years ago, the State Department set up a "back channel" to encourage dissent from the field, but little use has been made of it. In 1979, Congress set up a new agency, the Merit System Protection Board, to (among other things) defend whistle-blowers from retaliation by their superiors, but the board has discovered that whistle-blowers are in short supply. The problem is that people who are drawn to the career service, though admirable in many respects, are not inclined to go out on limbs—even when there is a safety net below. They may realize that they can't be fired, but they still don't want to do anything to jeopardize their regular promotions.

How do we deal with this problem? The Peace Corps experience is instructive. The reason we got candid criticism from our volunteers is that they had no careers to protect. They were in for only two years, and then they were going to do something else with their lives. They could be completely fearless in saying what we were doing wrong.

We ought to have many more public employees who are in for only a short time and thus have no careers to protect and nothing to be cautious about. Short-term jobs are also likely to attract the kind of person who has the self-confidence to think that he can easily get another job when this one ends and thus is not afraid to speak up.

I propose that we take roughly half the positions under civil service and, as they become vacant through attrition, turn them into short-term appointments with the same term of service that worked so well for the Peace Corps staff—two and a half years, renewable (but only once) for another two and a half years. This would give an infusion of new blood to a government that badly needs it. (The commercials that got Federal Express going—the ones about those bored and indifferent postal clerks—worked because they were recognizably close to the truth.)

As a bonus, when the short-term employees return to private life, they will take with them real knowledge of how the government works—where there is fat that can be trimmed and which programs need more support. As they spread the word, democracy will work better because the public will be better informed.

It also would help to make a substantial number of these short-term appointments explicitly political. I don't mean that the people appointed would not have to be qualified—you couldn't make your sister Susie your secretary if she couldn't type—but the president and his appointees, rather than civil servants, would pick them. If democracy means that we are governed by the people we elect and the people they appoint, then it is sad that the president can now choose fewer than one-tenth of one percent of the people who serve under him. By the way, the same is increasingly true of governors and mayors because of the growth of civil service systems at the state and local levels. In Los Angeles, the mayor can't even choose his department heads.

If those jobs were available as a reward for people who participate in politics, more good people would participate in politics. Today, about all campaign volunteers can look forward to is a certificate of appreciation from the League of Women Voters. This is why their number is declining and why most campaign workers now have to be paid. If we don't want a system that requires candidates to raise money for their workers' salaries, then we have to provide some other kind of reward to the workers. If we could offer those who push the doorbells, man the telephones, and hand out the leaflets the opportunity to come to Washington or the state house or city hall and help put into effect the programs they have campaigned for, we would not only make elections less dependent on money but attract higher caliber people to politics.

The main objection to a patronage system is that incompetent or crooked elected officials would appoint incompetent or crooked subordinates. In addition, serious students of government worry that institutional memory will be lost (which already happens with each White House turnover) if there is a wholesale change of bureaucrats after every election.

As to the first objection, it is true that accountable

government will work only if there are accountable voters who realize the importance of making the right choice when they turn those levers on the voting machine. But it seems to me that the more citizens there are who have had experience in government, the more likely the electorate is to make the right choice. Certainly, we are more likely to vote carefully if we know that the people we choose will actually run the government instead of acting as temporary figureheads presiding over a permanent bureaucracy of unaccountable civil servants. As for the institutional memory point, recall that I would have half the jobs under civil service—which, by the way, would mean putting more civil servants in the White House.

If the approach I recommend had been in effect for even the past decade, the nation would today be far better equipped than it is to make the sophisticated judgments about the budget that will be necessary in the years to come. We would know which programs need to be strengthened and which should be reduced or eliminated. And there would be more people in government who, because they'd spent most of their lives on the outside, would have genuine empathy for the problems of the average citizen. The lack of this empathy is the most glaring deficiency of the bureaucracy in Washington.

Those who were alive in the thirties will remember that the post office used to deliver packages intact and letters on time—twice a day, in fact. That postal system was political. If the mail didn't come on time, people could complain to their congressman, and if he wanted to be reelected, he would arrange for a new local postmaster. The postal system was gradually depoliticized, becoming completely nonpolitical in 1968. What has happened to the mail since then? What happens when people complain? Many don't even bother—they call Federal Express instead. But the poor can't afford Federal Express. So it is they who suffer the most from inept civil servants, just as they suffer the most from poor public school teachers.

Of all the messages I have tried to get across in the *Monthly*, none has had less impact than this campaign to give government back to the people. I understand why the rest of the world is leery of politics in government, because I used to be, too. Not only was I an ardent advocate of civil service when I was in the West Virginia legislature, but I was so embarrassed about being a political appointee at the Peace Corps that I did not display my autographed picture of John Kennedy until November 23, 1963.

For most of us, politics has become a bad word—you may have noticed that when people mean politics but want it to sound respectable, they call it "the political process"—and politician is an even worse one. I no longer feel that way, but almost all of the educated elite—conservative and liberal—still do. They simply don't believe in government by the people. They are closet Coriolanuses, who, instead of identifying with the people, look down on them.

One of the great differences between today and when I was a boy in the thirties is that, then, the millions of people like my mother and father who had come from rural America to make it in the towns and cities continued to identify with their friends and relatives back on the farm. Today, their counterparts emulate the upper class, reading those magazines that tell them about the right wines, the right restaurants, the right places to vacation, and the right paintings to buy, and watching television shows that take them inside the homes and lives of the wealthy—or if they're watching PBS, of the British aristocracy.

Because they identify with the wealthy, money—both as a measure of status and as a means of acquiring the objects needed to demonstrate one's taste—is dominating the lives of people who should know better. Steven Rattner, a talented young reporter for the *New York Times*, deserted his opportunity to serve the public interest in journalism to pursue a morally marginal million-dollar income on Wall Street. Ivanhoe Donaldson, one of the brightest young black public officials in the nation, went to jail because he had taken bribes to support his attempt to imitate the life-styles of the rich and famous.

During World War II, FDR proposed a limit on all incomes. He saw the danger that people would lose the idealism of the struggle against depression and tyranny and become preoccupied with personal gain—that they would begin to forget about the national interest in pursuit of their own. He may have been wrong in thinking that people shouldn't have the opportunity to get rich if they so choose. But he was sublimely right in understanding that they shouldn't forget their nation and their fellow man in the process. People who place a high value on money usually place a low value on jobs that help others, jobs that are often far more satisfying than many that pay high salaries. Because how much money they make is important to them, they are not free to do work they believe in when it doesn't pay well.

There is no advice I can give that is more important than Do Work You Believe In. I was reminded of just how crucial that advice is when, a few years ago, a treasured friend of mine died. He was a good and thoughtful man whose time on this earth gave pleasure to all who knew him. But he was in one sense a very unhappy man. He never enjoyed his work. He spent his life dutifully managing family businesses that he had inherited. At times he talked about doing other things, such as becoming a doctor, and one could sense his excitement at the prospect. But he never made the break. Finally it was too late.

Thinking about him makes me sad. It also makes me

angry at myself for not having tried harder to persuade him to do what he wanted to do while there was still time. I don't want to make that mistake again. So if there is anyone out there reading this book who is still doing work he or she does not like and respect, please get out now. You can be in your thirties—even your forties or fifties—and it's not too late.

I know it can be done because I've done it, changing the kind of work I did three times in my adult life: leaving the theater to enter law and politics at twenty-seven, leaving law to become a Peace Corps bureaucrat at thirty-four, and leaving government to start *The Washington Monthly* at forty-one. The last change in particular was filled with anxiety and peril, but I am glad I made it, as I have been glad I made the others, for each step was taken in search of work that would use more fully whatever abilities I possessed.

Suppose you became a lawyer because your parents wanted you to do something respectable. Or suppose you went into investment banking because it seemed to be where the glamour and excitement were going to be in the eighties. Now you find yourself doing something that is either boring or unworthy or both. What should you do? Get out! Now.

What can you do? One possibility is teaching. It is work that many have found they love. Or you could become a nurse—there is a severe shortage of Sadie Stouts and Mary Ianzettis these days—or a reporter or a civil servant in an agency that's doing something important. All are jobs where good people are needed and where good people can make a difference.

Perhaps you have a suppressed yearning for a career in the arts that is stronger than mine was. Or maybe you would like to start your own enterprise and make a good product and give people jobs. Just because my friend didn't like business doesn't mean that you wouldn't find the life of the entrepreneur exhilarating.

Whatever you decide to do, the point is to decide and move. Don't let yourself be trapped in the wrong work. Don't wait, as my friend did, until it's too late.

Above all don't betray your potential in life for the sake of money. Even if you find yourself unpersuaded by the other doctrines of neoliberalism, embrace its indifference to wealth. Jesus Christ and Mahatma Gandhi are better spiritual guides than Ronald Reagan.

"I'll cut your taxes" was the trumpet call Reagan sounded as the Me Decade came to a close, challenging America to be even more selfish in the eighties. The nation responded with a fervor that should be an everlasting embarrassment to us all.

Of course, "What's in it for me?" has always been a thought not very far from the center of our national consciousness. But in the seventies and eighties it became an obsession. Perhaps we were freed from it by the lessons of October 19, 1987. I hope so. There is a better side to our character. We need a leader who appeals to it, who calls for the best within us instead of the worst. Woodrow Wilson once said, "They call me an idealist. That's how I know I'm an American." The words sound absurd today, but in my heart I know they're true. Even if the right leader doesn't come along, we can all decide that we're sick of greed and status-seeking, that we want to be part of a community in which we all do our part, that we want being an American to mean being an idealist.

But our idealism doesn't have to be heavy or righteous. Neoliberalism may be the first political movement in history to have humor as a plank in its platform. Humor is important to us, not merely because we want to entertain but because it's basic to our view of life. Remember the roles played by Jean Arthur and Katharine

Hepburn and those other actresses I admired as a boy? They were like Rosalind in *As You Like It*, in that they were caring and affirmative at the same time that they saw what was ridiculous about the world and about themselves. It is a comment on our time that the dominant female star of the eighties has been Meryl Streep, most of whose roles are characterized by a kind of anguished self-absorption.

In many ways, life was much tougher in the thirties, but there was a lot more sunshine in the soul and laughter in the land. We need that laughter today. We need to laugh, above all, at ourselves. If we don't, we will never overcome the politics of self-righteous, self-pitying interest groups and begin to listen to one another, to rebuild community, and to take the risks that can produce a just and prosperous and democratic society.

# Chapter Notes

**CHAPTER ONE**

*page 1*
down the Kanawha:
Soon after they had passed Kanawha Falls, which was a few miles above Charleston and the last natural obstacle to navigation, the pioneers would halt to cut down trees and build wooden flatboats that would carry them, their furniture, mules, chickens, and families down the river to wherever they chose to settle. There they would tear up the flatboats and use the lumber to construct their first dwellings.

*page 15*
*Mr. Smith Goes to Washington,* by Sidney Buchman, can be found in *Twenty Best Film Plays,* John Gassner, ed. (Crown, 1943).

*page 17*
Henderson Peebles:
Many big-city sophisticates assume that all small-town insurance salesmen are insensitive hustlers. This was not the case with Henderson Peebles. During the severe depression I experienced while I was in law school (see page 86), I happened to run into him when I was home for a visit. He sensed my condition and proceeded to take the time, just a few days before his death, to write me a long letter of encouragement, which

ranks in my life with the letter I received from Theodore White at a moment almost as dark in 1969 (see page 173).


## CHAPTER TWO

*page 40*
I became a socialist:
In 1945, the argument for government control of private enterprise was considerably more convincing than it is today. Both the post office and the TVA were models of efficiency and service, which, alas, is no longer the case with either.


## CHAPTER THREE

*page 43*
*Teacher in America,* by Jacques Barzun (Little, Brown, 1945).

*page 44*
required to take courses:
Among the authors we had to read in just the first term were Homer, Aristotle, Plato, Sophocles, Euripides, Aeschylus, Aristophanes, Herodotus, Thucydides, Virgil, and St. Augustine.

inexpensive French and Italian restaurants:
Unfortunately, in the fifties, Barbetta's was gussied up and became expensive, and Le Champlain was demolished in the sixties, along with a lot of other good, moderate-priced restaurants in the West Forties and Fifties, to make way for the westward expansion of Rockefeller Center.

*page 51*
Harry Golden:
*Only in America* (World Publishing, 1958) and *For 2 Cents Plain* (World Publishing, 1959) were Harry's most successful books.

*page 56*
Herbert Huncke:
Huncke later followed Ginsberg and Kerouac into the world of literature. See his *The Evening Sun Turned Crimson* (Cherry Valley Edition, 1970), and the forthcoming *Guilty of Everything,* to be published by Paragon Press.

**page 61**
Mark Van Doren:
An example of his work is *Shakespeare* (Holt, 1939). See especially his essay on "As You Like It."

**page 62**
Thomson grabbed:
I know some readers will be saying, "It was *Hank* Thompson, not Bobby Thomson, at third base for the Giants in 1951." This was true for part of the season, but not for the period I write about. Then, Bobby Thomson was on third, and his usual outfield positions were filled by Monte Irvin, Willie Mays, and Don Mueller.

## CHAPTER FOUR

**page 73**
Professor Krutch:
For insight into the quality of Krutch's mind, see his essay on Cervantes in *Five Masters* (Jonathan Cape and Harrison Smith, 1930), which was reprinted in *This Is My Best*, Whit Burnett, ed. (Dial Press, 1943).

**page 74**
stretch it out for a little more than two years:
I did take leave from graduate school from January through August 1950 to direct four plays for the Kanawha Players and to do another season of summer stock in Charleston. That summer we broke even again. We should have done better, since our gross income increased by $600. But success inspired carelessness about expenses—we actually had a real phone instead of the pay phone.

**page 75**
consistent hard work:
One of the best tests of whether a career interest is vocational or avocational is how hard you are willing to work at it day in and day out over a long period of time.

**pages 75–76**
Russian postwar behavior in Eastern Europe:
The Russian invasion of Finland in the fall of 1939 was another factor in my lingering hostility toward the Soviet Union. The

intense sympathy Americans felt for Finland was captured in a play, *There Shall Be No Night*, written in 1940 by Roosevelt's chief speechwriter, Robert Sherwood.

### page 76
Lionel Trilling:
See especially *The Middle of the Journey* (Viking, 1947), and *The Liberal Imagination: Essays on Literature and Society* (Viking, 1950).

### page 77
campaign of Rudolph Halley:
Who was Rudolph Halley? He had become prominent as the counsel for the Kefauver committee, which in 1951 had given the nation its first televised glimpse into organized crime.

### page 79
William Faulkner:
During rehearsals, Faulkner visited the studio with his mistress, a sensitive and talented writer named Joan Williams, and Joan and I struck up a friendship. I sublet her apartment at 55 Horatio Street in the Village while she was home in Memphis. I met Faulkner again when I dropped by to see her after she returned to New York and resumed occupancy of the apartment. Several years later, while I was in Charlottesville, a fairly remarkable coincidence occurred. I was invited to a party by one of my law school classmates, who happened to be married to Faulkner's daughter, Jill. She was the apple of her father's eye and not at all likely to know about her father's mistress. Faulkner was visiting her at the time. When I walked in the door, a look of panic appeared on the great man's face, as he must have been thinking that I might be so indiscreet as to mention Joan in front of his daughter. I was tempted to nudge him in the ribs and wink but managed to restrain myself.

### CHAPTER FIVE

### page 84
An article I wrote:
I explained my theory of the establishment clause by using the GI Bill as an example of its proper effect. Under the GI Bill, the government offered to pay my tuition at the college of my choice. In fact it was Columbia. But it could have been Notre

Dame. Had the government's money been paid to Notre Dame, either through me or directly, the effect of the transaction would have been to aid religion. But is this enough to make it unconstitutional? Although the Supreme Court has never confronted the question because of its rules barring certain types of suits in federal courts, the ACLU and many state courts that have considered similar issues would answer yes. If this is unconstitutional, then would it not also be unconstitutional for a government employee to give any part of his salary to his church? Of course, you can argue that the salary is paid for services performed under contract, whereas the tuition is a gift; there are no strings on how the salary money is to be spent, but the tuition money must go for education.

But if the fact that the scholarship is a gift would make its use at a Catholic school unconstitutional, a veteran's bonus would be unconstitutional to the extent that the veteran contributed it to religion. And if the fact that there is a restriction on how the money is to be used is enough to make it unconstitutional, using public money for a fire department would also be unconstitutional to the extent that the fire department used it to protect sectarian property.

If a church catches fire, putting out the fire will aid religion. But if government refuses to put out the fire, it will be denying church property the protection it gives all other property. If religious schools and buildings are denied the fire protection and financial assistance government gives to all other schools and buildings, then the government is hampering the free exercise of religion. Veterans who want to go to Sectarian U. will have to attend Agnostic Tech because they can't get GI benefits if they go to Sectarian U.—and the place will have burned down anyway.

The purpose of the First Amendment's religion provision— the free exercise and establishment clause—is to keep government from doing anything that influences people's opinions in the realm of religion. This purpose can be accomplished only by forbidding government to single out religion, or a religion, for help or harm and by keeping the government from encouraging any person to be religious or not to be religious or to be a Catholic or not to be a Catholic.

There are sensible reasons for arguing that public money should be used only for public schools. But it's about time we took the sanctimony of constitutional principle out of the argument. Those who remain confused by the "wall of separation" metaphor should know that it does not appear in the Constitution or the Bill of Rights or any of the debates preceding the adoption of the First Amendment. Unfortunately, the confused include a large number of judges who continue to reach wrong decisions as they try to protect a wall that the Founding Fathers never intended to erect.

**page 97**
the judge will be biased:
Other reasons for judicial prejudice against the poor and in favor of the wealthy are: (1) that it is usually the rich and their lawyers whom the judge knows socially and sees at his country club, and (2) that, in the event his judicial career comes to an end, he would like to be welcomed as a partner by the more affluent firms, whose favor is not likely to be bestowed upon vigorous defenders of the rights of the poor.

**CHAPTER SIX**

**page 109**
Stanislavski:
For a more reliable version of the method, see *A Dream of Passion: The Development of the Method*, by Lee Strasburg (Little, Brown, 1987).

**page 113**
bill establishing a state human rights commission:
This bill was an example of failed "foot-in-the-door" liberalism. State Senator Paul Kaufman and I, who were its cosponsors, reasoned that we would get the commission established first and give it enforcement powers later. But the powers were never added; future civil rights progress in the state was due less to our commission than to the progress that was being made through federal law.

**page 114**
my father's air pollution bill:
Theodore White nailed my "realism" with this comment about a similar episode in his own life in the fifties: "A self-censorship, imposed not by government but by prudence, circumscribed me as it circumscribed countless others." *In Search of History*, by Theodore H. White (Harper & Row, 1978).

## CHAPTER SEVEN

**pages 117–29**
Evaluation in the Peace Corps is described in Richard Rovere's introduction to *Inside the System*, Timothy Adams and Charles Peters, eds. (Praeger, 1970); *A Moment in History*, by Brent Ashabranner (Doubleday, 1972); *The Bold Experiment: JFK's Peace Corps*, by Gerard Rice (Notre Dame Press, 1985); and *Come As You Are: The Peace Corps Story*, by Coates Redmon (Harcourt Brace Jovanovich, 1986). It was also discussed in *Keeping Kennedy's Promise—The Peace Corps: Unmet Hope of the New Frontier*, by Kevin Lowther and C.P. Lucas (Westview Press, 1978), for which the evaluation reports were a major source, as they were for *Agents of Change: A Close Look at the Peace Corps*, by Meridan Bennett and David Hapgood (Little, Brown, 1968). Evaluation was abolished by the Nixon administration.

**page 128**
confined themselves to the capital city:
"Never Leave the Cities Where the Good Bars Are," I later realized, was a guiding principle of behavior in the State Department and the CIA, as well as among our foreign correspondents. It helped account for the almost continuous series of surprises that Third World grass-roots rebellions provided our government and press.

**page 131**
Chester Bowles:
For an account of the Kennedy treatment of Bowles, see "You're Right Chet. You're Right, and You're Fired," by Harris Wofford, *The Washington Monthly*, July–August 1980.

**page 133**
Kennedy did not have this kind of machismo:
See "Cuban Missiles and Kennedy Macho: New Evidence to Dispel the Myth," by Graham Allison, *The Washington Monthly*, October 1972.

**page 134**
"I knew right away":
Doris Kearns Goodwin, *The Fitzgeralds and the Kennedys* (Simon and Schuster, 1987).

one writer:
*The Founding Father,* by Richard J. Whalen (New American Library, 1964).

**CHAPTER EIGHT**

*page 141*
Johnson was better on civil rights:
I respect what Robert Kennedy's Justice Department did for civil rights, but I was ashamed of John Kennedy's failure to march to the Lincoln Memorial with Martin Luther King in August 1963. (Most of white Washington joined the president in hiding out that day. Downtown was deserted.)

*pages 141–42*
examine the operation of a government agency:
The General Accounting Office could do what Peace Corps Evaluation did, but it seldom has (see "The One-Eyed Watchdog of Congress," by Richard F. Kaufman, *The Washington Monthly,* February 1971; and "The Best Job in Washington," by Thomas N. Bethell, *The Washington Monthly,* April 1980). So could the inspectors general in various agencies around the government, but they, too, rarely achieve the potential their positions offer (see "Inspectors General: The Fraud in Fighting Fraud," by Joseph Nocera, *The Washington Monthly,* February 1979, and "Watching the Watchdogs," by John Eisendrath, *The Washington Monthly,* July–August 1986). The closest thing to Peace Corps Evaluation was the inspector general's office in Sargent Shriver's Office of Economic Opportunity, established by William Haddad and directed by Edgar May from 1964 to 1967 (see "The Shriver Prescription," by Jack Gonzalez and John Rothchild, *The Washington Monthly,* November 1972).

*page 144*
Social scientists wrote:
Among the pioneer social scientists were David Reisman, author of *The Lonely Crowd* (Yale University Press, 1950), and Wallace S. Sayre and Herbert Kaufman, who wrote *Governing New York City* (Russell Sage Foundation, 1960). In the seventies, the psychiatrist and anthropologist Michael Maccoby established himself as a perceptive observer of organizational behavior; see *The Gamesman* (Simon and Schuster, 1976). Many more would join them in the eighties. On the whole, until then,

the participation of social scientists in this area was miserable. In fact, one of the best early books on the subject, *The Organization Man* (Simon and Schuster, 1956), was written not by a social scientist but by the journalist William Whyte. The most prolific early critic of business organizations was the management consultant Peter Drucker.

### page 145
enriched by a novelist's feel:
Before Theodore White, Tom Wolfe, and Truman Capote came along, life usually entered journalism only through the feature story, often in the form of the "sob sister" sidebar to an article about some crime or other disaster, in which the reporter, often a woman, would provide a colorful and moving account of how the condemned killer or his wife spent his or her last hours. An exception was Murray Kempton, who by the early fifties was proving that the usually dry column of the op-ed page could be made to come alive with humor and human insight. In the sixties, Clay Felker, as editor of the *New York Herald Tribune* Sunday supplement and *New York* magazine, did much to encourage Wolfe and others in the practice of the new journalism.

### page 148
a large dinner party:
Several years later, I told Katharine Graham this story, adding that I had felt like the country boy at a fancy party. Her comment was that the real secret of understanding the self-pity of Washingtonians is that almost all of us think of ourselves as insecure outsiders. Although I still think I'm more of a country boy than she is a country girl, there is undeniable wisdom in her observation.

### page 152
editorial advisory board:
In the early seventies, I asked James David Barber and Graham Allison to join the board. They were the academics who seemed most sensitive to our emphasis on understanding the interaction of character and bureaucracy in government. In October 1969, we had published the article, "Analyzing Presidents," that led to Barber's landmark book, *The Presidential Character* (Prentice-Hall, 1971). (Barber, by the way, was also born in Charleston; his father was my family's doctor.)

255

In the mid-seventies, Baker had to leave the board because of a *New York Times* policy against such involvement with other publications. James C. Thomson, Jr., resigned when he became director of the Nieman program at Harvard. They were replaced by Richard Reeves, who was the *Monthly*'s regular book reviewer for several years, and David Halberstam (see page 198).

### page 154
Seymour Hersh and Robert Kuttner:
See "The Rusty Fair Employment Machine," by Robert Kuttner, and "The Military Committees," by Seymour Hersh, in the April 1969 *Washington Monthly*. Hersh would soon become celebrated for his revelations about My Lai. Kuttner's reputation would take longer to establish, but by the eighties he was considered a leading spokesman for the conventional left (see *The Life of the Party*, by Robert Kuttner [Viking, 1987]), along with Michael Harrington (see *Decade of Decision* [Simon and Schuster, 1980]). Kuttner's article for the *Monthly* in 1969 was a perfect example of an issue on which old and new liberals can agree. It was about the failure of government—the Pentagon— to pursue a desirable social goal in a case where the government could have done the job, and done it well, by using existing laws to require that defense contractors not discriminate against blacks and other minorities.

### page 162
shortage of great leaders:
After the murders of Robert Kennedy and Martin Luther King, there was only one inspiring figure left in American public life— Ralph Nader. For the next few years he, more than anyone else, carried the banner of idealism and devotion to the public inter- est (see "Ralph Nader Reconsidered," by Jonathan Rowe, *The Washington Monthly*, March 1985). He was a great influence on *The Washington Monthly* and on many of the people who worked for it. At one time or another, Rowe, James Fallows, Michael Kinsley, and Taylor Branch worked on Nader projects.

the war dominated our table of contents:
Among the Vietnam articles we published in the years 1969– 72 were: "The Stupidity of Intelligence," by Ariel, September 1969; "The Only Alternative—A Reply to President Nixon on Vietnam," by Frank Church, December 1969; "The Nuremberg

Suggestion," by Townsend Hoopes, January 1970; "The Other Side of the Table," by Tran Van Dinh, January 1970; "The Politics of Peace," by Sam Brown, August 1970; "The Diplomacy of Intervention and Extraction," by Arthur Schlesinger, March 1971; a special Indochina Section in April 1971, including "Maximizing Cobra Utilization," by Jeffrey Record, "The Vietnamization of Cambodia," by Peter A. Poole, "No Victory Parades," by Murray Polner, the first article about the plight of the Vietnam veterans, and "The Burn Ward," by Ronald J. Glasser; "The Wild Blue Yonder over Laos," by Fred Branfman, July 1971; "Cooing Down the War: The Senate's Lame Doves," by John Rothchild, August 1971; "Working Up to Killing," by Oriana Fallaci, February 1972; "The Red Badge of Literature," by William Styron, March 1972; "The Ugly American and the Flexible Response," by Taylor Branch, April 1972; "Let Those Hillbillies Go Get Shot," by Suzannah Lessard, April 1972; "Our Bombs Fall on People," by George Wald, May 1972; and "Prisoners of War, Prisoners of Peace," by Taylor Branch, August 1972. After the last American troops were withdrawn, articles on the war appeared less often. Among them were: "We Knew What We Were Doing When We Went into Vietnam," by Henry Fairlie, May 1973; "Mary McCarthy—The Blinders She Wears," by James Fallows, May 1974; "What Did You Do in the Class War, Daddy?" by James Fallows, October 1975; "The Case for Intervention," by Stephen Young, November 1976; "The CIA in Vietnam," by Joseph Burkholder Smith, February 1978.

#### page 163
people who were psychologically ready to resign:
This concern of ours was to lead to a book, *Blowing the Whistle: Dissent in the Public Interest*, Charles Peters and Taylor Branch, eds. (Praeger, 1972). It was also reflected in other books during this period, including, most notably, *Exit, Voice and Loyalty*, by Albert O. Hirschman (Harvard University Press, 1970), which was excerpted in the December 1969 issue of *The Washington Monthly; Whistle Blowing*, by Ralph Nader (Grossman, 1972); and *Resignation in Protest*, by Thomas M. Franck and Edward Weisband (Grossman, 1975).

#### page 164
macho element . . . feminist revolution:
Among the early *Washington Monthly* articles were: "Spock-

lash: Age, Sex and Revolution," by Philip E. Slater, February 1970; "Violence and Masculinity," by Lucy Komisar, July 1970; "Gay Is Good for Us All," by Suzannah Lessard, December 1970; "Is Camelot Dead? A New Look at JFK," by Suzannah Lessard, October 1971; "The *Ms.* Click! The Decter Anguish, the Vilar Vulgarity," by Suzannah Lessard, January 1973. The most recent were: "The Politics of Motherhood," by Deborah Fallows, June 1985, and "Has *Ms.* Undergone a Sex Change?" by Susan Milligan, October 1986.

What has happened, of course, is that too many women have imitated the worst in men. A recent study sponsored by the American Council on Education showed that the number of women who wanted to make lots of money had grown from 30 percent in 1967 to 72 percent in 1987.

### page 166
an escaping plane:
Almost everyone who has read this has said, "You mean helicopter, don't you?" No, I mean plane. The only photograph of Vietnamese being kicked away from an aircraft door was not of a helicopter but of a plane leaving some airstrip in the provinces.

### page 167
an article about Mary McCarthy:
In the October 17, 1974, issue of the *New York Review of Books*, Harold Rosenberg, who was a close friend of Mary McCarthy, wrote the official response to Fallows's *Monthly* article ("Mary McCarthy—The Blinders She Wears," May 1974). It is a revealing statement of the disdainful attitude toward journalism that was then common among the New York intellectuals. Fallows had criticized McCarthy for failing to investigate the facts behind appearances she had clearly misjudged. Rosenberg seemed to feel that such reporting would be beneath the dignity of a leading intellectual.

### page 168
"Let Those Hillbillies Go Get Shot," by Suzannah Lessard, *The Washington Monthly*, April 1972.

### page 169
"What Did You Do in the Class War, Daddy?" by James Fallows, *The Washington Monthly*, October 1975.

## CHAPTER NINE

**page 171**
article about us:
See "Low-Keyed Muckrakers," *Time*, March 21, 1971; "Charlie Peters and His Gospel Singers," by Laurence Zuckerman, *Columbia Journalism Review*, September–October 1983; and "The Peters Principles," *Newsweek*, February 6, 1984. The first article about us in *Washington Journalism Review* was in May 1983.

**page 176**
I.F. Stone:
I was in Stone's debt for two reasons. It was he who taught me the importance of being a demonic clipper of newspapers. He was also responsible for our receiving the George Polk Award for 1970. Had he not called me to suggest that we put out a press release on the article that won it for us—"CONUS Intelligence: The Army Watches Civilian Politics," by Christopher Pyle, January 1970—I, who have a very poor news sense, would never have thought to publicize the article. Stone's wife, Esther, taught me the principle of management that must govern an understaffed magazine: concentrate on what has to be done today.

**page 177**
average journalist's ignorance of both business and the law:
Chapter XI proceedings, when not treated as going-out-of-business bankruptcies, were almost always described as "reorganizations," which they were not. For an indication of the depth at which business journalism operated in the early seventies, see the following *Washington Monthly* articles: "Oily Reprints at the *Times*," by Richard Karp, November 1970; and "Kay, Otis and Newby: They Sell Out Too," by Walter Shapiro, December 1973.

**page 183**
better for us and for other struggling businesses:
Lest anyone think that I am advocating relief from Social Security taxes—or incentives for new investment (see page 182)—just for the sake of *The Washington Monthly*, I should emphasize that I would want the reforms that I urge even if the *Monthly* were excluded from both.

*page 185*
we were alone among liberal magazines:
During the seventies, we published the following articles about entrepreneurship and business: "Do Entrepreneurs Have More Fun?" by Suzannah Lessard, December 1972; "A Radical Proposal: Free Enterprise," by Michael Rappeport and Christine Van Lenten, May 1973; "How We Can Survive the Seventies," by James Fallows, February 1974; "How We Can Bring Back Quality—Sharing a Piece of the Action," by Marjorie Boyd, February 1974; "Big Is Bad for Us All," by John Winslow, June 1974; "Putting Yourself on the Line," by Charles Peters, October 1974; "How Not to Help Small Business," by Walter Shapiro, October 1974; "Wall Street—The Entrepreneur's Worst Friend," by Thomas Redburn, March 1976; "The Bankers Attack on Free Enterprise," by John Winslow, June 1976; "The Myth of Corporate Democracy," by Ralph Nader, Mark Green, et al., July–August 1976; "A Harvard Man Discovers Free Enterprise," by James Glassman, October 1976; "Why Other Harvards Aren't," by Charles Peters, October 1976; "Off-Off-Broadway—Lessons for Us All," by Nicholas Lemann, December 1976; "The Government vs. Small Business," by John Kenneth Galbraith, September 1978; "Independent Oilmen—Why They Take More Risks," by Nicholas Lemann, November 1978; and "The Merger Mania," by Thomas Redburn, February 1979.

We began the eighties with "Pie-Slicers vs. Pie-Enlargers," by Robert Reich, September 1980, and continued with "Meet the Master of Risk-Free Enterprise," by Eric Pianin, April 1981; "How Congress Spoils Small Business," by Bill Keller, March 1982; "Merger Mongers," by Joseph Nocera, December 1982; "What's Right with Big Business," by Thomas J. Peters and Robert H. Waterman, December 1982; "Confessions of a Socialist Entrepreneur," by Peter Barnes, October 1983; "Weirton Steel: Buying Out the Bosses," by Jonathan Rowe, January 1984; "Hello Sweetheart, Get Me Mergers and Acquisitions," Philip Weiss, May 1986; and "Paradise Tossed: How a Chance to Save American Capitalism Was Sabotaged at Eastern Airlines," Alex Gibney, June 1986.

*page 186*
tenure can entrap:
See the following *Washington Monthly* articles: "The Terms of Tenure," by Suzannah Lessard, September 1971; "The Trouble

with Tenure," by Mark Nadel, January 1978; and "I Turned Down Tenure," by David Helfand, June 1986.

finance college and a professional education:
See the following *Washington Monthly* articles: "New Hope for Parents—A Way to Beat the High Cost of College," by Walter Shapiro, April 1974; "Let the Students Pay," by Robert M. Kaus, March 1979; and "Highbrow Robbery," by Timothy Noah, July–August 1983.

### page 191
[Taylor Branch] began work:
Taylor did everything from setting type to raising money to checking newsstands to make sure they were carrying the *Monthly*. Only Phillip Keisling (1982–84) rivaled him among our editors in willingness to do anything for the cause.

Suki was the most intellectually daring:
Among her articles for *The Washington Monthly*: "America's Time Traps: The Youth Cult, the Work Prison, the Emptiness of Age," February 1971; "Busting Our Mental Blocks on Drugs and Crime," June 1971; "The Terms of Tenure," September 1971; "Is Camelot Dead: A New Look at John Kennedy," October 1971; "Rehnquist, Powell, and the Cult of the Pro," February 1972; "What Do People Do All Day," March 1972; "Let Those Hillbillies Go Get Shot," April 1972; "Aborting a Fetus: The Legal Right, the Personal Choice," August 1972; "An Ulsterman's Irishman, An Arab's Jew," October 1972; "Do Entrepreneurs Have More Fun?" December 1972; "The *Ms.* Click! The Decter Anguish, the Vilar Vulgarity," January 1973; "America the Featherbedded," February 1973; "The Hidden Injuries of Class," March 1973; "Moral Myopia: *The New York Review* and the New York Intellectuals," November 1973; "Why Johhny Can't Work: The Snobbery Factor," November 1974; "Taste, Class, and Mary Tyler Moore," March 1975; "Kennedy's Woman Problem, Women's Kennedy Problem," December 1979.

In terms of courage, all of the *Monthly*'s young editors rank high, but I would place James Fallows, Joseph Nocera, and Timothy Noah next to Lessard. Each of them did what few journalists are willing to do—criticize a potential employer. Each wrote tough articles about the *Washington Post* ("Ben Bradlee and His All-Star Review," by James Fallows, January

1975; "Making It at the Post," by Joseph Nocera, January 1979; "The Washington Post: Monopoly Profits and Broken Promises," by Timothy Noah, January 1984). It is to the credit of Katharine Graham that even though she was angered by Noah's article—she spent an entire lunch berating me for it—he ultimately was hired by *Newsweek*, which is owned by the *Post*.

John is the author:
"Cooing Down the War: The Senate's Lame Doves," by John Rothchild, *The Washington Monthly*, August 1971.

**page 192**
Michael Kinsley:
My favorite Kinsley line was, "Is it a conflict of interest for a mother to have a second child?" ("The Conflict of Interest Craze," *The Washington Monthly*, November 1978).

**page 194**
"How Walter Shapiro Sank, Riding the Wave of Popular Support for Acid, Amnesty, and Abortion," *The Washington Monthly*, December 1972.

**page 196**
Warren Buffett called me with a tip:
Warren had another idea that we have endorsed instead of ignored. It is to tax at 100 percent all capital gains on stocks held less than a year. In other words, short-term traders would make zero profit. This proposal would end speculative abuse on Wall Street. Perhaps that's why so little is written about it.

**page 197**
energy crisis was over:
I had felt that gasoline rationing was necessary to break OPEC's stranglehold. Easterbrook convinced me that excess supply was already doing the job. But I still think the president should have standby rationing authority so that we will never again be faced with short-term shortages—which are always possible for political and other reasons, even though the basic supply is more than adequate—that cause the kind of double-digit inflation we twice endured in the seventies.

**page 198**
shoehorn into their articles:
Art Levine exposed all my unfortunate tendencies in "Do You

Have What It Takes to Write for *The Washington Monthly*?" in our February 1979 issue.

### page 200
Don't Say Anything Bad About the Good Guys:
Conservatives also have good guys about whom they are loath to say anything bad—businessmen, the military, the police, and the clergy, except for the social activists. In other words, their good guys are the same as the liberals' bad guys.

### page 201
steel:
See "What's Left of Big Steel," David Ignatius, *Washington Post,* March 20, 1988, C1, and his similar March 1979 *Monthly* article.

### pages 201–2
number of Indians dwindled:
The historic turning point in the Indians-to-chiefs ratio in the federal government occurred in 1978, when the civil servants at the top—GS-18s—began to outnumber the GS-1s at the bottom.

### page 202
prejudices against the police:
See the two articles called "Two Cops Talk Turkey": "Letting Rizzo Do the Thinking," by Christopher Wrenn, and "Thinking for Ourselves—Questions We Can Start With," by Donald Graham—in the December 1973 issue of *The Washington Monthly.* I was not to get the hard-line article on violent crime that I wanted until I hired the only certifiable conservative ever to serve on the *Monthly* staff—right-wing Tom Bethell (as distinguished from left-wing Thomas N. Bethell, who also served as one of our editors). Tom wrote "Criminals Belong in Jail" for our January 1976 issue.

### page 203
National Bank of Washington:
As a West Virginian, I was haunted by my knowledge of what their bosses and their union did to the miners. See the following *Washington Monthly* articles: "Conspiracy in Coal," by Thomas N. Bethell, February 1969; "Secretary Shultz and the Miners," by Robert Walters, February 1970; "Manslaughter on Buffalo Creek," by Thomas N. Bethell and Davitt McAteer, May

1972; "You Can't Buy Safety at the Company Store," by Davitt McAteer, November 1972; "The Unions—How Much Can a Good Man Do?" by Curtis Seltzer, June 1974; "The UMW: Now More than Ever," by Thomas N. Bethell, March 1978. The bosses, especially in the early days, were worse, but later on the union was almost as bad.

**page 204**
staunchly liberal . . . *Washington Post*:
"Clean Thoughts and Dirty Water," by Dirk van Loon, *The Washington Monthly*, December 1970; and "The Washington Post: Monopoly Profits and Broken Promises," by Timothy Noah, *The Washington Monthly*, January 1984.

another example of liberal hypocrisy:
"The Floating Plantation," by Timothy Ingram, *The Washington Monthly*, October 1970.

**page 205**
another inconsistency:
"The Odd Couple: Ellsberg and Otepka," by Taylor Branch, *The Washington Monthly*, October 1971.

a long article about the *Monthly*:
"Dept. of Evaluation—A Magazine Watches the Government Closely," by Garrett Epps, *The Washington Post*, February 25, 1979.

**page 206**
Lionel Trilling:
Among the Marxists of the thirties who, like Trilling, became disillusioned with the Soviet Union, there were two typical reactions. One was to become, as did Whittaker Chambers, a conservative, solely concerned with fighting communism. The other, of which Richard Rovere was an example, was also to oppose communism but at the same time to remain faithful to the old liberal causes. The Chamberses anticipated neoconservatism as the Roveres did neoliberalism.

As the sixties approached, John and Robert Kennedy were departing from conventional liberalism in their willingness to take on corrupt labor unions. And when John Kennedy showed that he also could take on the villains of business, like Big Steel, he proved he was a neoliberal at heart. The intellectuals who supported the Kennedys (and took considerable heat from their peers for doing so)—John Kenneth Galbraith and Arthur Schlesinger, Jr.—were displaying at least some desire to free liberalism from its old automatic responses. Galbraith was among the first to perceive how big labor and big business were conspiring to produce inflation for the rest of us. Schlesinger now seems torn between dismissing neoliberalism and claiming that he and Galbraith invented it (see "The Old Idea of 'New Ideas,'" *New Republic*, May 27, 1985). By 1969, another intellectual, Theodore Lowi, had written in *An End to Liberalism* (Norton, 1969) the pioneering analysis of interest-group liberalism, opposition to which was a cornerstone of neoliberalism. Like Schlesinger, Lowi is now unenthusiastic about the movement he helped anticipate. See Theodore Lowi, "What's New in Neoliberalism," *Washington Post Book World*, June 16, 1985. Oddly, neither Lowi's article nor Schlesinger's, part of which was repeated in his book *The Cycles of American History* (Houghton Mifflin, 1986), dealt with the two major themes of *The Washington Monthly*'s neoliberalism—taking the risk and sharing the burden.


## CHAPTER TEN

**page 207**
article, by Randall Rothenberg . . . later turned it into a book: "The Neoliberal Club," by Randall Rothenberg, *Esquire*, February 1982; and *The Neoliberals*, by Randall Rothenberg (Simon and Schuster, 1984).

**page 208**
the average journalist's notion of neoliberalism:
As an example of the kind of misunderstanding we have to deal with, here is Paul Taylor, generally a good reporter, writing in the *Washington Post*, January 7, 1988:

> In the early 1980s, Gephardt, like Hart and Gore, was loosely identified with a group of so-called neoliberal or Atari Democrats fascinated by technology and next-generation industries, skeptical of Great Society spending programs, and inclined more toward economic policies that would bring growth rather than redistribution or entitlements.

This was half-right, but it was crucially misleading to those who thought it described *The Washington Monthly*'s kind of neoliberalism. We have never been Atari Democrats, fascinated by next-generation industries. Although we were skeptical of Great Society spending, we were sympathetic to its objectives. And we were just as interested in redistribution as we were in growth. Our criticism of the entitlement programs is redistributionist; in that sense, we are much more liberal than the conventional liberals.

One of the reasons for Randall Rothenberg's middle-of-the-roadism is that he wanted to define a politically feasible movement, so that, although he was personally sympathetic and always quite kind to me, he was troubled by my more bizarre stands. While I tried to be pragmatic in the sense of offering workable solutions, I was not at all concerned about being pragmatic or realistic in the sense of compromising my positions to make them politically palatable. In addition, Rothenberg disagreed with our critique of American education. In this case, he had his own Amtrak (see the paragraph beginning "This is not easy" on page 208)—his mother was a public school teacher.

*The Washington Monthly* version of neoliberalism:
See "A Platform for the Seventies," by Thomas Redburn, *The Washington Monthly*, October 1974; "A Platform for the Nineteen Eighties," by Charles Peters, *The Washington Monthly*, February 1979; "A Neoliberal's Manifesto," by Charles Peters, *Washington Post*, Outlook section, September 7, 1982; and "A Neoliberal's Manifesto," by Charles Peters, *The Washington Monthly*, May 1983. See, also, "The Man Who Put Neo in Neoliberal," by William E. Farrell, *New York Times*, November 1, 1984, B12; *A New Road for America*, by Phillip Keisling and Charles Peters (Madison Books, 1984); and "What's Happening to Your Politics—A Neoliberal [Charles Peters] and A Radical Democrat [Robert Kuttner] Face Off," by David Osborne, *Mother Jones*, May 1985.

Neoliberalism is not solely an American movement. Its British version in the eighties has been the Social Democratic Party (see *Washington Monthly* articles: "Britain's Radical Center," by Laurence Grafstein, September 1984; and "The Rise and the Fall of Britain's Neoliberals," by Polly Toynbee, November 1987). There's even a French neoliberal, the sociologist Michael Crozier; see his book, *The Trouble with America* (University of California Press, 1985). The most intriguing fact about the British SDP is that before it self-destructed in 1987, polls showed that more than half of British voters would have supported it if they had thought it had a chance of attaining power.

*page 209*
the Shavian corollary:
Shaw's version of the Golden Rule can be found in "The Revolutionist's Handbook," appended to *Man and Superman* in *Nine Plays*, by George Bernard Shaw (Dodd, Mead, 1946).

*page 211*
The upper middle class and the rich have not shared the burden:
Under Lyndon Johnson, the upper class could buy draft deferment for their young simply by paying the tuition for graduate school. Protests about the inequity of this practice led to the institution of a lottery in 1969, so that members of the educated elite, like Fallows, had to resort to feigning insanity or to losing a lot of weight to evade serving. I am proud that my own position on the draft has been constant. In the Lyndon B. Johnson Library at the University of Texas is a White House memo from Hayes Redmon to Bill Moyers describing a call I made to Hayes complaining about the unfairness of the Vietnam draft. It was written in 1965, just as the Westmoreland escalation was beginning.

*page 212*
get rid of the law:
The last draft was abolished in 1973. Earlier drafts were terminated at the ends of World Wars I and II.

*page 213*
national service draft:
For more on our national service proposal, see Timothy Noah's article in *The Washington Monthly*: "We Need You: National Service, An Idea Whose Time Has Come," November 1986. Also see "Draft the Rich," by William Greider, Richard Harwood, and Charles Peters, *The Washington Monthly*, April 1980. The latter article was in the form of a debate. A longer version of Greider's views, titled "The Draft Is a Terrible Idea," appeared in the *Washington Post* on February 25, 1979. In support of that position, Greider quoted my son, who was then a teenager and whom Greider was shrewd enough to interview, rightly suspecting that there might be intrafamilial discord on this issue.

**page 214**
1987 in New York City:
"Metro Matters—Racial Barriers: Private Schools Confront Reality," by Sam Roberts, *New York Times,* June 15, 1987, B1.

Skelly Wright decision:
*Smuck v. Hobson,* 408 F.2d 175 (1969).


**page 217**
articles on education:
"Saving the Schools from Teachers Unions," by Joseph Nocera, May 1979; "The Class War We Can't Afford to Lose," by Phillip Keisling, June 1982; and "Yes, But Where Are Your Credits in Recess Management 101?" by Susan Ohanian, April 1984.

answer to inferior public schools:
I concede that some urban private parochial schools, in addition to providing a better education than the public schools, have a more democratic mixture of students (see "Lessons from America's Best Run Schools," by Danielle Schultz, *The Washington Monthly,* November 1983). I also concede that voucher proposals can be useful as a threat to make the public schools reform. But my hope is that they will reform and the vouchers will never be used.

That the problems that became clear in Washington's public schools in the seventies persist in other urban areas is demonstrated in "New York's School System an Intractable Mess," by Howard Kurtz, *Washington Post,* January 2, 1988, A1; and "Carnegie Report Urges Crusade for 'Bypassed Urban Schools,'" Edward B. Fiske, *New York Times,* March 16, 1988, A1.


**page 220**
explosion of snobbery:
The reason snobbery is so insidious is that, instead of encouraging us to reach out to find common ground with our fellow man, it excludes people who don't fit the right mold. It is an expression of concern, not for real substance but for how we look to the world. It makes us nervous about the things that don't count and thus detracts from the commitment to do the things that will make the world a better place, which is the commitment that should govern our lives.

city magazines . . . sprang up:
See "From World War II to Clay Felker: How America Bought Its Way to Happiness," by Nicholas Lemann, *The Washington Monthly*, March 1977.

**page 221**
other publications . . . and greatly expanded lifestyle sections:
See "Wooing the Wealthy Reader," *New York Times*, October 14, 1987, D1. Major newspaper lifestyle sections began to feature issues such as where to eat and vacation and what was "in" in the arts. Most had their own wine critics, who became important personages. The *New York Times* even chose its wine critic, Frank Prial, to be its Paris correspondent. And R. W. Apple, as the *New York Times* London correspondent from 1975 to 1985, devoted much of his time to covering cultural and culinary matters in Europe. Mitterand and Thatcher became less important than choosing the right burgundy and knowing where the best Francesca frescoes are.

The role of taste in determining class was first explored in the *Monthly* by Suzannah Lessard in "Taste, Class, and Mary Tyler Moore," March 1975. Subsequent articles on this and related topics included "The Halstonization of America," by Nicholas Lemann, July–August 1978; "Who's a Snob and Who's Not," by James Fallows, June 1979; "The Age of the Artful Put-Down," by Alex Heard, May 1982; and "Selling Out with a Smirk: Lessons from David Letterman, Susan Sontag, and David Byrne," by William McGowan, March 1986.

**pages 221–23**
Credentialism:
See the following *Washington Monthly* articles: "Diplomaism: How We Zone People," by David Hapgood, May 1969; "The Health Professionals," by David Hapgood, June 1969; "Degrees: The Case for Abolition," by David Hapgood, August 1969; "Inside the Educational Testing Service," by Eric Rodriguez, March 1974; "Success in America," by Nicholas Lemann, July–August 1977; "Let the Nurses Do It," by Nicholas Lemann, April 1979; "Sheepskins Are for Sheep," by James Fallows, March 1981; "White Slaves—Why Nurses Lose Patience," by Donna Fenn, November 1981; "How SATs Are Ruining the GNP—The Merit Racket," by Nicholas Lemann, December 1981; "Artistic Licenses," by Philip Weiss, October 1982; "Yes, But Where Are Your Credits in Recess Management 101?" by Susan Ohanian,

April 1984; "The Pre-Med Machine," by Paul Barrett, May 1985; "The Recommendation Racket," by Paul Barrett, November 1985.

**page 222**
cab drivers were asked:
*Washington Post*, July 25, 1987, D1.

**pages 222–23**
"Anthropologists of the next century":
"Now You're Thinking Like a Lawyer," by Michael Kinsley and Charles Peters, *The Washington Monthly*, November 1975.

**pages 224–25**
Alger Hiss and the Rosenbergs:
Although I believe the Rosenbergs were guilty, I do not think they should have been electrocuted. The failure to commute their sentences remains a terrible blot on the record of Dwight Eisenhower.

**page 225**
Irving Kristol:
Kristol and I were attending a conference, "The U.S.A.—How Significant Is Neo-Conservatism in the Making of Domestic and Foreign Policy?" at the Aspen Institute Berlin in May 1983. I disagree with Kristol on many issues, but like him as a person and have nothing but admiration for two books by his wife, Gertrude Himmelfarb—*The Idea of Poverty* (Knopf, 1984) and *The New History and the Old* (Bellknap, 1987).

Cuban missile crisis:
*Thirteen Days* (Norton, 1969), Robert Kennedy's book on the Cuban missile crisis, told about his secret offer to Ambassador Dobrynin to withdraw our missiles from Cuba. The story of Rusk's revelation in 1987 that John Kennedy had been willing to go public with the offer is contained in "Class Reunion: Kennedy's Men Relive the Cuban Missile Crisis," by J. Anthony Lukas, *New York Times Magazine*, August 30, 1987.

**page 226**
legislative goof:
The liberals, in trying to protect labor union PACs, opened the door to the corporate variety.

television commercials:
Of course, the greatest reduction in political spending could be achieved by banning the manufactured political commercials. Half the money spent on campaigns goes for time and production costs. The commercials always gild the lily, making the candidate look better than he is. It would not interfere with his free speech to allow him to buy whatever television time he wants if it's used just to show him speaking. The danger that he would spend too much would be guarded against by his and his supporters' fear that his unadorned speeches would bore the public into voting against him.

**pages 226–27**
a rebirth of idealism:
See "The New Idealism" issue of *The Washington Monthly,* March 1980; and "We Do Our Part," a speech by Charles Peters at the Conference on Neoliberalism, October 21–23, 1983, reprinted in "Tilting at Windmills," *The Washington Monthly,* December 1983.

**page 227**
Social Security:
See the following *Washington Monthly* articles: "Social Security: The Poor Man's Welfare Payment to the Middle Class," by Milton Friedman, May 1972; "Pat Moynihan's Ship of Fools," by Taylor Branch, January 1973; "A Platform for the Seventies," by Thomas Redburn, October 1974, p. 10; "Anti-Social Security," by Nicholas Lemann, January 1978; "A Platform for the Eighties," by Charles Peters, February 1979, p. 10; and "A Neoliberal's Manifesto," by Charles Peters, May 1983, p. 12.

**page 228**
This consolidated program:
In addition to this program, we need to address the values of the underclass. Financial help and employment opportunities must be accompanied by moral leadership that ridicules the pimps and the pushers and makes them seem like losers to everyone else in the ghetto. See, also, "The Origins of the Underclass," by Nicholas Lemann, *Atlantic,* June and July, 1986; "Saving the Underclass," Ken Auletta interviewing Charles Murray, *The Washington Monthly,* September 1985; "The Work Ethic," by Mickey Kaus, *New Republic,* July 7,

1986; and "Start Helping the Underclass," by Jason DeParle, *The Washington Monthly*, March 1988.

Social Security is financed:
See *Born to Pay: The New Politics of Aging in America*, by Phillip Longman (Houghton Mifflin, 1987); "Scaling Back Hikes in Social Security," by Peter J. Ferrara, *New York Times*, January 25, 1987; "Social Security Tax Rates Rise at Least 5% Friday," *New York Times*, December 28, 1987, B10; "Social Security: It's Enough to Make You Die Laughing," *Money*, March 1988.

**pages 228–29**
arguments against the changes:
For the arguments for keeping Social Security as it is, see *The Life of the Party*, by Robert Kuttner (Viking, 1987); and "Bite the Deficit, Not Social Security," by Henry J. Aaron and Robert D. Reischauer, *Washington Post* op-ed page, December 14, 1987.

**page 229**
government *can* make distinctions:
For the Pierre, South Dakota–New York City distinction, see "Tilting at Windmills," by Charles Peters, *The Washington Monthly*, July–August 1986, p. 7. The government has also been able to make distinctions in pay on the basis of when workers such as engineers are in short supply and have to be offered higher salaries to be attracted to federal service (see "The Federal Diary," *Washington Post*, September 24, 1987). But more reform still is needed in the civil service to make salaries reflect actual competitive rates in the private sector, which are sometimes higher but are more often *lower* than the federal government pays; see "Inflated Pay," by Stephen Chapman, *The Washington Monthly*, April 1977, and "The Great Federal Gravy Train Robbery," by Leonard Reed, *The Washington Monthly*, February 1980. Also, federal wage increases are given far too automatically to all employees rather than to only those who deserve them. The "merit" increase, for example, goes to 99 percent of those eligible each year.

Perhaps the greatest need for this kind of distinction is in retirement pay, where the unfunded liability of federal, state, and local governments is now in the trillions of dollars and threatens to make the federal deficit of the eighties look like peanuts. By 1985, for federal pensions alone, that unfunded liability was $528 billion for civil service and $709 billion for military. These unfunded amounts will have to be paid for by future taxpayers, just as future workers will have to pay for the Social Security that was badly underfunded for present retirees. The great majority of today's Social Security recipients were paid back their own contributions, plus their employers', plus interest within three years of retirement. Thus, when they say they're entitled to their Social Security because they paid for it, they are telling the truth about only their first three years as beneficiaries.

One reason for all this is that, although most private pensions do not provide full cost-of-living adjustments, Social Security and civil service and military pensions do—even to the point of being above the inflation rate. Thus, a civil servant who retired in 1965 with a pension of $400 a month now receives $1,608. Carl Albert, the former Speaker of the House, retired in 1976 with a pension of $51,000. By 1983, his pension was $85,000. As with many federal retirees, he was being paid more not to work than he ever had been paid for working. But in addition to the generous COLA, pension costs are inflated by rules that permit retirement at an early age—after just twenty years' service in the military and thirty years in the civil service. Here is where the need to make distinctions comes into play. Policemen, firemen, and military personnel are permitted to retire with as little as twenty years' service on the assumption that they have been exhausted by their physically arduous duties. But most of the military and many of the police and firemen are deskbound or have other soft jobs for most of their careers. They have lots of work left in them, which most of them prove by getting other jobs when they retire. The justification for early retirement by civilian employees has been that it makes up for the fact that they were underpaid for years. This, though once a good argument, no longer is because of a series of pay raises that began in the early sixties and because of inflated job descriptions. If you've read about those "comparability" surveys that say federal workers are underpaid by 20 percent or so, remember that the surveys are based on comparing actual jobs in private industry with the "job descriptions" in government, which are often written by the jobholders themselves and which can endow a clerk with the apparent duties of a prime minister. By 1984, the median federal salary was twice that of the rest of us (see "How to End the Federal Pension Scandal," by Timothy Noah, *The Washington Monthly*, May 1984). An idea of the total unfunded pension burden at the

state and local levels can be gathered from the fact that it is
$3.4 billion in the District of Columbia and $8.4 billion in
Massachusetts.

**page 230**
a black man was elected:
In March 1988, Jesse Jackson won the Democratic presidential
primary in Virginia.

**page 232**
National defense:
*The Washington Monthly*'s articles on national defense began
with our second issue; they include: "How the Pentagon Can
Save $9 Billion," by Robert Benson, March 1969; "Washington's
Whispered Issue: Our First-Strike Capability," by Morton Kon-
dracke, June 1969; "The Loneliest Man in the Pentagon," by
Barbara Newman, July 1969; "National Security: Are We Ask-
ing the Right Questions?" by Paul Warnke, October 1969;
"American Arms Abroad," by George Thayer, January 1970;
"The Scorpions in the Bottle," by Robert L. Rothstein, January
1970; "The Oldest Established Permanent Floating Anachron-
ism on the Sea," by John Wicklein, February 1970; "Paying for
NATO," by Senator Charles Percy, July 1970; "Gilbert Fitz-
hugh's Golden Fleece," by Ernest Fitzgerald, November 1970;
"Tac Nukes—A More Personal Delivery," by Donald May, De-
cember 1970; "You Can't Keep a Deadly Weapon Down," by
Arthur Kanegis, December 1970; "Reserves and Guard: A More
Selective Service," by Adam Hochschild, January 1971; "The
Electronic Battlefield," by Paul Dickson and John Rothchild,
May 1971; "The Military Continues to Prepare for World War
II," by Col. James A. Donovan, December 1971; "Waiting for
Disarmament: Weapons We Can Live With—and Without," by
Robert Zelnick, May 1973; "Grumman Couldn't Bear It: The
F-14 Story," by Duane Yorke, July–August 1973; "Shooting at
Empty Silos," by Pat Schroeder, May 1974; "7,000 Toys for
Generals," by Paul Warnke, May 1974; "An Island Paradise for
the Admirals," by Gene LaRocque, May 1974; "Graduate School
for the Generals," by Maureen Mylander, October 1974; "P-38
Where Are You?" by William D. White, December 1974; "The
Air Force's Secret War on Unemployment," by Peter Ognibene,
July–August 1975; "National Defense: The Dodos and the Pla-
typuses," by Henry Fairlie, February 1976; "The Robot Air
Force," by Paul Dickson, May 1976; "How the Condor Was

Killed," by Greg Rushford, December 1976; "How the Defense Department Can Save Billions without Worrying about National Security," by Greg Rushford, March 1977; "The Better Cheaper Plane the Pentagon Didn't Want," by George Hopkins, March 1977; "The Navy We Need vs. the Navy We Got," by Clayton Fritchey, March 1977; "The Corrupt Military: A Case History," by Jim Henderson, September 1977; "How the Conglomerates Get Free Money from the Navy," by John F. Winslow, November 1977; "Thinking Like a Captain: How to Make General," by Nicholas Lemann, May 1978; "The Trident: Our Pre-Sunk Supercarrier," by Frank Packard, October 1978; "'Hello Central, Get Me NATO': The Computer That Can't," by James North, July–August 1979; "Death of the Devil's Advocate," by Eric Schnurer, July–August 1979; "Miss Hot Kiss Sells the Bomb," by James E. Cohen, November 1979; "Make Our 'Allies' Pay," by Vincent Wilson, November 1979; "The Spruce Goose of Outer Space," by Gregg Easterbrook, April 1980; "The Attack of the Atomic Tidal Wave," by Bill Keller, May 1980; "Moscow's *Real* Secret Weapon," by Jason Whitmire, June 1980; "The Case Against NATO," by George Ott, December 1980; "Another A-Bomb Coverup," by Raymond E. Brim and Patricia Condon, January 1981; ". . . And If This Is Just Another Job Then I'm A Sorry Suck-Egg Mule," by James Fallows, April 1981; "How to Bring Our Allies to Their Knees," by William R. Schulz, June 1981; "All Aboard Air Oblivion," by Gregg Easterbrook, September 1981; "From Sputnik to the Flying Submarine," by Gregg Easterbrook, October 1981; "Thirty-Five Ways to Cut the Defense Budget," by Jonathan Alter and Phillip Keisling, April 1982; "The Bradley Fighting Vehicle," by John Fialka, April 1982; "The Viper," by C. T. Hanson, April 1982; "Forget the Persian Gulf," by George Ott, April 1982; "Draft the Rich," by the editors, April 1972; "Get Out of Europe," by the editors, April 1982; "Thinking About the Next War," by Paul Warnke, January 1983; "Soldiers of Fortune," by Phillip Keisling, May 1983; "Bureaucracy of the Bomb," by Fred Kaplan, May 1983; "Dress Blues and Bleeding Mohawks: Scenes from the Modern Navy," by Scott Shuger, November 1983; "Misled and Underworked," by Phillip Keisling, February 1984; "The Army's $800,000 Model Airplane," by Gregg Easterbrook, July–August 1984; "What Caspar Weinberger Could Have Learned from the Falklands," by Gregg Easterbrook, September 1984; "Fighting World War III with Quarters," by Josh Martin, October 1984; "Can Our Public Affairs

Officer Help?" by Fred Reed, October 1984; "Why DIVAD Wouldn't Die," by Gregg Easterbrook, November 1984; "Why Star Wars Is Not Like the Manhattan Project," by John Tierney, March 1985; "Colonels in Every Corner," by Edward Luttwak, April 1985; "I Negotiated Contracts for the U.S. Navy," by Jamie Beckett, April 1985; "The 99% Fallacy," by David Evins, October 1985; "The Navy's Plane Stupidity," by Scott Shuger, October 1985; "The Pentagon's Blueprint for Lobbying Congress," by Dina Rasor, December 1985; "Grenada: Scenes from an Invasion," by Richard Gabriel, February 1986; "Sack Weinberger, Bankrupt General Dynamics, and Other Procurement Reforms," by Gregg Easterbrook, January, 1987; "Nuts, Bolts, and Death," by Harry Summers, January 1987; "The First Chrysler Bail-Out—The M-1 Tank," by Richard Mendel, February 1987; "The Door SDI Won't Shut," by Charles Hammer, March 1987; "The Sinking of a Supercarrier," by Joseph Enright and James Ryan, May 1987; "The Dark Secret of the Black Budget," by Tim Weiner, May 1987; and "The Case Against the Air Force," by Robert Coram, July–August 1987. See, also, *National Defense*, by James Fallows (Random House, 1981).

**pages 232–33**
growing awareness:
Regarding the reduction of wages, see "Tight Rein on Cost of Labor," *New York Times*, August 4, 1987, D1. And for the failure to cut executive pay, see "Millionaire Club Is Growing Today," *Washington Times*, December 28, 1987, B6, which notes: "There are . . . instances where executives are handsomely paid—even when their efforts result in the company losing money."

**page 233**
decline in the status of law degrees:
See "The Faster Track, Leaving the Law for Wall Street," *New York Times Magazine*, August 10, 1986, and "Fewer Applicants to Law School," *New York Times*, December 7, 1987, D2. I am afraid the decline in law school enrollment that occurred in the first half of the eighties may be reversed by the popularity of one of the hottest shows in television during the decade's second half. "L.A. Law" seems to be an exposé of the profession. *Newsweek* (November 16, 1987) says it delivers "a devastating, behind-the-bar portrait of what makes the legal world go round: deceit, avarice, domination, manipulation, backstabbing, loop-

276

hole leaping, and just about every form of lust, including bestiality." But I fear it is the same kind of exposé that "The Huckster" was of advertising, making whatever sins that are depicted very glamorous indeed. (My foreboding was confirmed when, as this book was going to the printer, the *Wall Street Journal* reported on February 23, 1988, that law school applications are up 17 percent for fall 1988 admission, attributing the rise in part to "L.A. Law.")

Fallows carried our concern:
See "Bad for Business: The Case Against Credentialism," by James Fallows, *Atlantic*, December 1985; "DIVAD," by Gregg Easterbrook. *Atlantic*, October 1982; "Why Boone Can't Lose," by Joseph Nocera, *Texas Monthly*, April 1985; "The Coming of the 'We' Decade," by Paul Taylor, *Washington Post* Outlook section, July 20, 1986; and "Do Americans Still Believe in Sharing the Burden," by Robert B. Reich, *Washington Post* Outlook section, April 26, 1987.

merger mania:
See "The Merger Mania," by Thomas Redburn, *The Washington Monthly*, February 1979.

**pages 233–34**
articles on unions:
See "The Class War We Can't Afford to Lose," by Phillip Keisling, *The Washington Monthly*, June 1982; "Industrial America's Suicide Pact," by Phillip Keisling, *The Washington Monthly*, December 1982; "The Trouble with Unions," by Robert M. Kaus, *Harper's*, June 1983; and "Voting for Unemployment," by Gregg Easterbrook, *Atlantic*, May 1983.

**page 234**
Art Levine:
In the history of the *Monthly*, Art deserves special recognition as the funniest of us all. For proof, see his articles: "The Final Days of the Third Reich as Told to Woodward and Bernstein," September 1976; "The President and the Senator's Wife," October 1977; "Do You Have What It Takes to Write for *The Washington Monthly*?" February 1979; and "Gandhi's Girls," July–August 1987.

corporate culture:
On just one day, February 4, 1988, two articles using the anthropological approach to business—"Infighting on Rise at Troubled Firm After Stock Plunge" and "Latest Turf Battle Pits SEC Against CFTC"—appeared in the *New York Times* (pages 1 and D1, respectively), which twenty years earlier was not publishing such articles at all.

**page 235**
taxes were enacted:
The tax enacted was on half the Social Security received by individuals earning more than $25,000 a year. Full taxation of benefits was one of the options most seriously considered by the deficit-cutting congressional conference committee in late 1987. It finally lost on a threat from the organized elderly to make the tax a major issue in the next election. However, a poll taken by *Newsweek* (November 23, 1987) showed that the tax would be supported by the public by a margin of 55 percent to 40 percent. I was delighted to see that it was also supported by an editorial in the *Washington Post* (November 9, 1987), because over the years I have been driven crazy by the *Post*'s failure to take means testing seriously as a way of dealing with the problem of Social Security. When I once asked Spencer Rich, the *Post* reporter who covered Social Security, why he wouldn't take means testing seriously, he replied, "The chances of that ever happening are zilch." The Spencer Riches of journalism have been one of the reasons why Social Security reform has taken so long. It was not until 1983, when Peter Peterson proposed means testing in the respectable forum of the *New York Times Magazine,* that it began to be taken seriously by the respectable press. My guess is that it will continue to have rough sledding politically so long as organizations like the American Association of Retired Persons succeed in portraying *all* the elderly as needy. The only way to counter this propaganda is for the large circulation magazines and newspapers to take up the cause, as was done by Robert S. Samuelson in "The Elderly Aren't Needy," which was published in both *Newsweek*, March 21, 1988, and the *Washington Post*, March 15, 1988.

**pages 235–36**
depressing failure:
"The Spruce Goose of Outer Space," by Gregg Easterbrook, April 1980. Earlier, we had expressed our skepticism about

278

various aspects of the manned space program in "The Space Shuttle: Conceived in PR and Dedicated to the Preservation of NASA," by Les Aspin, September 1972, and "Why We Went to the Moon," by Hugo Young, Bryan Silcock, and Peter Dunn, April 1970. The Manned Orbiting Laboratory was criticized in "How the Pentagon Can Save $9 Billion," by Robert Benson, March 1969.

**page 236**
Another of our disappointments was Jimmy Carter:
See "Why Carter Fails: Taking the Politics Out of Government," by Nicholas Lemann, *The Washington Monthly*, September 1978; "The Passionless Presidency," a two-part series, by James Fallows, *Atlantic*, May and June 1979; and "How to Be a One-Term President," by Charles Peters, *Harper's*, December 1982.

**pages 237–38**
The great master of the art:
See *One Third of a Nation: Lorena Hickock Reports on the Great Depression*, Richard Lowitt and Maurine Beasley, eds., (University of Illinois Press, 1981); *Roosevelt: The Lion and the Fox*, by James MacGregor Burns (Harcourt, Brace, 1956); *A Thousand Days: John F. Kennedy in the White House*, by Arthur M. Schlesinger, Jr. (Houghton Mifflin, 1965); and *Kennedy*, by Theodore C. Sorensen (Harper & Row, 1965).

**page 238**
the communications problem:
Herbert Kaufman has written an excellent, if unenticingly entitled, monograph on this problem (see *Administrative Feedback*, Brookings, 1973).

Often, when I talk about the government's information problem—perhaps because people associate the subject with words like administrative feedback—I notice eyes glazing over. But I'm not talking about something academic. Consider the case of NASA. Why had the top NASA officials who decided to launch the fatal *Challenger* flight not been told of the concerns of the people down below, such as Allan McDonald and the other worried engineers at Morton Thiokol? The view expressed by Deke Slayton, the former astronaut, when he was asked about the failure of middle-level managers to tell top NASA officials about the problems they were encountering was: "You depend on managers to make a decision based on the information they have. If they had to transmit all the fine detail to the top people, it wouldn't get launched but once every ten years." The point is not without merit. It is easy for large organizations to fall into "once every ten years" habits. Leaders who want to avoid that danger learn to set goals and communicate a sense of urgency about meeting them. But what many of them never learn is that once you set those goals, you have to guard against the tendency of those down below to spare you not only "all the fine detail" but essential facts about significant problems.

In NASA's case, chances had been taken with the shuttle from the beginning—the insulating thermal tiles had not gone through a reentry test before the first shuttle crew risked their lives to try them out—but in recent years the pressure to cut corners had increased markedly. Competition with the European Ariane rocket and the Reagan administration's desire to see agencies like NASA run as if they were private businesses have led to a speedup in the launch schedule, with a goal of twenty-four by 1988.

Under pressures like these, the NASA launch team watched *Columbia*, after seven delays, fall about a month behind schedule and then saw *Challenger* delayed, first by bad weather, then by damaged door handles, and then by bad weather again. Little wonder that Lawrence Mulloy, when he heard the warnings from the Thiokol engineers, burst out: "My God, Thiokol, when do you want me to launch? Next April?"

With NASA's senior officials, the conviction that everything was A-OK was fortified by skillful public relations. Julian Scheer began a tradition of inspired PR that endured until *Challenger*. These were men who could sell air conditioning in Murmansk. The trouble is they also sold their bosses the same air conditioning. Every organization has a tendency to believe its own PR—NASA's walls are lined with glamorizing posters and photographs of the shuttle and other space machines—and usually the top man is the most thoroughly seduced because, after all, it reflects the most glory on him.

Favorable publicity and how to get it is therefore the dominant subject of Washington staff meetings. The minutes of the Nuclear Regulatory Commission show that when the reactor was about to melt down at Three Mile Island, the commissioners were worried less about what to do to fix the reactor than they were about what they were going to say to the press.

One of the hottest rumors around Washington at the time

of the *Challenger* launch was that the White House had put pressure on NASA to launch so that the president could point with pride to the teacher in space during his State of the Union speech. The White House denies this story, but (and this is fact, not rumor) NASA had put pressure on itself by asking the president to mention Christa McAuliffe. In a memorandum dated January 8, NASA proposed that the president say:

Tonight while I am speaking to you, a young elementary school teacher from Concord, New Hampshire, is taking us all on the ultimate field trip as she orbits the earth as the first citizen passenger on the space shuttle. Christa McAuliffe's journey is a prelude to the journeys of other Americans living and working together in a permanently manned space station in the mid-1990s. Mrs. McAuliffe's week in space is just one of the achievements in space we have planned for the coming year.

The flight was scheduled for January 23. It was postponed and postponed again. Now it was January 28, the morning of the day the speech was to be delivered, the last chance for the launch to take place in time to have it mentioned by the president. NASA officials must have feared that they were about to lose a PR opportunity of stunning magnitude, an opportunity to impress not only the media and the public but the agency's two most important constituencies: the White House and the Congress. Wouldn't you feel pressure to get that launch off this morning so that the president could talk about it tonight?

A 1983 reorganization at NASA shifted the responsibility for monitoring flight safety from the chief engineer in Washington to the field. This may sound good. "We're not going to micromanage," said James M. Beggs, then the NASA administrator. But the catch is that if you decentralize, you must maintain the flow of information from the field to the top so that the organization's leader will know what those decentralized managers are doing. What NASA's reorganization did, according to Mark Tapscott of the *Washington Times*, was to close off "an independent channel with authority to make things happen at the top."

I suspect that what happened was that the top NASA administrators, who were pressuring employees down below to dramatically increase the number of launches, either consciously or unconsciously did not want to be confronted with the dangers they were thereby risking.

When NASA's George Hardy told Thiokol engineers that he was appalled by their verbal recommendation that the launch be postponed and asked Thiokol to reconsider and make another recommendation, Thiokol, which Hardy well knew was worried about losing its shuttle contract, was in effect being told, "Don't tell me" or "Don't tell me officially, so I won't have to pass bad news along and my bosses will have deniability."

In addition to the leader himself, others must be concerned with making him face the bad news. This includes subordinates. Their having the courage to speak out about what is wrong is crucial, and people like Richard Cook of NASA and Allan McDonald of Thiokol deserve great credit for having done so. But it is a fact that none of the subordinates who knew the danger to the shuttle took the next step and resigned in protest so that the public could find out what was going on in time to prevent disaster. The almost universal tendency to place one's own career above one's moral responsibility to take a stand on such matters has to be one of the most depressing facts about bureaucratic culture today.

Even when the issue was simply providing facts for an internal NASA investigation after the disaster, this is the state of mind Cook described: "Another [NASA employee] told me to step away from his doorway while he searched for a document in his filing cabinet so that no one would see me in his office and suspect that he'd been the one I'd gotten it from."

Merit System Protection Board:
It is also possible that the board's Office of Special Counsel has been less than diligent in seeking to help whistleblowers.

**page 240**
most campaign workers now have to be paid:
One of the problems with the paid campaign workers is that those whose political activity is inspired by money rather than by conviction are prone to cynicism and the sins that follow in its wake—for example, paid Dole workers forged signatures to get Dole on the Texas primary ballot in 1988. See "Dole Hits Bush, Plays Down Problem of Texas Petitions," *Washington Post*, January 10, 1988.

**page 243**
Steven Rattner:
See "Hello, Sweetheart, Get Me Mergers and Acquisitions: The

Rise of Steve Rattner," by Philip Weiss, *The Washington Monthly*, May 1986. Rattner's own version of Wall Street can be found in "A View from the Trenches," by Steven Rattner, *Newsweek*, December 14, 1987, p. 80.

Ivanhoe Donaldson:
Donaldson, who was Mayor Marion Barry's top assistant and political guru, spent too much of his time not using his brain to help meet the terrible problems of the city's poor black population but instead figuring out how to steal money from the taxpayers to finance his taste in fancy cars and restaurants.

FDR proposed a limit:
FDR's proposal to limit income to $25,000 a year is described in *Roosevelt, The Soldier of Freedom*, by James MacGregor Burns (Harcourt Brace Jovanovich, 1970), pp. 307 and 362.

*page 244*
it's not too late:
I'm painfully aware that for some people it is too late—or impossible, for other very good reasons—to change jobs, and that some don't even have a job. For them my words can only be a cruel reminder of their fate. But most people do have the freedom to change their work and do something that they enjoy and believe in, and it is for their sake that I feel I must risk injury to the feelings of those who don't have such freedom.

become a nurse:
Of all the jobs that I would like to see more good people enter, nursing best symbolizes the rejection of status, power, and money in favor of helping others. Anyone who has ever been hurt or sick enough to be put in the hospital knows why nurses are important. For further explanation, see *Nurse*, by Peggy Anderson (St. Martins, 1981). For a way to make nursing a better profession for the nurses, see "White Slaves," by Donna Fenn, *The Washington Monthly*, November 1981. Even if we want nurses to lead the rest of us in rejecting the values of the affluent society, they are entitled to a decent income, which most of them aren't getting now. A nurse in a New York City hospital with seven years' experience makes $4,000 less than her policeman brother with four years' experience (see Colman McCarthy, "Breakdown at Bellevue," *Washington Post*, March 19, 1988, A23.

**page 245**
I hope so:
On January 4, 1988, *Newsweek* decreed that my hopes had come true with a cover story that proclaimed, "The 80's Are Over," subtitled "Greed Goes Out of Style." But then, on January 15, came the results of a study conducted by the American Council of Education, headlined "Freshman Found Stressing Wealth" in the *New York Times* and "Making Big Bucks, Goal of Most Freshmen" in the *Charleston Gazette*. The *Los Angeles Times* began its account of the study, "Some social commentators talk about the end of the materialistic Yuppie Generation, but such speculation is contradicted by a newly released study."

# Index of Names

Thomson, James C., Jr., 146, 152–153, 160
Three Deuces, 44
Three Stooges, 15
Thurow, Lester, 207
*Time* magazine, 22, 26, 78, 142, 157, 171
Toynbee, Polly, 194
  *A Working Life*, 194
Tracy, Spencer, 66
Transportation, Department of, 204–205
Treasury Department, 192
*Trial, The*, 61
Trillin, Calvin, 139, 160
Trilling, Lionel, 43, 47, 76, 206
Trueblood, Carol, 154, 155, 172, 174, 178
Truman, Bess, 133
Truman, Harry, 66, 75, 133, 204
Twain, Mark, 153, 195, 209

Uhl, John, 46
Union Carbide, 69, 77
United Mine Workers, 111, 203

Vanderbilt, Arthur, 84–85
Vandermeer, Johnny, 17
Van Doren, Mark, 43, 61, 76
*Vanity Fair*, 221
Vassar College, 88, 89, 148
Vaughn, Jack, 135, 136, 142, 148, 150
Vietnam War, 132, 141, 146, 149, 157, 161, 162–164, 166–167, 168–169, 191–192, 202, 205, 211, 224, 232
Virginia, University of, Law School, 82–87, 223
VISTA, 213

Wallace, George, 161
Wallace, Henry, 75, 76
Walters, Bucky, 17
Walton, William, 104
War on Poverty, 139–140

Washington and Lee University, 4, 15–16
*Washingtonian*, 220–221
*Washington Monthly, The*, 142–206, 208, 217, 222–223, 225, 226, 228, 231, 232–236, 242, 244
*Washington Post*, 148, 197, 204, 205, 233
Waterman, Robert, *In Search of Excellence* (with Tom Peters), 231
Webster, Stanley, 12
West, James, 167–168
Westmoreland, William, 225
West Point, 16, 88, 163
West Virginia House of Delegates, 99, 100, 111–114
West Virginia University, 16, 187
  Law School, 82
Wheeler and Woolsey, 15
White, Theodore, 145, 160, 173
White House Fellows, 153–154, 157
White House mess, 204
Williams, Bob, 46, 49
Williams, Tennessee, 59
Williston and Corbin, *Restatement of the Law of Contracts*, 85
Wilson, Teddy, 29
Wilson, Woodrow, 18, 245
Wirth, Timothy, 154
Wolfe, Tom, 145, 160
Woodward, Bob, *The Brethren*, 144
World's Fair (Chicago, 1934), 12
World's Fair (New York, 1939–1940), 51
World War I, 4, 14, 89
World War II, 10, 31, 32–33, 35, 39, 46, 89–90, 100–101, 106, 115, 130–131, 144, 219, 226–227, 243
Worth, William Jenkins (General), 89
Wright, Skelly, 214, 215
*Wrong Man, The* (film), 93–94

293